D1258012

WITHDRAWN
WILLIAM F. MAAG LIBRARY
YOUNGSTOWN STATE UNIVERSITY

REFERENCE GUIDES IN LITERATURE

Ronald Gottesman, *Editor*

# THEODORE ROETHKE'S CAREER: AN ANNOTATED BIBLIOGRAPHY

Keith R. Moul

WITHDRAWN

G. K. HALL & CO., 70 LINCOLN STREET, BOSTON, MASS.

Copyright © 1977 by Keith R. Moul

Moul, Keith R
   Theodore Roethke's career.

   (Reference guides in literature)
   Includes index.
   1.  Roethke, Theodore, 1908-1963--Bibliography.
I.  Title.
Z8753.4.M68  (PS3535.039)    016.811'5'4   76-50593
ISBN 0-8161-7892-5

*This publication is printed on permanent/durable acid-free paper*
MANUFACTURED IN THE UNITED STATES OF AMERICA

Z
8753.4
.M68

# Contents

WILLIAM F. MAAG LIBRARY
YOUNGSTOWN STATE UNIVERSITY

# Introduction

As with any work, that which follows has undergone numerous revisions to become what you see. Rather than repeat the sketchy Theodore Roethke biography habitual with secondary material aimed at the uninitiated, I will assume that most who read this are familiar with Allan Seager's The Glass House, and proceed to an innocent question asked by a person with whom I have worked most closely during the late stages before printing, yet who prefers anonymity. The question caused me mild irritation, but after that had passed, I examined my own motives in producing this compilation and the biases influencing me as I read each review, article, book, etc. to excerpt the insightful, the purposeful, the insensitive and the merely entertaining.

The question involved the inclusion of inconsequential material, i.e. oft-repeated announcements of various kinds and considerable numbers of "short, favorable" reviews, that could contribute little to researchers using the book. My initial response was to pass the buck to my predecessors, editors of similar series as the one into which this work will fit, or James McLeod, compiler of Theodore Roethke: A Bibliography, because they obviously have felt the inclusion of such references necessary. My task had been to locate and account for every burp by reviewers, reporters and various hangers on who had read, heard or digested incompletely a Roethke poem, essay, book, reading or second-hand dream. We have little enough time to contemplate the act or thought of consequence, I agreed, so why burden harried researchers or students with innumerable announcements of prizes awarded, awards prized, or admissions in print that Roethke was indeed a "good" or a "bad" poet?

Sarcasm is one response to the question, but it makes no answer. By far the most copious resource for Roethke study is the University of Washington's collection of a dead man's nonsenses and treasures. As it has generated already other reports (articles and a book so far), it gave me the rationale for including the inconsequential in this volume and knowing the necessity of doing so. Roethke himself was the collector, item by item, from the fatuous to the profound. Karl Shapiro has reviewed Ralph Mills' selection of the letters and David Wagoner's arrangement of notebook fragments and seen a man's vulgarity and shameless connivance. Of course ample self-celebration may be found there, but I see more too that leads me to believe that Roethke was painfully conscious of the need for cooperation between poet and critic if a successful poem is to be created. "Cooperation," "critic," "successful poem," all of these topics assume their meanings during the course of my discussion. The poet's concern for the seemingly inconsequential is what will generate my remarks.

Whether to challenge convention or for some other reason, I had considered foregoing an introduction. My research progressed with the noblest purpose and references with their annotations began to accumulate. I became aware of thematic repetition, critical jargonese, and superficial treatment that colored a giant task with futility. As this awareness increased, I felt that my biases could be made plain by the manner in which I summarized the material I read, or the re-marks I chose to excerpt. Certainly I did not need to be openly deri-sive of the slight or irrelevant. Without derogating material of value, I decided to give adequate space to the worthless. This might prove to be commentary enough were the quality of remaining criticism sufficiently high. Although much of it is excellent, there are areas of concern that as a poet I feel deserve more attention. Landmark essays in Roethke criticism are rare. Therefore my purpose has changed; in the following remarks I will try at least to provoke further examination of these areas of concern.

Treatments of theme and style are numerous; opinions on these topics fall into patterns and evolve eventually into discrete com-plexities, in which elaboration of one demands no mention of the other. Unfortunately, ideas echoed too easily become "themes" and style is for too many an end that when described becomes definitive. Style is too superficial a subject to qualify or make clear the essen-tial nature of any poet's work, particularly Roethke's, who changed writing styles with every narrowing or widening of men's lapels. However as Roethke was able to use variants of numerous styles as a means to communication, he became a more effective poet. I hope to explain this contention later. Instead of dwelling on theme and style there are three additional topics basic to an understanding of Roethke's achievement that have received only partial and sporadic attention in the body of secondary material referenced here: Roethke's conception of higher criticism; Roethke's "careerism"; and Roethke's poetic consciousness.

Elaboration of these topics requires only casual tracing of evi-dence through specific poems and essays, mainly because Roethke's conception of higher criticism seems to be an unstated, unquestioned, almost a priori operating principle; his "careerism" has been imposed on him from without, mainly after his death, and he did not acknowl-edge it during his life; and his poetic consciousness overwhelms in its diversity any individual poem or sequence of poems. If these are excuses for lax scholarship, very well, but to them must be added much that I impute to Roethke's personality from what I interpret as anal-ogous in my own experience. I will not dress up my opinions to make them sound objective, but an apology is due to those who take comfort in the presence of recognizable critical apparatus.

Paradoxically, Roethke was suspicious of critics and criticism. He early came to consciousness regarding the function of both, primarily because of his own sensitivity to language and an ideal manner in which it _ought_ to be handled.  The mistreatment of language made of Roethke a critic, a teacher; and to call him early in his writing life a critic may be more just than calling him a poet.  Yet he seldom displayed trust for those who reviewed his poems because he measured them against his own ideal.

Generosity, not as to compliments, but as to interest in the process of communication, was for Roethke probably the first important criterion for criticism.  The function of criticism of the live writer/artist is to discern potential ideas from which an idiom and direction may be established; this function is organic, contributory in the best sense, and provides nurturing by making available experience of a new perspective that may be assimilated by the writer/artist. The cooperation or sharing unselfishly and immediately of ideas by such critics as John Holmes, Louise Bogan, Rolphe Humphries, and especially Kenneth Burke supplied Roethke with an impetus toward successful communication that belies totally any suspicions of criticism.  His gravitation toward teaching as a profession, and the reputation he acquired in it, serve as a further manifestation of his critical generosity and a further contradiction of his apparent distrust.

The intellectual equipment both to complement and challenge the writer/artist is the second criterion to make creation work.  By the sheer number of "brief, favorable" reviews dotting this compilation, I discerned seldom the challenge Roethke, any poet, would crave from a truly audacious reader.  Assuming that important poems are not of the occasional type, they represent a necessary response to some aspect of the poet's experience.  No less should a reader feel compelled in turn to make his necessary response.  Audacity should widen and deepen communication and no limitation ever should be placed on the potential of meaning.

As a teacher, Roethke knew these truths as second nature.  He played it spontaneously, he beat his students with contrivance, he hated and loved, made himself impertinent, an imposition, the symbol of a student's terror, but he generated the will to make the necessary response.

I do not know why, but for some reason in Roethke's role as poet generous criticism did not survive.  That he was consumed with self-love, or overly competitive are absurd answers.  But, the fact remains that after a few early reviews Roethke saved his energy for his own poems and allowed the critical function to be borne entirely by those who recognized and supported the quality of his work.  As he was for others, he became his own provacateur, filling his notebooks with lines and phrases, and demanding of himself the concentration to cultivate them until they could be productive. In some, selfishness becomes obsession; in Roethke it more favorably became dedication to his own private thought. The results have been fortunate. As the function of criticism of the dead writer's work is to tabulate the number of successful ideas that inform his direction; and to comment on the relative success of those ideas at describing the organization of the writer's mind, whether significant or insignificant, Roethke has been an ample provider. The propensity to be lastingly supportive in the face of the inarticulate, to be patient or sympathetic with what prove to be the writer's failings, may well be among the final criteria for criticism.

According to some of his notable detractors (such as Karl Shapiro), however, Roethke went too far and caught himself in the "prideless transactions of the poet as ninny" (1968.B71); he made himself a career poet of a disreputable kind. Self-promotion, manipulation of friends and editors, a most aggressive salesmanship: Shapiro finds too much evidence of these things in Roethke's private life. to leave the poetic accomplishment untainted.

Allan Seager, who said "Ted was like a turtle who worked at ornamenting his own shell," (The Glass House p. 84) damns Roethke unintentionally by the candor of his biography and his ambivalence toward facts that he was the first to announce. The simile above works as well out of context as in, thereby leaving Roethke defenseless to any inference we can make. I do not fault Seager as misleading, or doubt that Roethke "confected versions of likelihood that sprang from wishes and hopes," (The Glass House p. 83) rather I challenge the surface images that sparkle in well-chosen words and fall short of substance or psychological motivation. If we put too much weight on the back of a turtle simile, we'll not penetrate to the heart of Roethke; instead we'll break through to the soft tissue that supports most rhetoric. Probably, given the opportunity of acquaintance with Roethke over many years, most of us would have felt similar frustration at reconciling an apparently loud-mouthed self-promoter with a poet almost enshrined for his own self-sacrifice.

For several years during the 1930's Roethke enjoyed the peculiar good fortune of having Dorothy Gordon as a correspondent in England. Although The Glass House makes no mention of her, Mrs. Gordon occupied a position to Roethke as literary agent, apparently with much energy and goodwill. She enabled a very young poet to publish his poems with extraordinary frequency in important British journals without the inconvenience of cajoling and plea-bargaining on his own behalf. However, the effect of success on Roethke seems to have been that he assumed an arrogance totally inappropriate in such a young man, while displaying it against a loyal disciple and willing servant, Mrs. Gordon. His letters to her, as well as others selected by Ralph J. Mills, Jr., embarrass reviewers such as Seymour Krim (1970.B13) as they do tend

to display a rather amateurish understanding of human relationships.
Certainly Roethke must be faulted for the cruel manipulation of
Mrs. Gordon when he writes:

> I remember I. A. Richards saying that Huxley was a very good
> second-rate, that he got much of his best stuff from repeat-
> ing conversations of his brilliant friends.
>
> How dull this all is, - but it's a dull day.
>
> I hope some editor has been foolish enough to take something.
>
> Theodore Roethke
>
> Lord, what a boor I am! What a way to end a letter! But
> I'm in an awful period of self-disgust. I seem to have
> lost my self-respect.

Her graciousness may well have allowed her to overlook such obvious ingratiation. But youth, the uncertainties common to a writer
who requires the reinforcement publication gives, a burgeoning com-
petitiveness not unique with Roethke, plus the realistic (although
crass) conviction that sufficient smoothness of style and persistence
of salesmanship will result in a market opening up are their own
excuses. Not that salesmanship was a strong point with Roethke--he
probably tended to oversell his wares--but rather that he discerned
rightly its necessity and effectiveness, although his enlarging critical perceptivity must have suffered at how infrequently he could
rely on editors to identify quality.

> It seems to me that nowadays when you're a young buck you
> have to eat more than your share of dung.
>
> But I'm so damned tired of guys who aren't on the up and
> up.
>
> (Selected Letters p. 16)

Writing here to Rolphe Humphries, Roethke speaks the truth of his
circumstances, but well or ill for his conscience does not admit his
hypocrisy. Yet I infer in "up and up" the higher conception of criticism mentioned already and infer also that Humphries, an honest con-
fidante, knows well to what Roethke alludes. That remarks excerpted
from the privacy of letters change is true too; we as readers see
them in isolation as emblems, as fragments that we would piece together with others into a larger, more comprehensible design. Because
of this, and because we lack the consciousness of the person to whom
the letters have been written, the thoughts continued or elaborated,
as well as the confidence of a predictable effect the remarks will
make on a chosen reader, we really possess little more authority to
criticize them than a voyeur peeking through a window.

# Theodore Roethke's Career: An Annotated Bibliography

I place the letters and many of the notebook jottings ignored by
Roethke in his final poems in a category conveniently thought of as
spontaneous communications.  He does not seem to have been well
suited for business transactions or social intercourse not requiring
full exploitation of his profundity; these circumstances made him uneasy, clumsy like a bear, overly self-conscious.  Accounts prove that
his wit could be extraordinary and his suavity fine but these roles
drained him of energy severely.  Sherman Paul (1969.B42) discerns cor-
rectly that the Roethke of <u>The Glass House</u> and <u>Selected Letters</u> cor-
relates only obliquely to him of the poems.  Those works report the
training necessary for "success" in a conventional world, the world
in which celebration is important, and costly.  Struggle with it as
much as he did, Roethke most likely never became agitated by that
world to a degree so significant that it imposed itself on his poetic
consciousness.  Spontaneous communication was doubtful, untrustworthy;
Roethke felt privacy and patience of mind to be far more deserving of
scrutiny by his critics and the greatest commitment by himself, because from that source came the greatest reward.

To reveal Roethke's frailties should have a cathartic effect.
For some of his critics Roethke has been changed, for infringement on
their private ideals has scarred <u>them</u>.  But the ideal conception of
the poet under which they must labor obviously is an unnatural one.
Men will create their own heros, but perhaps the true measure of a
hero is the height he achieves in his work in relation to his necessary grounding in human vulgarity.  That which he creates and pre-
serves reflects his dedication to perfection, not the trauma of his
obsession with life.

Satisfying all of his particular critics should be no poet's concern; he writes to those few who challenge him deeply and cannot in
conscience be ignored.  John Wain, (1958.B38) for example, denies
Roethke a unique place in the literary market because of his lack of
unmistakable identity.  Wain's assumption is that Roethke aspired to
unmistakable identity as surely all poets must!  The attainment of
singularity is all important!  I do not limit Roethke to journeyman
status when I try to contradict Wain, rather let me suggest that pur-
suing uniqueness may prove a detriment to personal expansion.  However, it is true that Roethke's considerable accomplishment as
multi-faceted poet (the biggest of his generation) hurts rather than
helps his stock in the market place because it is not so easily pack-
aged and sold.

To emphasize the strength Roethke derived from his continuing
compulsion to encounter uncertainty, the always new and exciting
prospect, makes him what Arnold Stein (1965.A3) calls a "perpetual
beginner."  In truth this does describe his spirit.  Too it goes far
toward countering John Wain's complaint.  The desire to face uncertainty for many is impenetrable, yet Roethke's capacity to do this,
again and again, has made him for James Dickey the greatest American
poet (1968.B29) because of the way he could define and enrich a place,

a situation, by his own presence there: "...so vividly and evoca-
tively, waking unheard of exchanges between the place and human re-
sponsiveness at its most creative." In one critic's eye, a variety
of these insightful responses has become fragmentary, while in another
critic's eye that variety reveals genius manifesting itself on itself.

Roethke wanted to be recognized by bartenders, not as a profligate,
but as a notable personality for whose achievement he could be loved.
This desire falls in the tradition of the trubador or bard (See
1963.B32) and should establish for Roethke a sympathetic image. It
calls Balder to mind for one writer (1962.B41) and highlights the
incongruity of Roethke as showman and shaman. He trained his voice
although he could not train his stomach, and the anxiety over an
imminent public performance made him vomit. As he believed poetry
should be an auditory experience, he in effect auditioned at every
reading, most frequently achieving not obscurity in his poems, but
mystery. He knew the method to be correct, but like the rest of us,
he never was certain of his own capacity to bring it off. He read
the poems in the confidence of their rhythms and word selection, then
joked with self-conscious asides, uneasily a target. The psychic cost
is high. As he was no priest, Roethke could not give of himself and
expect nothing in return; rather he wanted our recognition (something
more than indifference) first and finally our necessary response.

Because of this, his craft was militant. By 1934, John Holmes
already could say that Roethke "had fought off and defeated the loose
and ordinary phrase." Abstractions such as "duty" and "mercy" arise
in my mind and seem totally accurate in relation to Roethke's sweated-
for triumph over his own human limitations. Although it does not
demand our admiration, careerism is no crime; it merely reflects the
passing of gentlemen's literature as one more instance of competitive
social evolution.

Under these circumstances, Roethke's literary arrogance is not
pride. He practices no tricks that I can detect, no fortuitous strat-
agems that will not advance his craft toward meaning; even a lucky
accident, from whatever source, might be impetus that wakes his consciousness. The potential of any experience to be a revelation, a
revolution, is a portion of Roethke's knowledge. It does not call
for self-congratulation, only the continual awareness that distances
deceive, perspective alters, time brings on both growing and diminish-
ing; and awareness that control of these things, circles within circles, must be tentative. Psychologists cannot explain how it happens,
nor can I, but Roethke's poetry is the synthesis of his frailties and
terrors with his own commitment to explore them for their meaning.
Babette Deutsch (1941.B24) comments on how Roethke writes about the
"mind as awareness grows on it," hopefully a revelation with the
power to convert the reader to seeing with the poet. Following the
lead of others, such as Rolph Humphries (1941.B29), I accept this as
a kind of courage.

# Theodore Roethke's Career: An Annotated Bibliography

A. Alvarez has stated: "Roethke's art was a matter of sensibility rather than style" (1965.B18). The single most negative aspect of the body of criticism collected here is that Roethke failed to assimilate numerous influences, including Eleanor Wylie, John Clare, William Wordsworth, T. S. Eliot, W. B. Yeats, Dylan Thomas, Lewis Carroll and Walt Whitman, among others. The insight of Alvarez answers the "imitation" critics, for it is true that a personality can filter itself through any outside influence to avoid absolute subjectivity. To make this statement clear, I will discuss some particulars that illuminate for me Roethke's poetic consciousness.

Generally speaking, Roethke's personality is that of a disorganized investigator, who with child-like vanity assumes first a temporary fascination for a subject or object, until it develops into a clue or private correlative. Stephen Spender characterizes this habit as "innocent, rather clumsy" in the poems, but it is no persona as this particular trait marks Roethke's wide range of styles with consistency. Spender had in mind the sequence of regressive poems from The Lost Son, but all of Roethke's poems strike us as excursions into unfamiliar territory, full of surprises and valuable for their excited mood if for no other quality.

By this means, a sense of anarchy is imparted to almost every line Roethke ever retained, mainly because the predictable rarely survives. However, a paradox emerges because of the severely self-disciplined control he maintains over each uninhibited exploration. Rather than anarchic, Roethke's personality is essentially the epitome of objective classification and organization; his impulse is toward the constant definition of his place, his psychological condition at present, and the events of his past influencing the present; plus, of course, the numerous possible futures logically to result from his current combination of circumstances.

This is his impulse, but it is diverted by his naturally supersensitive imagination and investigative intelligence that complicates the original impulse and results, seemingly, in chaos. Most of Roethke's poems begin simply enough and could, would his sensibility allow it, progress toward conclusive fulfillment. Rarely does he deceive us with a trick atmosphere or mood, run away and leave us lost. Instead, he establishes us with him in a believable circumstance and expands it into its conceivable ramifications, each one more than likely discrete from the other, and some requiring a large imaginative leap to appreciate fully. Usually the controlling impulse reasserts itself to organize the experience. Or at least Roethke hoped this happened because certainly he believed that poetry has as one of its functions to find its own order and reach its own fulfillment. No man's judgment in these matters is faultless, but Roethke's ratio of success/failure indicates both that he did not fear the gamble and that his intuition seldom disappointed him.

To describe this method or tendency, many critics have retreated into the safety of referring to it as "obscure." Edwin Muir (1958.B31) speaks more rightly of Roethke's attraction to the "enigmatic." An enigma can be the obsession of a lifetime and therefore of interest to most readers for the various responses made to it. Confusion and obscurity well may be part of the poet's response to the enigma, but selecting to use "enigmatic" eliminates the derogatory connotations and provides a kind of credibility. Man facing his own private enigma is a universal experience; Roethke's militancy stands him in good stead in his battle, but there will be few reinforcements upon which to draw.

I had thought at this point to discuss several of the numerous veins that Roethke mined, but realize now that to do so would create in the reader certain points of reference, perhaps too personal to myself and therefore misleading, that would when linked form an over-view of thematic concern. Ranking of poets is for the lazy of mind and I see no reason to classify or aim at the broad appraisal of Roethke's achievement except for the purpose of ranking him. Rather, I will allow myself some further discussion on his capacity to learn from himself and others.

In Roethke's life, explosions occurred periodically, explosions attributable only to the mind's inability to correlate further the minutae of forces building up as his experience expanded. As a learner, Roethke was a merciless profligate; he strained the mind as well as the tissue, not self-consciously, but as obligatory. Fre-quently, to judge by his necessary rest periods, he failed his own tests and fell into self-doubt. Yet only, it appears, after all avenues from which to research his objective had been exhausted. I am not speaking of ordinary stamina or perseverance, for Roethke did not merely get tired; instead he ran out of mind to contemplate. As a result, some critics complain of lapses in his development, as though no life were complete without continuity. It may be valuable to think some obstacles were too high or deep for Roethke to get over or through and survive. On such occasions he recognized the need to alter his course, adopt new styles, themes, inspirations, and begin again. This is not to imply that anything learned, psychologically, philosophically, or artistically, was abandoned. On the contrary, his wisdom became partial source for his new determination to continue.

The psychology of the Self, the establishment of a personal myth, a philosophy of expansion, irony, regression, the madness tradition of literature, love literature, formal conventions such as trimeter lines, doggerel, attitudinizing, the trite or fortuitous, etc., all these things are part of reality that did not belong to Roethke, but were used by him as part of his private arsenal; they represent the collection of objective restraints on his subjectivity that Roethke found manageable after a long process of eliminating others. The presence of the "me" in his poems is so strong that some of his crit-ics are prepared to dismiss him as a neurotic crank. They should not be so hasty, because Roethke's ability to assimilate the "not me" represents a profound departure from conventional psychology and conventional literature. No word, line, open space, verse paragraph, or poem existed in a vacuum for this man. On the contrary, every smudge on white paper, each nuance of meaning, or slight grammatical alteration resonated through his poetic consciousness as he tried to understand the effect gained or the change that might be registered in the combination of potentials comprising his poems. As a reader of Roethke, if you find a phrase too facile (in his later work particularly), you will be closer to the truth of that language if you assume responsibility for the error, rather than attributing it to Roethke. I may disagree with his choice of tools to make his meaning clear, but I do not doubt that he has considered numerous options before making his choice.

For a man to burden himself with the weight of continual self-control, in marked contrast to the lack of self-discipline that characterizes the mass of humanity throughout history, represents an achievement of a unique kind. I do not wish to suggest that Roethke disdained his fellow creatures for their weaknesses. On the contrary, his contempt and disgust normally were aimed at his own failures. He seems to have felt reasonably comfortable with the human condition, in which he shared, to the extent that he accepted pain, death, and other trials as the necessary pre-conditions to triumph over them. As a teacher, he knew that self-trust, even braggadocio, when tempered with mercy can be an adequate defense against chaos. Yet he had no faith that chaos would be conquered, removed as an obstacle; he foresaw no paradise; he preferred an almost debilitating fear, that compelled him to respond, to a style of contentment.

Because of this, Roethke's actual position in Twentieth Century American literature should correspond to the one he occupied in his personal relationships. Roethke is the originator, the source of ideas and energies to which the rest of us react: he initiates direction, we follow. Even a cursory look at the primary and secondary materials that follow reveals that, although many of the finest minds of America and England are represented, the impulse of communication is almost entirely from Roethke outward. Unless the passage of years can show that Roethke generated his poetry in response to letters and other private thoughts put to him by friends and colleagues, he will win by default. Few of his prominent contemporaries have kept silent on Roethke.

"Many meditations destroy," Roethke tells us (Straw for the Fire, p. 151). As we meditate to plumb purpose and design, we not infrequently break in upon the uncontrollable that is beyond our ability to reduce to numbers, geometrical shapes, or imaginative images; most of our meditations (TM proponents must admit) produce that which makes no lasting bond in our experience of the objective world, or that which augurs incoherency in the subjective world. Yet, characteristically, this particular truth did not make it into the Roethke canon.

# Introduction

Some writers would reduce his work to the madman's therapy. But as
with many things of value, that which enables us to create paradoxically dooms us at the same time. Certainly Roethke used his poems
as a means to make him whole, to provide that which he lacked, but
the mirror took his wholeness, and more, back again.

This is part of Roethke's humanity and how he functions for me as
a provocateur. The lesson of his notebook fragments gives insight
into his morality. Experience of life generally is not pleasant,
beautiful, good, etc.--but it is more than worthwhile because it
exercises and educates us to our own capacity. Learning this, we
hopefully feel some obligation to train ourselves to love life,
because love in life is what marks us as human.

Roethke achieves knowledge in his poems and the question of how
he does so is relevant here. Surely, as some scholars have made
clear, his method of composition at times was by juxtaposition of divergent lines or rhythms to see if one had the chemistry to act as
catalyst to the other. The reaction gave the direction to his poem,
but it was one if recorded scientifically would evidence causality;
he would follow one reaction hoping it would lead to another and a
chain with definite links concluding in its own stability. But, as
analogy is the only way to speak of this process, no amount of worldly
rational experience will enable the instigator, or creator, to assign
qualitative significance to it. Another way to think of "Words for
the Wind" is as the poetic equivalent to atomic fission. What god-
like being the poet is to decide that his poem serves humanity!

Since the completion of the main body of this work, at least two
additional books making Roethke their subject have appeared: Theodore
Roethke's Dynamic Vision, by Richard Allen Blessing, Bloomington &
London: Indiana University Press, 1974; and Theodore Roethke: The
Garden Master, by Rosemary Sullivan, Seattle: University of Washing-
ton Press, 1976.

All references preceded by an asterisk (*) have proven unlocate-
able and are cited from various unconfirmed sources.

# Acknowledgments

The preparatory stages of a project such as this one consist almost entirely of the efforts of others. Needless to say, my grateful thanks go out to all of them. Claudia Drum of McKissick Memorial Library, University of South Carolina, was of special assistance during the correspondence stage. Charles W. Mann, Louise K. Kelly and John H. Fulzer of Pattee Library, Pennsylvania State University, gave generously of their time and resources. Karyl Winn, Suzallo Library, University of Washington, has been most gracious in allowing me access to the Roethke collection.

Many others provided information without signing their names. The following people helped with from one to several references, most often in a congenial way. I appreciated their good natures as much as their assistance:

Charlotte Patterson, Pacifica, California

Phoebe Harris, Seattle Public Library

David Wagoner, University of Washington

Frances Green, University of Washington Daily

Beverly Russell, The Seattle Times

Sylvia Sanderlin, Harvard College Library

Ralph J., Mills, Jr., University of Illinois at Chicago Circle

Greg Kuzma, Pebble and The Best Cellar Press

Daphne Dunbar, The Malahat Review

Sharon Steinhoff, Doubleday & Co.

Radcliffe Squires, Michigan Quarterly Review

Zulfikar Ghose, University of Texas

Irene Moran, The Bancroft Library, University of California

Sandy Whitelay, Yale University Library

R. G. Smith, University Library, University of Illinois at
    Urbana-Champaign

Linda T. Zehner, Worcester State College Library

Lillian Newman, McCain Library, Agnes Scott College

Kathryn Samuel, Williams College

Robert Huff, Western Washington State College

Maxine Cushing Gray, _Argus_

Robert D. Monroe, Suzallo Library, University of Washington

Jane L. Houston, Idaho State Library

Marie Morris, Woodruff Library, Emory University

Alice E. Wolff, Kirkus Service, Inc.

Daniel A. Evans, David Bishop Skillman Library, Lafayette College

Judith Bunting, King County (Washington) Library System

Robert D. Stevick, Chairman, Department of English, University
    of Washington

Patricia Bartkowski, Wayne State University

Marjorie Carpenter, Northwestern University Library

James L. Bingham, University of California Library

Marjorie Donker, Western Washington State College

Cameron G. Northouse, South Carolina

Jonathan Barker, Poetry Book Society, The Arts Council of Great
    Britain

X. J. Kennedy, _Countermeasures_

My wife, Sylvia, and my daughter Ianthe, know by this time how
much they contribute to everything I do. To them I say, with this
the work is almost finished.

# Abbreviations of
# Theodore Roethke's Work

CP     The Collected Poems of Theodore Roethke

DD     Dirty Dinky and Other Creatures: Poems for Children

EX     The Exorcism: A Portfolio of Poems

FF     The Far Field

I Am     I Am! Says the Lamb

LS     The Lost Son and Other Poems

OH     Open House

PC     On the Poet and His Craft: Selected Prose of Theodore Roethke

PE     Praise to the End!

PZ     Party at the Zoo

SF     Straw for the Fire: From the Notebooks of Theodore Roethke, 1943–63

SL     Selected Letters of Theodore Roethke

S, SM     Sequence, Sometimes Metaphysical

SP     Selected Poems of Theodore Roethke

WA     The Waking: Poems 1933–1953

WW     Words for the Wind

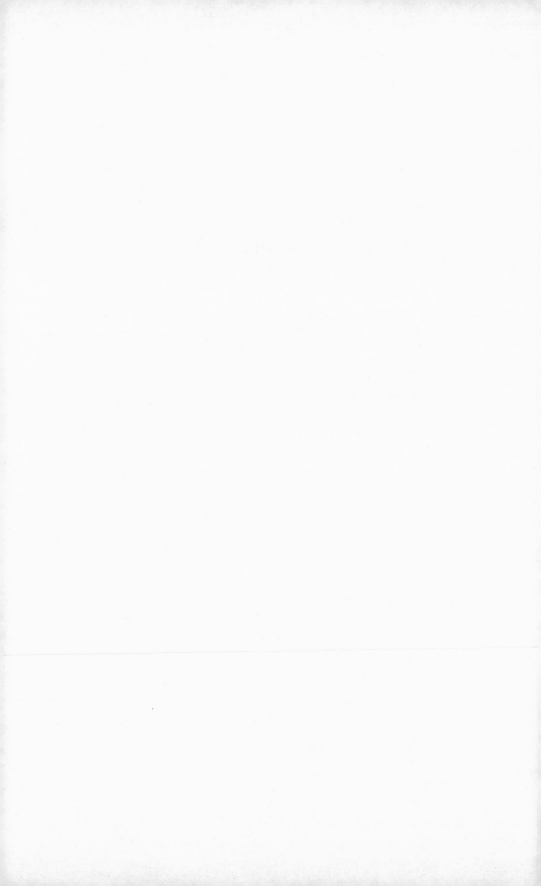

# Writings by Theodore Roethke

**BOOKS**

Open House  New York:  Alfred A. Knopf, 1941.

The Lost Son and Other Poems  Garden City, New York:  Doubleday & Co.,
    1948; London:  John Lehmann, 1949.

Praise to the End!  Garden City, New York:  Doubleday & Co., 1951.

The Waking:  Poems 1933-1953  Garden City, New York:  Doubleday & Co.,
    1954.

The Exorcism:  A Portfolio of Poems  San Francisco:  Mallette Dean,
    1957.  A limited edition of 1150 copies.

Words for the Wind  London:  Secker & Warburg, 1957; Garden City,
    New York:  Doubleday & Co., 1958; Bloomington, Indiana:  Indiana
    University Press, 1961.

I Am! Says the Lamb  Garden City, New York:  Doubleday & Co., 1961.
    With drawings by Robert Leydenfrost.

Party at the Zoo  New York:  Crowell-Collier, Modern Masters Book
    for Children, 1963.  Illustrated by Al Swiller.

Sequence, Sometimes Metaphysical  Iowa City, Iowa:  Stone Wall Press,
    1963.  Limited edition of 330 copies; with wood engravings by
    John Roy.

The Far Field  Garden City, New York:  Doubleday & Co., 1964; London:
    Faber & Faber, 1965.

On The Poet and His Craft:  Selected Prose of Theodore Roethke
    Edited by Ralph J. Mills, Jr.  Seattle and London:  University
    of Washington Press, 1965.

The Collected Poems of Theodore Roethke  Garden City, New York:
    Doubleday & Co., 1966; London:  Faber, 1968.

Selected Letters of Theodore Roethke  Edited by Ralph J. Mills, Jr.
    Seattle and London:  University of Washington Press, 1968;
    London:  Faber, 1970.

Selected Poems of Theodore Roethke  Edited by Beatrice Roethke.
    London:  Faber, 1969.

Straw for the Fire:  From the Notebooks of Theodore Roethke, 1943-63
    Edited and arranged by David Wagoner.  Garden City, New York:
    Doubleday & Co., 1972.

Dirty Dinky and Other Creatures:  Poems for Children  Selected by
    Beatrice Roethke and Stephen Lushington.  Garden City, New York:
    Doubleday & Co., 1973.


## ESSAYS AND NONFICTION

### 1936

"Some Poetry in Review."  New Republic, LXXXVII (July 15), 305.  A
    review of Ideas of Order by Wallace Stevens.

"Books in Brief."  New Republic, LXXXVII (July 22), 333.  A review
    of This Modern Poetry by Babette Deutsch.  Signed "T.R."

"Books in Brief."  New Republic, LXXXVIII (August 26), 83-84.  A review
    of A Spectacle for Scholars by Winnifred Welles.  Signed "T.R."

### 1937

"Poets' Corner."  New Republic, XCIII (November 17), 52.  A review of
    The Last Look and Other Poems by Mark Van Doren.  (Reprinted PC.)

"Poets' Page."  New Republic, XCIII (December 29), 234.  A review
    of Country Men by James Hearst.  Signed "T.R."

### 1938

"Facing the Guns."  Poetry, LII (April), 43-46.  A review of And
    Spain Sings:  Fifty Loyalist Ballads, edited by M. J. Benardete
    and Rolfe Humphries.  (Reprinted PC.)

### 1939

"Evidence of Growth."  Poetry, LIII (March), 336-338.  A review of
    Concerning the Young by Willard Maas.  (Reprinted PC.)

"Ben Belitt's First Volume"  Poetry, LIII (January), 214-217.  A
    review of The Five-Fold Mesh.  (Reprinted PC).

2

## Writings by Theodore Roethke

"Verse in Rehearsal."  Portfolio (Pennsylvania State University), I
     (September), 3, 15-16.  (Reprinted PC.)


### 1942

"Obiter Dicta."  Poetry, LX (May), 109-110.  A review of The Alert
     by Wilfrid Gibson; and Gautama The Enlightened by John Masefield.
     (Reprinted PC.)


### 1946

"Meditations of a Sensitive Man."  Poetry, LXVII (January), 218-221.
     A review of A Lost Season by Roy Fuller.  (Reprinted PC.)


### 1947

"Integrity of Spirit."  Poetry, LXIX (January), 220-223.  A review of
     The Earth-Bound by Janet Lewis.  (Reprinted PC.)


### 1950

"Last Class."  Botteghe Oscure (Rome), V, 400-406.  (Reprinted PC.)

"Open Letter."  In Mid-Century American Poets.  Edited by John Ciardi.
     New York:  Twayne Publishers, pp. 67-72.


### 1952

"One Ring-tailed Roarer to Another."  Poetry, LXXXI (December),
     184-186.  A review of In Country Sleep and Other Poems by Dylan
     Thomas.  Signed "Winterset Rothberg."  (Reprinted PC; and Dylan
     Thomas:  The Legend and the Poet:  A Collection of Biographical
     and Critical Essays.  Edited by E. W. Tedlock.  London:
     Heinemann.)

"The Teaching Poet."  Poetry, LXXIX (February), 250-255.  (Reprinted
     PC.)


### 1953

"Five American Poets."  New World Writing:  Fourth Mentor Selection.
     New York:  The New American Library, pp. 83-85.  (Reprinted PC.)

"An American Poet Introduces Himself and His Poems."  BBC Broadcast,
     July 30, Disc #SLO 34254.  (Reprinted PC.)

## 1954

"Dylan Thomas: Elegy," as part of "Dylan Thomas: Memories and
Appreciations." Encounter, II (January), 11. (Reprinted PC;
and without title in Dylan Thomas: The Legend and the Poet: A
Collection of Biographical and Critical Essays. Edited by
E. W. Tedlock. London: Heinemann.)

"I Cry Love! Love!," a reading and commentary, recorded by KPFA in
Berkeley, California, March 24 and 25. (Partially reprinted in
McLeod, James R., "Bibliographic Notes on the Creative Process
and Sources of Roethke's 'The Lost Son' Sequence." Northwest
Review, XI [Summer 1971], 99.)

## 1955

"Theodore Roethke." Twentieth Century Authors, First Supplement.
Edited by Stanley J. Kunitz. New York: H. W. Wildon, pp. 837-
838. (Reprinted PC.)

## 1957

"Last Class." College English, XVIII (May), 383-386. (Reprinted
PC.)

"Theodore Roethke Writes...." Poetry Book Society Bulletin (London),
No. 16 (December), unpaginated (front page). (Reprinted PC.)

"Richard Selig," as part of "Tribute to Richard Selig--1929-1957."
Gemini: Oxford and Cambridge Magazine, I (Winter 1957-1958),
62-63. (Reprinted PC.)

## 1959

"How to Write Like Somebody Else." Yale Review, XLVIII (March),
336-343. (Reprinted PC.)

## 1960

"How to Write Like Somebody Else." London Magazine, VII (October),
49-55. (Reprinted PC.)

"Some Remarks on Rhythm." Poetry, XCVII (October), 35-46. (Reprinted
PC; and untitled in Brooks, Cleanth and Robert Penn Warren, eds.
Conversations on the Craft of Poetry. New York: Holt, Rinehart
and Winston, 1961. Pp. 48-62.)

## 1961

"The Poetry of Louise Bogan." Critical Quarterly, III (Summer),
142-150. (Reprinted PC.)

"Theodore Roethke--Comment," as part of "The Poet and His Critics:
A Symposium edited by Anthony Ostroff." New World Writing,
Number 19. Philadelphia: J. B. Lippincott, pp. 214-219.
(Reprinted The Contemporary Poet as Artist and Critic. Edited
by Anthony Ostroff. Boston: Little, Brown, 1964. Pp. 49-53.)

## 1962

Introduction to "Words for the Wind." Poet's Choice. Edited by Paul
Engle and Joseph T. Langland. New York: Dial Press, pp. 96-100.

## 1963

"A Tirade Turning." Encounter, XXI (December), 44-45. Signed
"Winterset Rothberg." (Reprinted PC.)

## 1965

"On Identity," as part of "Roethke Remembered." Show, V (May),
11-12, 15. (Reprinted PC.)

"Some Self-Analysis," as part of "Roethke Remembered." Show, V
(May), 11. (Reprinted PC.)

"What Do I Like," excerpt from "Some Remarks on Rhythm." The Structure of Verse: Modern Essays on Prosody. Edited by H. S. Gross.
Greenwich, Conn.: Fawcett Publications, pp. 218-232.

"A Word to the Instructor." Published for the first time. On The
Poet and His Craft: Selected Prose of Theodore Roethke,
pp. 52-56.

## 1967

"The Poetry of Louise Bogan." Michigan Quarterly Review, VI (Fall),
246-251. (Reprinted PC.)

## POETRY

### 1930

"Lost," as part of "Three Poems." The Harp, VI (May/June), 8.

"Method," as part of "Three Poems." The Harp, VI (May/June), 8.
    (Reprinted The Glass House, p. 66.)

"To Darkness," as part of "Three Poems." The Harp, VI (May/June), 8.
    (Reprinted The Glass House, p. 66.)

### 1931

"The Conqueror." Commonweal, XIV (October 7), 544.

### 1932

"Bound," as part of "Two Poems." Poetry, XL (September), 316.

"Epidermal Macabre." Saturday Review of Literature, VIII (May 7),
    709. (Reprinted OH; Wa; WW; CP.)

"Fugitive," as part of "Two Poems." Poetry, XL (September), 316-317.

"Second Version." Sewanee Review, XL (January/March), 88.

"Silence." New Republic, LXIX (January 20), 263. (Reprinted OH; CP.)

### 1933

"The Buds Now Stretch." The Adelphi, VI (April), 9.

### 1934

"Autumnal." The Adelphi, VIII (September), 409. (Reprinted, with
    slight revision, as part 3 of "The Coming of the Cold" in OH; CP.)

"Death Piece." Nation, CXXXVIII (May 2), 511. (Reprinted OH; Wa;
    WW; CP.)

"Essay." American Poetry Journal, 17th monthly issue (November),
    p. 5.

"Exhortation." American Poetry Journal, 17th monthly issue
    (November), p. 6.

"Genius." Atlantic Monthly, CLIII (May), 550.

"I Sought a Measure." American Poetry Journal, 17th monthly issue
    (November), p. 4. (Printed under original title, "Unessential
    Truth," SL, p. 23.)

"No Bird." Atlantic Monthly, CLIV (November), 543. Reprinted OH;
    Wa; WW; CP.)

"Now We the Two." American Poetry Journal, 17th monthly issue
    (November), p. 5.

"Prepare Thyself for Change." American Poetry Journal, 17th monthly
    issue (November), p. 6.

"Some Day I'll Step." American Poetry Journal, 17th monthly issue
    (November), p. 4. (Printed under original title, "More Pure Than
    Flight," SL, pp. 23-24.)

"The Knowing Heart." American Poetry Journal, 17th monthly issue
    (November), p. 6.

"This Light." American Poetry Journal, 17th monthly issue (November)
    p. 3. (Reprinted The Poet's Work. Edited by John Holmes. New
    York: Oxford University Press, 1938; as "This Various Light,"
    SL, p. 10.)

"To My Sister." The Adelphi, VIII (August), 300; New York Herald
    Tribune, September 2, Sect. II, p. 8. (Reprinted OH; Wa; WW; CP.)


## 1935

"Feud." New Republic, LXXXIV (September 11), 123. (Reprinted OH;
    CP.)

"Prayer." New Republic, LXXXIII (July 10), 242. (Reprinted OH; Wa;
    WW; CP.)

"The Fugitive." Trial Balances. Edited by Ann Winslow. New York:
    MacMillan. (Reprinted SL, p. 25.)


## 1936

"Genesis." Nation, CXLII (June 24), 807. (Reprinted OH; CP.)

WILLIAM F. MAAG LIBRARY
YOUNGSTOWN STATE UNIVERSITY

"'Long Live the Weeds.'" Poetry, XLVIII (July), 203. (Earlier version, "Hurray for Weeds," in SL, p. 33. Reprinted OH; Wa; WW; CP.)

"Open House." See "Strange Distortion."

"Strange Distortion." Scribner's Magazine, XCIX (May), 311. (Reprinted as "Open House," OH; Wa; WW; CP.)

## 1937

"Autumnal," as part of "Two Poems." New Republic, XCII (September 1), 96. (Reprinted as part 2 of "The Coming of the Cold" in OH; CP.)

"Hay-Fever Lament." New Yorker, XIII (August 14), 58. (Reprinted SL, p. 43.)

"In Praise of Prairie." New Republic, XCVIII (December 22), 203. (Reprinted OH; CP.)

"In the Time of Change." Atlantic Monthly, CLIX (January), 47.

"Lines Upon Leaving a Sanitarium." New Yorker, XIII (March 13), 30. (Reprinted CP.)

"Meditation in Hydrotherapy." New Yorker, XIII (May 15), 87. (Reprinted CP.)

"Prayer Before Study." New Yorker, XIII (August 28), 45. (Reprinted OH; CP.)

"Reply to Censure." Poetry, LI (November), 80. (Reprinted OH; CP.)

"Statement." Commonweal, XXVII (December 31), 261. (Reprinted SL, pp. 57-58.)

"The Coming of the Cold." For three parts, see "Autumnnal," 1934, 1937, 1938.

"The Heron," as part of "Two Poems." New Republic, XCII (September 1), 96; New York Herald Tribune, September 12, Sect. II, p. 10. (Reprinted OH; Wa; WW; I Am; CP; DD.)

## 1938

"Against Disaster," as part of "Seven Poems." Poetry, LIII (December), 140. (Reprinted OH; CP.)

"Autumnal." <u>Christian Science Monitor</u>, September 8, p. 9. (Reprinted as part 1 of "The Coming of the Cold," <u>OH</u>; <u>CP</u>.)

"Hay-Fever Lament." <u>The Woman's Journal</u>, (June), page unknown. (Reprinted <u>SL</u>, p. 43.)

"Interlude." <u>New Republic</u>, XCVIII (February 2), 361. (Reprinted <u>OH</u>; <u>Wa</u>; <u>WW</u>; <u>CP</u>.)

"Prognosis," as part of "Seven Poems." <u>Poetry</u>, LIII (December), 138. (Reprinted <u>OH</u>; <u>CP</u>.)

"Sign Though No Sign." <u>Sewanee Review</u>, XLVI (January/March), 3.

"The Bat." <u>New Republic</u>, XCV (May 18), 51. (Reprinted <u>OH</u>; <u>Wa</u>; <u>WW</u>; <u>I Am</u>; <u>CP</u>; <u>DD</u>.)

"The Bringer of Tidings," as part of "Seven Poems." <u>Poetry</u>, LIII (December), 141-142. (Reprinted <u>SL</u>, p. 46.)

"The Buds Now Stretch." <u>New York Times</u>, November 9, p. 22.

"The Light Comes Brighter." <u>Atlantic Monthly</u>, CLXI (March), 340; <u>New York Herald Tribune</u>, February 20, Sect. II, p. 10. (Reprinted <u>OH</u>; <u>CP</u>.)

"The Pause," as part of "Seven Poems." <u>Poetry</u>, LIII (December), 141.

"The Reckoning," as part of "Seven Poems." <u>Poetry</u>, LIII (December), 139. (Reprinted <u>OH</u>; <u>CP</u>.)

"The Signals," as part of "Seven Poems." <u>Poetry</u>, LIII (December), 139-140. (Reprinted <u>OH</u>; <u>CP</u>.)

"The Summons," as part of "Seven Poems." <u>Poetry</u>, LIII (December), 142-143. (Reprinted <u>SL</u>, pp. 54-55.)

"The Unextinguished." <u>Saturday Review of Literature</u>, XVIII (July 23), 7. (Reprinted <u>OH</u>; <u>CP</u>.)

"The Victims." <u>Twentieth Century Verse</u> (London), XII/XIII (September/October), 105-106. (Reprinted <u>SL</u>, p. 67.)

"Verse with Allusions." <u>Atlantic Monthly</u>, CLXI (May), 700. (Reprinted <u>OH</u>; <u>CP</u>.)


## 1939

"Academic." <u>New Verse</u> (London), NS I (May 1939), 41; <u>Partisan Review</u>, VI (Winter), 39. (Reprinted <u>OH</u>; <u>Wa</u>; <u>WW</u>; <u>CP</u>.)

"After Loss." New York Times, September 27, p. 24.

"Ballad of the Clairvoyant Widow." Partisan Review, VI (Fall),
    18-19. (Reprinted OH; CP.)

"For an Amorous Lady." New Yorker, XIV (January 7), 25. (Reprinted
    OH; CP.)

"Idyll." New Yorker, XV (August 26), 51. (Reprinted OH; CP.)

"Poetaster." New Republic, CI (November 29), 164. (Reprinted OH;
    CP.)

"Praise." New Republic, CI (December 20), 254.

"Random Political Reflections." New Republic, XCVIII, (March 1), 98.

"Slow Season." Yale Review, XXIX (Summer), 89. (Reprinted OH; CP;
    earlier version SL, 95.)

"Summer Wind." New Yorker, XV (July 22, 1939), 58. (Printed as
    "Windy Weather," SL, p. 66.)

"The Auction." Poetry, LIV (May 1939), 69. (Reprinted OH; CP.)

"The Bat." New York Times, May 24, 1939, p. 22. (Reprinted OH; Wa;
    WW: I Am; CP; DD.)


1940

"Highway: Michigan." New Republic, CII (May 6, 1939), 608.
    (Reprinted OH; CP.)

"Lull." New Republic, CII (February 12, 1940), 209. (Reprinted OH;
    CP.)

"Night Journey." New Yorker, XVI (June 8, 1940), 34. (Reprinted OH;
    Wa; WW; CP.)

"Orders for the Day." Poetry, LVI (May 1940), 75. (Reprinted OH; CP.)

"The Pure Poets." Childhood Education, XVII (November 1940), 134.

"The Search." American Prefaces, V (May 1940), 118.

"Vernal Sentiment." New Yorker, XVI (March 30, 1940), 65.
    (Reprinted OH; Wa; WW; I Am; CP.)

# Writings by Theodore Roethke

## 1941

"After Loss." Harrisburg (Penn.) Patriot, April 11, 1941, p. 22.

"City Limits." Partisan Review, VIII (November/December 1941), 459. (Reprinted SL, p. 93.)

"Mid-Country Blow." Open House. (Reprinted Wa; WW; CP.)

"My Dim-Wit Cousin." Open House. (Reprinted CP.)

"On the Road to Woodlawn." Open House. (Reprinted Wa; WW; CP; earlier, untitled version SL, p. 76.)

"Poem with a Dash of Houseman." New York Herald Tribune, March 5, p. 26, in "Sports Here and There" Column.

"Sale," as part of "Two Poems." Poetry, LVII (February), 292. (Reprinted OH; Wa; WW; CP.)

"Second Shadow," as part of "Two Poems." Poetry, LVII (February), 293. (Reprinted SL, pp. 94-95.)

"The Adamant." Open House. (Reprinted Wa; WW; CP.)

"The Cycle." Virginia Quarterly Review, XVII (Autumn), 538. (Reprinted LS; Wa; WW; CP.)

"The Favorite." Open House. (Reprinted CP.)

"The Gentle." Open House. (Reprinted CP.)

"The Premonition." Open House. (Reprinted CP.)

"The Reminder." Open House. (Reprinted CP.)

## 1942

"Dedicatory Poem." Centre Daily Times (State College, Penn.), April 13, p. 1; Mineral Industries, XI (May), 3.

"Double Feature." See "Episode Seven."

"Episode Seven." Commonweal, XXXVI (June 12), 179. (Reprinted as "Double Feature" in LS; CP. Early version of "Double Feature," SL, p. 94.)

"My Papa's Waltz." Harper's Bazaar, 2761 (February), p. 16. (Reprinted LS; Wa; WW; I Am; CP; DD.)

"The Minimal." Harper's Bazaar, 2271 (November), p. 103. (Reprinted
    LS; Wa; WW; CP.)

"Wind Over the City." Harper's Bazaar, 2764 (April), p. 114.


1943

"Dolor," as part of "Four Poems." Poetry, LXIII (November), 69-70.
    (Reprinted LS; Wa; WW; CP.)

"Elegy." Poetry Quarterly (England), V (Summer), 68. (Reprinted SL,
    p. 56.)

"Florist's Root Cellar," as part of "Four Poems." Poetry, LXIII
    (November), 69. (Reprinted as "Root Cellar," LS; Wa; WW; I Am;
    CP.)

"Germinal." New Yorker, XIX (April 3), 17. (Reprinted SL, p. 99.)

"Growth." American Mercury, LVI (March), 366.

"Pickle Belt." American Mercury, LVI (May), 618. (Reprinted LS; Wa;
    WW; CP.)

"River Incident." New Yorker, XIX (September 11), 67. (Reprinted
    LS; CP. Slightly different version, SL, p. 55.)

"Root Cellar." See "Florist's Root Cellar."

"Summer School Marms," as part of "Four Poems." Poetry, LXIII
    (November), 68-69.

"The Gossips," as part of "Four Poems." Poetry, LXIII (November),
    68.


1944

"Night Crow." Saturday Review, XXVII (November 11), 12. (Reprinted
    LS; Wa; WW; CP; DD.)


1946

"Carnations." New Republic, CXIV (February 18), 244. (Reprinted
    LS; Wa; WW; I Am; CP.)

"Child on Top of a Greenhouse." New Republic, CXIV (February 11),
    181. (Reprinted LS; Wa; WW; I Am; CP; DD.)

"Flower-Dump." New Republic, CXIV (February 11), 181. (Reprinted LS; Wa; WW; I Am; CP.)

"Forcing House." New Yorker, XXII (October 5), 79. (Reprinted LS; Wa; WW; I Am; CP.)

"Fruit Bin." New Republic, CXIV (February 11), 181.

"Last Words." Harper's Bazaar, 2812 (April), p. 239. (Reprinted LS; Wa; WW; CP.)

"Moss-Gathering." New Republic, CXIV (February 18), 244. (Reprinted LS; Wa; WW; I Am; CP.)

"Old Florist." Harper's, CXCII (February), 174. (Reprinted LS; Wa; WW; I Am; CP.)

"The Return." Poetry, LXVIII (August), 250. (Reprinted LS; Wa; WW; CP.)

"Weed Puller." New Republic, CXIV (February 25), 282. (Reprinted LS; Wa; WW; I Am; CP.)


## 1947

"Big Wind." American Scholar, XVII (Winter 1947/1948), 56-57. (Reprinted LS; Wa; WW; I Am; CP.)

"Judge Not." Sewanee Review, LV (Spring), 258-259. (Reprinted LS; CP.)

"The Long Alley." Poetry, LXX (July), 198-201. (Reprinted LS; PE; Wa; WW; CP.)

"The Lost Son." Sewanee Review, LV (Spring), 252-258. (Reprinted LS; PE; Wa; WW; CP. An excerpt from this poem, "The Shape of a Rat," reprinted I Am; DD.)

"The Shape of the Fire." Partisan Review, XIV (September/October), 486-488. (Reprinted LS; PE; Wa; WW; CP.)


## 1948

"A Field of Light." The Tiger's Eye, III (March 15), 15-16. (Reprinted LS; PE; Wa; WW; CP.)

"Cuttings." The Lost Son and Other Poems. (Reprinted Wa; WW; I Am; CP.)

"Cuttings (Later)." <u>Harper's Bazaar</u>, 2834 (February), p. 227.
(Entitled "Cuttings" in original periodical appearance. Reprinted as above in <u>LS</u>; <u>Wa</u>; <u>WW</u>; <u>I Am</u>; <u>CP</u>.)

"Orchids." <u>The Lost Son and Other Poems</u>. (Reprinted <u>Wa</u>; <u>WW</u>; <u>I Am</u>;
<u>CP</u>.)

"Praise to the End!" <u>Botteghe Oscure</u>, II, 288-291. (Reprinted <u>PE</u>;
<u>Wa</u>; <u>WW</u>; <u>CP</u>.)

"The Waking." <u>The Lost Son and Other Poems</u>. (Reprinted <u>CP</u>.)

"Transplanting." <u>Mademoiselle</u>, April, p. 148. (Reprinted <u>LS</u>; <u>Wa</u>;
<u>WW</u>; <u>I Am</u>; <u>CP</u>.)


<u>1949</u>

"Unfold! Unfold!" <u>Partisan Review</u>, XVI (November), 1098-1100.
(Reprinted <u>PE</u>; <u>Wa</u>; <u>WW</u>; <u>CP</u>.)


<u>1950</u>

"A Light Breather." <u>Kenyon Review</u>, XII (Summer), 475. (Reprinted
<u>Wa</u>; <u>WW</u>; <u>CP</u>.)

"Bring the Day!" <u>Botteghe Oscure</u>, VI, 445-447. (Printed here as
untitled Part II of "Give Way Ye Gates." Reprinted <u>PE</u>; <u>Wa</u>; <u>WW</u>;
<u>CP</u>.)

"Cuttings (Later)." <u>Arena: New Zealand and Overseas Writing,
American Poetry Number</u>. Edited by Gustav Davidson. XXIII, 12.
(Reprinted from <u>LS</u>. Reprinted <u>Wa</u>; <u>WW</u>; <u>I Am</u>; <u>CP</u>.)

"Elegy for Jane." <u>Kenyon Review</u>, XII (Summer), 476. (Reprinted
<u>Wa</u>; <u>WW</u>; <u>CP</u>.)

"Give Way Ye Gates." <u>Botteghe Oscure</u>, VI, 477-449. (Printed here
under this one title are three poems: the above; "Bring the
Day!"; and "I Need, I Need." Reprinted <u>PE</u>; <u>Wa</u>; <u>WW</u>; <u>CP</u>.)

"I Cry Love! Love!" <u>Hudson Review</u>, III (Summer), 217-218. (Reprinted
<u>PE</u>; <u>Wa</u>; <u>WW</u>; <u>CP</u>.)

"I Need, I Need." <u>Botteghe Oscure</u>, VI, 443-445. (Printed here as
untitled part I of "Give Way Ye Gates." Reprinted <u>PE</u>; <u>Wa</u>; <u>WW</u>;
<u>CP</u>. An excerpt from this poem, "A One Is, A Two Is," reprinted
<u>DD</u>.)

"Old Song." Lyric set to music by Douglas Moore. New York: Carl Fischer, Inc.

"Praise to the End!" Sewanee Review, LVIII (January/March), 114-117. (Reprinted PE; Wa; WW; CP.)

"The Ceiling," as part of "Four Children's Poems." Poetry, LXXVI (September), 332. (Reprinted I Am; CP.)

"The Chair," as part of "Four Children's Poems." Poetry, LXXVI (September), 332. (Reprinted I Am; CP.)

"The Cow," as part of "Four Children's Poems." Poetry, LXXVI (September), 332. (Reprinted WW; I Am; CP; DD.)

"The Kitty-Cat Bird," as part of "Fables in Song." Flair, I (May), 115. (Reprinted I Am; CP; DD.)

"The Lamb," as part of "Fables in Song." Flair, I (May), 115. (Reprinted I Am; CP; DD.)

"The Monotony Song," as part of "Fables in Song." Flair I (May), 115. (Reprinted I Am; CP.)

"The Serpent," as part of "Four Poems for Children." Poetry, LXXVI (September), 331. (Reprinted WW; I Am; CP; DD.)

"The Sloth," as part of "Fables in Song." Flair, I (May), 114. (Reprinted WW; I Am; CP; DD.)

"The Visitant." Sewanee Review, LVIII (January/March), 109-110. (Reprinted Wa; WW; CP.)

"Where Knock Is Open Wide." Sewanee Review, LVIII (January/March), 110-113. (Reprinted PE; Wa; WW; CP. An excerpt from this poem, "Once Upon a Tree," reprinted DD.)

## 1951

"Heard in a Violent Ward." See "Words in the Violent Ward."

"O Lull Me, Lull Me," as part of "Two Poems." Poetry, LXXVIII (September), 314-315. (Reprinted PE; Wa; WW; CP.)

"Sensibility! O La!," as part of "Two Poems." Poetry, LXXVIII (September), 311-313. (Reprinted PE; Wa; WW; CP.)

"Song." Botteghe Oscure, VIII, 282-283. (Reprinted CP.)

"The Lady and the Bear." Flair, II (January), 119. A slightly altered version reprinted WW; I Am; CP; DD.)

"The Waking." New York Times Book Review, February 11, p. 2.
(Reprinted from LS. Reprinted CP.)

"To an Anthologist," as part of "Two Epigrams." Poetry, LXXVII
(February), 262.

"Words in the Violent Ward," as part of "Two Epigrams." Poetry,
LXXVII (February), 262. (Reprinted as "Heard in a Violent Ward,"
FF; CP.)


## 1952

"Frau Bauman, Frau Schmidt, and Frau Schwartze." New Yorker, XXVIII
(March 29), 38. (Reprinted WW for the first time, as part of LS;
I Am; CP, some editions.)

"Goo-Girl," as part of "Poems for Children." New World Writing:
Second Mentor Selection. New York: The New American Library,
p. 224. (Reprinted I Am; CP.)

"Myrtle," as part of "Poems for Children." New World Writing: Second
Mentor Selection. New York: The New American Library, p. 224.
(Reprinted I Am; CP; DD.)

"Myrtle's Cousin," as part of "Poems for Children." New World Writing: Second Mentor Selection. New York: The New American
Library, p. 224. (Reprinted I Am; CP.)

"Old Lady's Winter Words." Kenyon Review, XIV (Winter), 60-62.
(Reprinted Wa; WW; CP.)

"O, Thou Opening, O." Poetry, LXXXI (October), 64-67. (Reprinted Wa
as part of PE; WW; CP.)

"The Boy and the Bush," as part of "Poems for Children." New World
Writing: Second Mentor Selection. New York: The New American
Library, p. 223. (Reprinted I Am; CP; DD.)

"The Bug." New Yorker, XXVIII (August 9), 30.

"The Changeling." Botteghe Oscure, X, 239-242. (Reprinted CP.)

"The Dance." Atlantic Monthly, CXC (November), 53. (Reprinted as
Sect. I of "Four for Sir John Davies," Wa; WW; CP.)

"The Partner." Partisan Review, XIX (September/October), 558.
(Reprinted as Sect. II of "Four for Sir John Davies," Wa; WW;
CP.)

"The Yak," as part of "Poems for Children." New World Writing:
Second Mentor Selection. New York: The New American Library,
p. 223. (Reprinted I Am; CP; DD.)


1953

"Dinky." Hudson Review, V (Winter), 516. (Reprinted WW; I Am; CP;
DD.)

"Pastorale." Nation, CLXXVI (May 9), 398. (Reprinted as "The
Siskins," WW; CP.)

"Song for the Squeeze Box." Hudson Review, V (Winter), 514-515.
(Reprinted WW; CP.)

"The Dance." New Statesman and Nation, November 7, p. 568. (Reprinted as Sect. I of "Four for Sir John Davies," Wa; WW; CP.)

"The Siskins." See "Pastorale."

"The Vigil." New World Writing: Fourth Mentor Selection. New York:
The New American Library, pp. 96-97. (Reprinted as Sect. IV of
"Four for Sir John Davies," Wa; WW; CP.)

"The Waking." New World Writing: Fourth Mentor Selection. New York:
The New American Library. Pp. 97-98; New York Times Book Review,
September 27, 1953, p. 2. (Reprinted Wa; WW; CP.)

"The Wraith." Hudson Review, V (Winter), 515-516. (Reprinted as
Sect. III of "Four for Sir John Davies," Wa; WW; CP.)

"Words for the Wind." Botteghe Oscure, XII, 211-214. (Reprinted
WW; CP.)


1954

"Elegy." Botteghe Oscure, XIV, 226. (Reprinted WW; CP.)

"Elegy for Jane." London Times Literary Supplement, Special Section,
"American Writing Today," September 17, p. liv.

"Follies of Adam." Partisan Review, XXI (November), 650-651.
(Reprinted CP.)

"Four for Sir John Davies." See individual sections, 1952 and 1953:
"The Dance," "The Partner," "The Wraith," and "The Vigil."

"I Knew a Woman." See "Poem."

"Love's Progress." Botteghe Oscure, XIV, 225-226. (Reprinted WW; CP.)

"Poem." London Times Literary Supplement, Special Section, "American Writing Today," September 17, p. lxvi; as part of "Four Poets on Love." Harper's Bazaar, 2917 (December), p. 101. (Reprinted as "I Knew a Woman," WW; CP.)

"'The Shimmer of Evil.'" Botteghe Oscure, XIV, 224. (Reprinted WW; CP.)

"The Visitant." Encounter, III (November), 58. (Reprinted Wa; WW; CP.)

"The Waking." London Times Literary Supplement, January 15, p. 35. (Reprinted Wa; WW; CP.)

"Transplanting." New York Times Book Review, April 25, p. 2. (Reprinted from Wa. Reprinted WW; CP.)

"Words for the Wind." Encounter, II (March), 16-17. (Reprinted WW; CP.)

## 1955

"All the Earth, All the Air." Hudson Review, VIII (Spring), 58-59; The Listener, September 8, p. 374. (Reprinted WW; CP.)

"A Rouse for Stevens: To Be Sung in a Young Poet's Saloon." Seven Arts, Number Three. Edited by Fernando Puma. Indian Hills, Colo.: The Falcon's Wing Press, p. 117. (Reprinted, with some revisions, CP.)

"Elegy." New Republic, CXXXIII (September 12), 19. (Reprinted WW; CP. Earlier version, entitled "The Stumbling," SL, pp. 197-198.)

"First Meditation." See "Old Woman's Meditation."

"His Words," as Sect. I of "The Dying Man." Encounter, V (December), 50. (Reprinted WW; CP.)

"Love's Progress." New Republic, CXXXII (April 11), 27. (Reprinted WW; CP.)

"Old Woman's Meditation." Partisan Review, XXII (Fall), 491-494. (Reprinted as "First Meditation," Sect. I of "Meditations of an Old Woman," WW; CP.)

"Pipling." New Pocket Anthology. Edited by Oscar Williams. Cleveland: World Publishing, p. 475. (Reprinted, with slight revisions, as Sect. I of "Three Epigrams," CP.)

"Snake." New Yorker, XXXI (September 17), 48. (Reprinted WW; I Am; CP; DD.)

"The Beast." Hudson Review, VIII (Spring), 60. (Reprinted WW; CP.)

"The Dream." New Yorker, XXXI (June 4), 34. (Reprinted WW; CP.)

"The Dying Man." See individual sections, 1955, 1956 and 1957: "His Words," "What Now?," "The Wall," "The Exulting," and "They Sing, They Sing."

"'The Shimmer of Evil.'" New Republic, CXXXIII (August 29), 19. (Reprinted WW; CP.)

"The Slug." New Republic, CXXXII (August 1), 18. (Reprinted as "Slug," WW; I Am; CP; DD.)

"The Song." Hudson Review, VIII (Spring), 59-60. (Reprinted WW; CP.)

"The Voice." New Yorker, XXXI (July 9), 28. (Reprinted WW; CP.)

"The Wall," as Sect. III of "The Dying Man." Encounter, V (December), 51. (Reprinted WW; CP.)

"What Now?," as Sect. II of "The Dying Man." Encounter, V (December), 50-51. (Reprinted WW; CP.)

"Words for the Wind." Harper's Bazaar, 2926 (September), pp. 90-91. (Reprinted WW; CP.)


## 1956

"First Meditation." See "Old Woman's Meditation."

"His Words," as Sect. I of "The Dying Man." Atlantic Monthly, CXCVII (May), 48. (Reprinted WW; CP.)

"I'm Here." New Yorker, XXXII (December 15), 39. (Reprinted as Sect. II of "Meditations of an Old Woman," WW; CP.)

"I Think the Dead are Tender. Shall We Kiss?" as I of "Two Poems." Kenyon Review, XVIII (Winter), 120. (Reprinted as "She," WW; CP.)

"I Waited." as II of "Two Poems." Kenyon Review, XVIII (Winter), 121. (Reprinted S,SM; FF; CP.)

"Meditations of an Old Woman." See individual sections, 1956, 1957 and 1958: "First Meditation," "I'm Here," "Her Becoming," "Third Meditation," "Fourth Meditation," "An Old Lady Muses," and "What Can I Tell My Bones?"

"Memory." Atlantic Monthly, CXCVII (April), 41.  (Reprinted WW; CP.)

"Old Woman's Meditation." London Magazine, III (June), 13-16.
   (Reprinted as "First Meditation," Sect. I of "Meditations of an
   Old Woman," WW; CP.)

"She." The Listener, November 29, p. 873; See also "I Think the
   Dead Are Tender.  Shall We Kiss?" (Reprinted WW; CP.)

"Song:  Under a Southern Wind." Criterion Book of American Verse.
   Edited by W. H. Auden.  New York:  Criterion, pp. 253-254.  (An
   excerpt from "Words for the Wind.")

"The Beast." New Statesman and Nation, March 17, p. 248.  (Reprinted
   WW; CP.)

"The Dream." London Times Literary Supplement, August 17, p. xxi.
   (Reprinted WW; CP.)

"The Dying Man." See individual sections, 1955, 1956 and 1957:
   "His Words," "What Now?" "The Wall," "The Exulting," and "They
   Sing, They Sing."

"The Exulting," as Sect. IV of "The Dying Man." Atlantic Monthly,
   CXCVII (May), 49.  (Reprinted WW; CP.)

"The Other." Botteghe Oscure, XVIII, 235-236.  (Reprinted WW; CP.)

"The Sententious Man." Poetry London-New York, I:2 (Winter), 27-28.
   (Reprinted WW; CP.)

"The Siskins." The Listener, October 18, p. 606.  (Reprinted WW; CP.)

"The Small." New Yorker, XXXII (September 8), 32.  (Reprinted WW;
   CP.)

"The Wall," as Sect. III of "The Dying Man." Atlantic Monthly,
   CXCVII (May), 49.  (Reprinted WW; CP.)

"They Sing." New Yorker, XXXII (August 18), 22.  (Reprinted as "They
   Sing, They Sing," Sect. V of "The Dying Man," WW; CP.)

"They Sing, They Sing." See "They Sing."

"What Now?," as Sect. II of "The Dying Man." Atlantic Monthly,
   CXCVII (May), 48.  (Reprinted WW; CP.)


1957

"An Old Lady Muses." Harper's Bazaar, 2950 (September), pp. 246-247.
   (Reprinted as "Fourth Meditation," WW; CP.)

# Writings by Theodore Roethke

"A Walk in Late Summer." New Yorker, XXXIII (September 7), 36.
   (Reprinted American edition only of WW; CP.)

"Elegy." London Magazine, IV (July), 13. (Reprinted WW; CP. Early
   version entitled "The Stumbling," SL, pp. 197-198.)

"Fourth Meditation." See "Third Meditation."

"Reply to a Lady Editor." Poetry London-New York, I:3 (Winter), 27.
   (Reprinted WW; CP.)

"The Cantankerous One." New Yorker, XXXIII (November 30), 50.
   (Reprinted as "The Surly One," WW; CP.)

"The Centaur." New Poems by American Poets, Number 2. Edited by
   Rolfe Humphries. New York: Ballantine Books, p. 135. (Re-
   printed, with slight revision, as Sect. III of "Three Epigrams,"
   CP.)

"The Exorcism." The Exorcism: A Portfolio of Poems. San Francisco:
   Mallette Dean. (Reprinted American edition only of WW; CP. For
   early material, later incorporated, see SL, p. 100.)

"The Exulting." London Times Literary Supplement, Special Section,
   "A Sense of Direction," August 16, p. xix. (Reprinted as Sect.
   IV of "The Dying Man," WW; CP.)

"The Mistake." New Poems by American Poets, Number 2. Edited by
   Rolfe Humphries. New York: Ballantine Books, p. 135. (Reprinted
   as Sect. II of "Three Epigrams," CP.)

"The Sensualists." New Poems by American Poets, Number 2. Edited
   by Rolfe Humphries. New York: Ballantine Books, pp. 133-134.
   (Reprinted WW; CP.)

"The Surley One." See "The Cantankerous One."

"Third Meditation." Botteghe Oscure, XIX, 207-210. (Reprinted in
   English edition as "Third Meditation," Sect. III, in American
   edition as "Fourth Meditation," Sect. IV, of "Meditations of an
   Old Woman," WW; CP.)

"What Can I Tell My Bones?:(An Old Lady Musing)." Partisan Review,
   XXIV (Summer), 359-362. (Reprinted as Sect. IV, English edition, and
   Sect. V, American edition, of "Meditations of an Old Woman," WW; CP.)

## 1958

"Her Becoming:(An Old Lady Muses)." Botteghe Oscure, XXI, 183-186.
   (Reprinted, American edition only, as Sect. III of "Meditations
   of an Old Woman," WW; CP.)

"Plaint." Tri-Quarterly, I (Fall), 24. (Reprinted American edition only WW; CP.)

"Snake." London Times Literary Supplement, Special Section, "Books in a Changing World," August 15, p. xxi. (Reprinted WW; I Am; CP; DD.)

"The Decision." Yale Review, XLVIII (September), 78. (Reprinted S,SM; FF; CP.)

"The Pure Fury." Partisan Review, XXV (Summer), 366. (Reprinted American edition only WW; CP.)

"The Renewal." New Yorker, XXXIV (April 26), 103; New Statesman, September 6, p. 292. (Reprinted American edition only WW; CP.)


## 1959

"Dirge." The American Scholar, XXVIII (Summer), 293–295. (Reprinted SL, pp. 223–234.)

"Many Arrivals." New Yorker, XXXV (July 25), 29. (Reprinted as "The Manifestation," FF; CP.)

"Saturday, Eight-O'clock." Ladies Home Journal, LXXVI (November), 130.

"The Decision." Observer (London), May 3, p. 23. (Reprinted S,SM; FF; CP.)

"The Early Flower." New Yorker, XXXV (April 25), 44. (Reprinted SL, pp. 232–233.)

"The Harsh Country." New Yorker, XXXV (April 18), 39. (Reprinted CP.)

"The Longing." London Times Literary Supplement, Special Section, "The American Imagination," November 6, p. xxxviii. (Reprinted FF; CP.)

"The Swan." Especially written for Poets and the Past. Edited by Dore Ashton. New York: Andre Emmerich Gallery, 1959. P. 24; New Statesman, July 4, p. 20. (Reprinted American edition only WW; CP.)


## 1960

"Advice to One Committed." Esquire, LIV (November), 138.

"Dirge." Hudson Review, XIII (Spring), 32. (Reprinted SL, p. 232.)

"Her Dream." Hudson Review, XIII (Spring), 30-31; Esquire, LIV (November), 138.

"In a Dark Time," as part of "Sequence." New Yorker, XXXV (January 16), 35. (Reprinted S,SM; FF; CP.)

"In Evening Air," as part of "Sequence." New Yorker, XXXV (January 16), 35. (Reprinted S,SM; FF; CP.)

"Meditation at Oyster River." New Yorker, XXXVI (November 19), 54. (Reprinted FF; CP.)

"Poem." The Listener, December 1, p. 976. (Reprinted as "The Manifestation," FF; CP.)

"The Dancing Man." Atlantic Monthly, CCVI (October), 77. (Reprinted, SL, pp. 234-236.)

"The Motion." Hudson Review, XIII (Spring), 31-32. (Reprinted S,SM; FF; CP.)

"The Restored," New Yorker, XXXVI (December 10), 58. (Reprinted S,SM; FF; CP.)

"The Sequel," as part of "Sequence." New Yorker, XXXV (January 16), 35; Observer (London), October 16, p. 23. (Reprinted S,SM; FF; CP.)

## 1961

"Advice to One Committed," as part of "Two Poems by Theodore Roethke." Spectator, March 24, p. 408.

"Elegy," as part of "Sequence." Encounter, XVI (January), 4. (Reprinted FF; CP.)

"From Whence." Yale Review, LI (December), 264. (Reprinted as "Song," FF; CP.)

"Gob Music," as part of "Pub Songs." Poetry, XCVIII (August), 284-285. (Reprinted CP.)

"In a Dark Time," as part of "Sequence." Encounter, XVI (January), 3. (Reprinted S,SM; FF; CP.)

"In Evening Air." New Statesman, March 31, p. 514. (Reprinted S,SM; FF; CP.)

"Journey to the Interior." New Yorker, XXXVI (January 7), 27. (Reprinted FF; CP.)

"Light Listened," as part of "Sequence." Encounter, XVI (January), 4. (Reprinted FF; CP.)

"Philander." I Am! Says the Lamb. (Reprinted CP.)

"Song." See "From Whence."

"The Donkey." I Am! Says the Lamb. (Reprinted CP; DD.)

"The Early Flower." The Listener, February 16, p. 317.

"The Gnu." I Am! Says the Lamb. (Reprinted CP.)

"The Hippo." I Am! Says the Lamb. (Reprinted CP; DD.)

"The Knowing." New Yorker, XXXVII (April 15), 38. (Reprinted SL, pp. 240-241.)

"The Lizard." I Am! Says the Lamb. (Reprinted CP; DD.)

"The Lizard." New Yorker, XXXVII (June 17), 36; as part of "Two Poems by Theodore Roethke." New Statesman, September 29, p. 430. (Reprinted FF; CP.)

"The Motion." New Statesman, January 27, p. 144. (Reprinted S,SM; FF; CP.)

"The Reply." New Yorker, XXXVII (July 1), 23. (Reprinted CP.)

"The Restored," as part of "Two Poems by Theodore Roethke." Spectator, March 24, p. 408. (Reprinted S,SM; FF; CP.)

"The Shy Man," as part of "Pub Songs." Poetry, XCVIII (August), 283. (Reprinted FF; CP.)

"The Storm." New Yorker, XXXVII (September 9), 48. (Reprinted FF; CP.)

"The Tree, The Bird." New Yorker, XXXVII (April 29), 40; as part of "Two Poems by Theodore Roethke." New Statesman, September 29, p. 430. (Reprinted S,SM; FF; CP.)

"The Wagtail." I Am! Says the Lamb. (Reprinted CP.)

"The Whale." I Am! Says the Lamb. (Reprinted CP; DD.)

"The Young Girl." Ladies Home Journal, LXXVIII (September), 85. (Reprinted FF; CP.)

# Writings by Theodore Roethke

1962

"Her Words," as part of "3 Love Poems by Theodore Roethke." Harper's
    Bazaar, 3005 (April), p. 130. (Reprinted FF; CP.)

"Her Wrath," as part of "3 Love Poems by Theodore Roethke." Harper's
    Bazaar, 3005 (April), p. 130. (Reprinted FF; CP.)

"I Like New England Men." Seattle Times, "Words and Music" Column,
    January 19, p. 13.

"Old Florist's Lament." Spectator, October 5, p. 530. (Reprinted
    as "The Old Florist's Lament," SL, pp. 226-227.)

"Once More, The Round." Encounter, XVIII (May), 45. (Reprinted,
    S,SM; FF; CP.)

"The Abyss." Encounter, XIX (October), 51-53. (Reprinted FF; CP.)

"The Apparition." New Yorker, XXXVII (February 10), 43. (Reprinted
    FF; CP.)

"The Far Field." Sewanee Review, LXX (Autumn), 609-612; London Times
    Literary Supplement, December 21, 1962, p. 992. (Reprinted FF;
    CP.)

"The Happy Three," as part of "3 Love Poems by Theodore Roethke."
    Harper's Bazaar, 3005 (April), p. 130. (Reprinted FF; CP.)

"The Longing." Saturday Review, XLV (August 11), 19; excerpt, Parts
    I, II only, XLIV (June 24, 1961), 46. (Reprinted FF; CP.)

"The Long Waters." New Yorker, XXXVIII (June 2), 34. (Reprinted
    FF; CP. An excerpt, "Whether the Bees Have Thoughts," reprinted
    DD.)

"The Marrow." New Yorker, XXXVIII (May 19), 42. (Reprinted S,SM;
    FF; CP.)

"The Saginaw Song." Encounter, XVIII (January), 94. (Reprinted CP.)

"Two for Cynthia." Harper's, CCXXIV (March), 54.

1963

"All Morning: An American Idyll." Observer (London), March 24,
    p. 22. (Reprinted as "All Morning," FF; CP.)

"A Wheeze for Wystan." Poetry, CIII: 1&2 (October/November), 88-89.

"Her Longing." <u>Atlantic Monthly</u>, CCXII (October), 101. (Reprinted <u>FF</u>; <u>CP</u>.)

"Her Reticence." <u>Hudson Review</u>, XVI (Spring), 52; <u>Observer</u> (London), October 20, 1963, p. 24. (Reprinted <u>FF</u>; <u>CP</u>.)

"Her Time," as part of "Six Poems." <u>New Yorker</u>, XXXIX (October 19), 50; <u>Observer</u> (London), October 20, p. 24. (Reprinted <u>FF</u>; <u>CP</u>.)

"His Foreboding." <u>Hudson Review</u>, XVI (Spring), 53; <u>New York Review of Books</u>, October 17, p. 21. (Reprinted <u>FF</u>; <u>CP</u>.)

"Infirmity," as part of "Six Poems." <u>New Yorker</u>, XXXIX (October 19), 50. (Reprinted <u>S,SM</u>; <u>FF</u>; <u>CP</u>.)

"I Waited," as part of "Two Poems." <u>New Statesman</u>, November 29, p. 789. (Reprinted <u>S,SM</u>; <u>FF</u>; <u>CP</u>.)

"Once More, The Round." <u>Harper's Bazaar</u>, 3014 (January), p. 117. (Reprinted <u>S,SM</u>; <u>FF</u>; <u>CP</u>.)

"Otto." <u>Partisan Review</u>, XXX (Spring), 56-57. (Reprinted <u>FF</u>; <u>CP</u>.)

"Song." <u>Poetry</u>, CIII: 1&2 (October/November), 87.

"Song: From Whence Cometh Song?" as part of "Three Poems." <u>New Statesman</u>, August 9, p. 176. (Reprinted as "Song," <u>FF</u>; <u>CP</u>.)

"Song: My Wrath, Where's the Edge." <u>Harper's</u>, CCXXVI (February), 44. (Reprinted as "Song," <u>FF</u>; <u>CP</u>.)

"Supper with Lindsay (1962)." <u>Poetry</u>, CIII: 1&2 (October/November), 85-86. (Reprinted <u>CP</u>.)

"The Abyss." <u>Harper's</u>, CCXXVII (November), 82-83. (Reprinted <u>FF</u>; <u>CP</u>.)

"The Advice," as part of "Three Poems." <u>New Statesman</u>, August 9, p. 176.

"The Apparition." <u>Observer</u> (London), October 20, p. 24. (Reprinted <u>FF</u>; <u>CP</u>.)

"The Chums." <u>New Statesman</u>, February 8, p. 202; <u>Saturday Review</u>, XLVI (December 21), 52. (Reprinted <u>FF</u>; <u>CP</u>.)

"The Geranium." <u>Partisan Review</u>, XXX (Spring), 55; <u>Agenda</u>, III (December 1963/January 1964), 9. (Reprinted <u>FF</u>; <u>CP</u>.)

"The Long Waters." <u>The Critical Quarterly</u>, V (Spring), 20-22. (Reprinted <u>FF</u>; <u>CP</u>. An excerpt, "Whether the Bees Have Thoughts," reprinted <u>DD</u>.)

"The Manifestation," as part of "Two Poems." New Statesman,
   November 29, p. 789. (Reprinted FF; CP.)

"The Marrow," as part of "Three Poems." New Statesman, August 9,
   p. 176. (Reprinted S,SM; FF; CP.)

"The Meadow Mouse," as part of "Six Poems." New Yorker, XXXIX
   (October 19), 50-51; Spectator, November 29, p. 719. (Reprinted
   FF; CP.)

"The Moment," as part of "Six Poems." New Yorker, XXXIX (October 19),
   51; Encounter, XXI (October), 68. (Reprinted FF; CP.)

"The Pike." Observer (London), May 5, p. 27; Saturday Review, XLVI
   (November 9), 42. (Reprinted FF; CP.)

"The Right Thing." Atlantic Monthly, CCXI (March), 51. (Reprinted
   S,SM; FF; CP.)

"The Rose." New Yorker, XXXIX (July 6), 26-27. (Reprinted FF; CP.)

"The Thing." Saturday Review, XLVI (March 9), 10. (Reprinted FF;
   CP.)

"The Tranced," as part of "Six Poems." New Yorker, (October 19), 51.
   (Reprinted FF; CP.)

"The Victorians." Observer (London), April 27, p. 15.

"The Young Girl." Observer (London), October 20, p. 24. (Reprinted
   FF; CP.)

"Wish for a Young Wife." Hudson Review, XVI (Spring), 52; as part of
   "Six Poems." New Yorker, XXXIX (October 19), 50-51. (Reprinted
   FF; CP.)

1964

"All Morning." Harper's Bazaar, 3028 (March), pp. 92-93. (Reprinted
   FF; CP.)

"Elegy." Poetry Northwest, V (Summer), 2. (Reprinted FF; CP.)

"Her Convalescence (An Old Lady Speaks)." Ladies Home Journal, LXXXI
   (April), 124.

"His Foreboding." London Magazine, NS IV (June), 55-56. (Reprinted
   FF; CP.)

"Infirmity." London Magazine, NS IV (June), 55-56. (Reprinted
   S,SM; FF; CP.)

"Journey to the Interior." Encounter, XXII (June), 50-51.
   (Reprinted FF; CP.)

"Light Listened." Harper's Bazaar, 3027 (February), p. 138.
   (Reprinted FF; CP.)

"On the Quay." The Far Field. (Reprinted CP.)

"Otto." London Times Literary Supplement, January 30, p. 89.
   (Reprinted FF; CP.)

"The Rose." Agenda, III (April), 1-4. (Reprinted FF; CP.)

"Wish for a Young Wife." London Magazine, NS IV (June), 54.
   (Reprinted FF; CP.)


## 1965

"Light Poem." New Yorker, XLI (July 10), 21. (Reprinted CP.)


## 1966

"Duet." Collected Poems.

"Supper with Lindsay." Encounter, XXXVII (October), 51-52.
   (Reprinted CP.)


## 1968

"Agrarian." Selected Letters, p. 79.

"Assailants Lurk Behind the Door..." Selected Letters, p. 36.

"Conscience." Selected Letters, pp. 38-39.

"Could I Spiral Like This..." Selected Letters, p. 118.

"Coward's Song." Selected Letters, pp. 62-63.

"Difficult Grief." Selected Letters, pp. 22-23.

"Evening Eye." Selected Letters, pp. 19-20.

"For the Sake of These..." Selected Letters, p. 86.

"Gooses." Selected Letters, p. 152.

"Like Walkers in an Unfamiliar Place..." Selected Letters, pp. 95-96.

"Love Curled in Many Laps..." Selected Letters, p. 100.

"Our Phantasies, Like Flies..." Selected Letters, p. 93.

"Pastoral." Selected Letters, pp. 93–94.

"Poem." Selected Letters, p. 96.

"Rune." Selected Letters, pp. 98–99.

"Side-Line Comment." Selected Letters, pp. 86–87.

"Song for Hemingway." Selected Letters, p. 34.

"Specialist." Selected Letters, p. 92.

"Suburbia: Michigan." Selected Letters, pp. 90–91.

"Suburban Lament." Selected Letters, pp. 84–85.

"The Cure." Selected Letters, p. 54.

"The Curious People." Selected Letters, p. 86.

"The Tribute." Selected Letters, p. 22.

"Three Poems on F. Prokosch." Selected Letters, p. 74.

## POEMS AND PROSE FRAGMENTS: FROM THE NOTEBOOKS

(All were arranged for publication by David Wagoner.)

### 1964

"Straw for the Fire." Poetry, CV (November), 113–118. (Reprinted
SF.)

### 1966

"In the Large Mind of Love." Hudson Review, XIX (Summer), 253–258.
(Reprinted SF.)

"The Plain Speech of a Crow." Southern Review, NS II (October),
906–910. (Reprinted SF.)

### 1968

"A Nest of Light." Tri-Quarterly, XII (Spring), 101–103.
(Reprinted SF.)

"In the Lap of a Dream." <u>Atlantic Monthly</u>, CCXXII (November), 58-62.
(Reprinted <u>SF</u>.)

"Proverbs of Purgatory." <u>Shenandoah</u>, XX (Autumn), 30-31. (Reprinted
<u>SF</u>.)

"The Stony Garden." <u>Poetry</u>, CXIII (November), 104-108. (Reprinted
<u>SF</u>.)

"The Things I Steal From Sleep." <u>Poetry Northwest</u>, IX (Spring), 3-6.
(Reprinted <u>SF</u>.)

"Words for Young Writers." <u>Saturday Review</u>, LI (June 29), 14-15, 42.
(Reprinted <u>SF</u>.)


## 1969

"Father-Stem and Mother-Root." <u>Denver Quarterly</u>, III (Winter),
81-84. (Reprinted <u>SF</u>.)

"First Class." <u>Antioch Review</u>, XXIX (Summer), 212-217. (Reprinted
<u>SF</u>.)

"In the Bush of Her Bones." <u>Southern Review</u>, NS V (January), 1-3.
(Reprinted <u>SF</u>.)

"The Loveless Provinces." <u>Yale Review</u>, LIX (October), 99-103.
(Reprinted <u>SF</u>.)

"The Right to Say Maybe." <u>Seattle Magazine</u>, VI (February), 27.
(Reprinted <u>SF</u>.)


## 1970

"I Teach Out of Love." <u>Shenandoah</u>, XXI (Spring), 141-149.
(Reprinted <u>SF</u>.)

"Roots of the Wind." <u>Mademoiselle</u>, LXX (March), 92-93. (Reprinted
<u>SF</u>.)

"The Dance of the One-Legged Man." <u>Poetry Northwest</u>, XI (Summer),
3-6. (Reprinted <u>SF</u>.)


## 1971

"The Dark Angel." <u>Northwest Review</u>, XI (Summer), 112-115.
(Reprinted <u>SF</u>.)

"The Poet's Business." <u>Northwest Review</u>, XI (Summer), 32–41.
    (Reprinted <u>SF</u>.)

"Heart, You Have No House." <u>Voyages</u>, III/IV (Spring 1971/Spring 1972),
    61–64. (Reprinted <u>SF</u>.)


<u>1972</u>

*"The Beautiful Disorder." <u>Pebble</u>, VIII (Spring), page unknown.
    (Reprinted <u>SF</u>.)

# Writings about Theodore Roethke, 1922-1973

1922 A BOOKS - NONE

1922 B SHORTER WRITINGS

1   ANON.   "Saginaw Youth's Address Now in World Languages:   Red
        Cross Translates Roethke's Speech Into 26 Tongues as World
        Propaganda."   The Saginaw News Courier, October 22, p. 6.
          Roethke gave his speech the preceding May when a Fresh-
        man at Arthur Hill High School.   The address is reproduced
        here.


1934 A BOOKS - NONE

1934 B SHORTER WRITINGS

1   ANON.   "Theodore Roethke Selected to Head College Publicity."
        The Lafayette, LXI (October 16), 1, 4.
          Roethke, English instructor and tennis coach, has been
        made Director of College Publicity.   His task will be to
        "keep Lafayette in the eyes of the public" by disseminating
        information of student accomplishments to newspapers in
        their hometown areas.

2   ANON.   "Poetry of Theodore Roethke Featured Recently by
        'American Poetry Journal.'"   The Lafayette, LXI (December
        14), 1, 3.
          An account of Roethke's recent significant publications
        in American and foreign journals, as well as two antholo-
        gies.   Some remarks are excerpted from John Holmes' intro-
        duction to Roethke's appearance in the American Poetry
        Journal.

3   HOLMES, JOHN.   "Theodore Roethke."   American Poetry Journal,
        17th monthly issue (November), 2.
          This first, perceptive evaluation of Roethke's work is
        quoted almost in full because it establishes a base for
        much of the later criticism.

1934

"Among younger poets coming into prominence, there are
very few who have the passionate patience of workmanship,
the subtly skilful ear for rhythms, and the savage alle-
giance to a high standard of poetic integrity, that mark
the poetry of Theodore Roethke. Publication of his work
from time to time in such magazines as the Adelphi, the
New Republic, the Atlantic Monthly, the Nation, and the
Saturday Review of Literature, has given him a group of
those readers who come to attention on finding in the
right line the word that is exact and extraordinary.
Roethke's theme is nearly always the conflict between
flesh and mind, between the confusions of earth and the
will toward pure identity of being. Even in his more
objective poetry, one is aware of an intensity with which
he has fought off and defeated the loose and ordinary
phrase. He has the meta-physical poet's reverence for
deity and its inherent mystery. Death haunts him with
its finality, and its utter quiet. But self-analysis
produces most of his poems, with every physical and mental
sense almost intolerably heightened and sharpened in the
onset. He refines these forces to their ultimates, and
makes them vibrate to an impulse of meter over which he
has a sure and delicate control.

Roethke likes to freight the small form with deep significance. In verbs and nouns of intensity and power, in
images burned pure, he seeks to convey the difficult
qualities of miracle, of terrible precision, of the swell
of sorrow, of lusty grace, of superior felicity. But the
rigor of this imagery is often warmed by fervent aspira-
tion, and sometimes by a native calmness in perception,
radiant and flushed with a pure light. Ecstasy cancels
the likelihood of merely metallic and enamelled statement.
His rhythm keeps its certainty: sometimes it is under a
heavy load of accumulated epithet, but rarely is it in
danger therefrom.

The present group of poems, excepting 'This Light,' is
representative of Roethke's earlier work, and scarcely
shows his variety of cadence and subject or fully exhibits
his sensitive manipulation of sounds within a pattern.
They do, however, include typical preoccupations. He
'appraises the purest substance'; he exhorts hope to rouse
the will 'with sudden miracle'; and he speaks of the soul
rising 'into Light in unbewildered flight.' It is poetry
of essences, crystal and dangerous in its extreme concentration. The poem 'This Light' belongs, in its style,
with several of his that have been lately published in
the Adelphi of London, and in these he makes his rhythm,
assonance, and imagery more effective than in anything

34

> he has done before. His more recent poems show that he
> can be objective, and they carry increased warmth for less
> complex things and feelings. His poetic growth is appar-
> ently in the first changing and vivid years of its
> majority."

## 1935 A BOOKS - NONE

## 1935 B SHORTER WRITINGS

1    BOGAN, LOUISE. "Stitched on Bone." Trial Balances, edited
    by Ann Winslow. New York: Macmillan, pp. 138-139.
        Roethke passes the tests of a young writer: resonant
    work and a movement toward clarification of emotion. He
    controls form without yielding to tricks of style, "he has
    a gift for form." Seven of Roethke's poems are included
    in this anthology.

2    HOLMES, JOHN. "Our Youngest American Poets." Boston Evening
    Transcript, October 5, "Book Section," p. 3.
        Review of Trial Balances, edited by Ann Winslow. Louise
    Bogan's remarks on Roethke are excerpted here to "sum up"
    the prospect the poets in this anthology indicate. Be-
    sides mentioning Roethke's "metaphysical note," the author
    says little more directly about him.

## 1936 A BOOKS - NONE

## 1936 B SHORTER WRITINGS

1    ANON. "English Department Member Called Promising Young Poet."
    The Daily Collegian (Penn State University), December 18,
    p. 1.
        Roethke, newly arrived at Penn State, is praised for his
    poetic accomplishments. Remarks by John Holmes in the
    Boston Transcript and Louis Untermeyer in American Mercury
    are reprinted.

## 1937 A BOOKS - NONE

## 1937 B SHORTER WRITINGS

1    ANON. "Penn State Author Praised Very Highly." Centre Daily
    Times (State College, Pa.), January 5, p. 3.

1937

> Roethke, new at Penn State, "is being hailed as one of the most promising of the younger poets in America." John Holmes and Louis Untermeyer are cited as authorities in support of this judgment.

2   ANON.  "Roethke Will Address Bell Staff Tomorrow." The Daily Collegian (Penn State University), October 12, p. 1.
     Roethke will speak on "The Younger American Poets."

3   ANON.  "Roethke to Judge in College Poet Contest." The Daily Collegian (Penn State University), December 14, p. 1.
     Roethke will select the winner of the "Witter-Bynner Award" in a contest sponsored by the "College Poetry Society of America."

1938 A BOOKS - NONE

1938 B SHORTER WRITINGS

1   ANON.  "Announcements--Tuesday: Woman's Club to Hear Poet." Centre Daily Times (State College, Pa.), February 11, p. 3.
     Roethke will speak on "Modern Poetry" to the "State College Woman's Club." He is described as the man who "writes the poetry commentary for the New Republic and is acting as the sole judge for one of the contests conducted by the College Poetry Society of America."

2   ANON.  "Roethke to Deliver Liberal Arts Lecture." Centre Daily Times (State College, Pa.), February 21, p. 1.
     Roethke's topic is not mentioned. Some of his accomplishments in poetry are listed.

3   ANON.  "Roethke to Give 3rd Liberal Arts Lecture." The Daily Collegian (Penn State University), February 22, p. 1.
     Roethke will speak on "Some New Poets." Publications in major magazines are listed.

4   ANON.  "Book Marks for Today." New York World-Telegram, December 6, p. 19.
     An incidental reference to the December issue of Poetry concludes with this remark: "...and closes with an important group of seven poems by Theodore Roethke."

5   HOLMES, JOHN.  "Forward Look at Poetry, Plus Anniversary Remarks." Boston Evening Transcript, October 5, Part III, p. 3.

> Of the poets included in Ann Winslow's <u>Trial Balances</u>,
> Roethke is here recognized as one who has "come forward
> with tremendous strides."

1939 A BOOKS - NONE

1939 B SHORTER WRITINGS

1   ANON.   "Roethke Will Coach Lion Tennis Team This Season:   Dink
        Stover Replaced by Ex-Mentor."  <u>Penn State Collegian</u>,
        March 28, p. 3.
            If Roethke is as successful a tennis coach as he is a
        poet, the team should do well.

2   ANON.   "Tennis Coach Bemoans Wet Weather Man."  <u>Centre Daily
        Times</u> (State College, Pa.), April 22, p. 6.
            Facing a rough tennis schedule, Roethke and his team
        have had to make due with many adverse conditions.

3   WERNER, W. L.  "Bookworm."  <u>Centre Daily Times</u> (State College,
        Pa.), January 13, p. 2.
            Article unsigned.  A comment on Roethke's poem "For an
        Amorous Lady" that appeared in a recent issue of the
        <u>New Yorker</u>.


1940 A BOOKS - NONE

1940 B SHORTER WRITINGS

1   ANON.   "Eight Roethke Poems Preserved in Collection at Buffalo
        Library."  <u>The Daily Collegian</u> (Penn State University),
        March 19, p. 1.
            Roethke work-drafts and typescripts of eight poems will
        be microfilmed and preserved in a collection of works by
        contemporary American poets at the Lockwood Memorial
        Library, University of Buffalo.

2   ANON.   "Roethke Starts 3rd Year as Tennis Coach Here."  <u>The
        Daily Collegian</u> (Penn State University), September 12,
        p. 12.
            Roethke, "as well as being an expert squash rackets and
        table tennis player, is recognized as one of the leading
        younger poets in America."

3   BERKLUND, CARL.  <u>New Michigan Verse</u>.  Ann Arbor: University
        of Michigan Press.

1940

> Brief biographical sketch refers to Roethke as "one of
> the most widely known of the younger American poets."
> Also included are ten poems, prior to their publication
> in Open House (1941): "The Light Comes Brighter," "High-
> way: Michigan," "The Heron," "Feud," "'Long Live the
> Weeds,'" "Autumnal" (Section III of "The Coming of the
> Cold"), "No Bird," "To My Sister," "Interlude," and "Slow
> Season."

1941 A BOOKS - NONE

1941 B SHORTER WRITINGS

1    ANON.   "Roethke and Auden...." Portfolio (Penn State Univer-
     sity), II:4 (February), 1, inside front cover.
        Auden is visiting the Penn State campus.  Roethke's first
     book, Open House, will soon be published.  The author ex-
     horts readers to make it a "best seller!"

2    ANON.   "Publishes New Book." Penn State Alumni News, XXVII
     (March), 14.
        Roethke has published Open House.  A brief biography is
     included, as well as critical remarks by John Holmes and
     excerpts from several of the poems.

3    ANON.   "Has New Book of Poems Published." Huntington (Pa.)
     News, March 7, page unknown (from the Roethke collection,
     University of Washington).
        Announcement of the publication of Open House.

4    ANON.   "Penn State Prof Publishes Poems." Jeanette (Pa.)
     News-Dispatch, March 7, page unknown (from the Roethke
     collection, University of Washington).
        Announcement of the publication of Open House.

5    ANON.   "Bibliography of the Published Work of Theodore
     Roethke." The Browse (Penn State University), No. 7,
     March 8, pp. 3-4.  (Attributed to John Hastings by McLeod
     in Theodore Roethke: A Bibliography.)
        Includes all poems in periodicals, anthologies and Open
     House, as well as Roethke's reviews of other poets' work.

6    ANON.   "Coach to Publish Book of Poetry." Latrobe (Pa.)
     Bulletin, March 8, page unknown (from the Roethke collec-
     tion, University of Washington).
        Announcement of the publication of Open House.

1941

7    ANON.    "Saginawian Publishes Collection of Poems; Wins Praise
     of Critic." The Saginaw News, March 9, p. 4.
        Mention is made of Roethke's mother, still living in
     Saginaw, some events in his own life and publishing his-
     tory. The notice concludes with a comment from Louis
     Untermeyer.

8    ANON.    "Theodore Roethke Has Book of Poems Published."
     Centre Daily Times (State College, Pa.), March 11, p. 5.
        Alfred A. Knopf has published Open House. Roethke's
     first collection consists of about 50 poems, some of them
     previously unpublished.

9    ANON.    "Open House." New Yorker, XVII (March 29), 64.
     (Ascribed to Louise Bogan on back cover of Words for the
     Wind, Indiana University Press paperback.)
        Roethke has fine lyric style, a bitter wit and a "feel-
     ing for the small and medium-sized, as well as for the
     large doings in the world about him."

10   ANON.    "Roethke Poems Lift Spirit Above Despair." Hartford
     (Conn.) Times, May 3, p. 7.
        Review of Open House. Roethke "speaks to the point. He
     writes in the English lyrical tradition and, though the
     form follows a similar pattern in many poems, it is epi-
     grammatic." He speaks the truth "transformed into vital
     experience, through interpretive words."

11   ANON.    "About Books and Authors." Newark News, May 17, p. 4.
        Review of Open House. Roethke writes poetry of "great
     distinction." "His style is clear and skillful and is
     tinged with genial humor." Sincerity of feeling and "gift
     of phrase" also make this first collection worthwhile.

12   ANON.    Review of Open House. Booklist, XXXVII (June 1), 461.
        Complete review--"Poems in modern style, intellectual
     and brittle in effect, and slight in emotional impact."

13   ANON.    Review of Open House. The Bookmark (New York State
     Library), II:5 (November), 10.
        Roethke's poems are "marked by wit and sensibility, a
     rhythmic quality and a careful craftsmanship stemming from
     the more traditional technic...."

14   ANON.    "Roethke Humor." Portfolio (Penn State University),
     III:2 (December). 8.
        Entire paragraph:
        When W. H. Auden, British poet, visited the campus
     last year, he had to itemize a bill for his services.

Roethke rescued him from the dilemma with: "Put down, 'one week as intellectual study.'"

15 "A. R. W." "The Daily Half Colyum." Centre Daily Times (State College, Pa.), March 12, p. 4.
An account of The Browse for March 1941, including W. H. Auden's review of Roethke's Open House (1941.B16) and a bibliography of Roethke's published works.

16 AUDEN, W. H. "Verse and the Times." Saturday Review, XXIII (April 5), 30-31.
Review of Open House. Roethke recognizes both chaos and order. He transforms life's humiliation. The book is a total success. The question is: where can he go from here?

17 BALDANZA, STEPHEN. "Books of the Week." Commonweal, XXXIV (June 13), 188.
Review of Open House. Roethke's self-revelation is incomplete; "it embodies a caution which is at the core of his poetic impulse." The poet is gifted, but he has "tapped only a vein of his talents."

18 BELITT, BEN. "Six Poets." Virginia Quarterly Review, XVII (Summer), 462-463.
Review of Open House. Roethke's work aims for a core, "or seminal cluster of insights and images which stand for the identity...." Yet he does not hit it consistently. And when he doesn't, his poems accept weak diction as a substitute.

19 BERGMAN, HAROLD. "Poet Theodore Roethke Prefers Drinking Beer to Talking Shop." The Burlington (Vermont) Free Press, September 10, p. 2.
The author interviewed Roethke at Breadloaf, which the latter was attending on a fellowship. "'Look,' he (Roethke) said, 'can't we just sit here and drink beer and forget about this business of an interview? After all, I'm just one of the small fellows. What I say won't cut any ice with anybody and besides how can a guy get through an interview without sounding pretentious? No kidding, let's have another beer.'" After this beginning, the author mentions the critical reception of the recently pub-lished Open House, some biographical information, and Roethke's attitudes about the teaching of verse writing. After boasting of his ability as a cook, Roethke comments thus on his work: "'There are some light, humorous ones,

some are intensely personal, some that deal with contemporary social problems, and some that sound pretty pontif-
ical. Any real poet, it seems to me, must have some social
consciousness but I don't mean that every poem must be
weighted with a propaganda message.  I guess I must be one
of the most naive guys in the world.  I actually believe
that such things as brotherhood of man and human justice
and decency are possible.  And what's more I'm a pigsty
isolationist and don't give a hoot whether it's fashion-
able or not.  But, hell, now I'm sounding oracular, just
because you give my ego a chance for a work-out.  Let's
have a beer and forget about the interview, shall we'?"

20  BERKLUND, C. E.  "Open House."  Michigan Alumnus Quarterly
    Review, XLVII (Spring), 287.
       This first book balances the difficult and familiar,
    standardized and modern, in poems of great range.  Roethke
    includes nature pieces, "poems intellectual in substance
    but passionate in expression," and poems of fastidious
    humor.  "He has set for himself a difficult goal and has
    reached it.  In the perfection of phrase and rhythm, in
    the clarity of design, in the expert handling of sound,
    it is not exaggeration to say that few, if any of the
    younger American poets are his superior.  At his best he
    is superb both as artist and craftsman."

21  BOIE, MILDRED.  "The Poetry Shelf."  Boston Herald, April 9,
    p. 28.
       Review of Open House.  Roethke sees clearly and directly.
    "The poems are tight, compact, strikingly simple; they
    show a fine, deft control of technique, but are never
    'difficult' through obscurity or arrogant modernity."

22  BONNER, AMY.  "The Poems of Theodore Roethke."  New York Times
    Book Review, October 5, pp. 9, 12.
       Review of Open House.  The reviewer stresses Roethke's
    strength and integrity in a confused, though known, world;
    and his vision of a never-seen-before world in nature.  He
    is a "scrupulous craftsman."  The absence of love poems in
    a first book also gets a comment.

23  "C. C. C."  "Some New Books of Verse for Poetry Shelf."
    St. Louis Globe-Democrat, April 19, Sect. II, p. 1B.
       Review of Open House.  "'Open House' (Knopf) is the first
    book of poems by a promising younger poet, Theodore Roethke.
    Some of the lyrics are light, others have an impressive
    strength and intensity, and all of them reveal a sensitive
    ear for rhythm."

1941

24    DEUTSCH, BABETTE. "Three Generations in Poetry." _Decision_,
        II (August), 60-61.
            Review of _Open House_. Roethke's verse is akin to the
        Metaphysicals--"less sensuous, more intellectualized."
        The poems deal with the interior landscape. Roethke
        "writes with particular acuteness about the mind as aware-
        ness grows on it."

25    DREW, ELIZABETH. Review of _Open House_. _Atlantic Monthly_,
        CLXVIII (August), uncertain pagination.
            Roethke's poems communicate a "sense of inner security
        and certainty." Technically his work is solid, no matter
        what his subject.

26    FORSTER, LOUIS. "A Lyric Realist." _Poetry_, LVIII (July),
        222-225. Review of _Open House_.
            Despite his limited technical range, Roethke is a poet
        of sincerity and fortitude, in a wide variety of honest
        emotions. "It is his power of eliciting a mood or a sud-
        den wave of feeling that constitutes Roethke's chief
        distinction, for a faithful portrayal of genuine emotion
        is always an original creation."

27    "H. L." "Roethke Commands Magic of Precision." _Buffalo Eve-_
        _ning News_, March 29, Magazine Section, p. 7.
            Review of _Open House_. The phrase "magic of precision"
        comes from John Drinkwater. Roethke's "tight-lipped"
        verse reminds the reviewer of Jonathan Swift.

28    HOLMES, JOHN. "Poems and Things." _Boston Evening Transcript_,
        March 24, p. 9.
            Review of _Open House_. Roethke's poetry has "enlarged,
        warmed, deepened, and strengthened" over the years, "until
        it flowers in this book as an integrated statement, matured
        and intensified, organized, edited, and shaped to a power-
        ful thrust through the intellect into the heart; a whole
        poet; a whole book." The author comments further on the
        arrangement of _Open House_ and individual poems. He also
        speaks of his early relationship as poet and colleague
        with Roethke. He speaks enthusiastically of Roethke the
        craftsman, "an angry poet, but exquisitely controlled in
        verbal performance."

29    HUMPHRIES, ROLPHE. "Inside Story." _New Republic_, CV (July 14),
        62.
            Review of _Open House_. Roethke's work is largely self-
        centered. But he is saved from the "sentimental, ordinary
        or painful results" by his "blunt and obdurate honesty of

statement, even at the cost of flexibility of technique, without embellishment or fancy business. He faces and acknowledges much that he knows or suspects to be wrong inside." "In the poems of nature and the visible world, with the weight of the theme less heavy, the music is richer, more sensuous and deeper; the observation, turned outward, is sensitive, delicate and perceptive, if not yet passionate and intense." He has both wit and humor, without frivolity.

30   KULP, MARGARET BECKER. Review of Open House in the "Chatter" Column. Harrisburg (Penn.) Patriot, April 11, p. 22.
  Roethke's poem "After Loss" is reprinted, eliciting the following responses. Roethke's physical agility, his masculinity, and his "fencer-like" wit receive adequate play here. Rising literary stature is conceded, but emphasised by excerpted remarks from Roethke's early critics, Louis Untermeyer and Robert Hillyer.

31   LANEY, AL. "Roethke, Penn State Tennis Coach, Author of Book of Verse." In "Sports Here and There" Column. New York Herald Tribune, March 5, p. 26.
  Roethke is both an able coach and poet, despite his modest attitudes on both subjects. The article announces his forthcoming book, Open House, and prints in its entirety "Poem with a Dash of Houseman," provided the author by a friend who took it from a locker room bulletin board.

32   MILLS, CLARK. "Documents on This Year." Voices, CVII (Autumn), 62.
  Review of Open House. "Having limited himself to the regular meters and the short form, Roethke has managed to perfect a technique amidst restrictions and difficulties almost as constraining as those of the French classicists. But his labor has borne fruit, in poems which cannot be called 'uneven,' or 'promising,' but which in idea and construction might be the work of a somewhat mellowed and modernized Housman."

33   MULDER, ARNOLD. "Library Adventures." Kalamazoo Gazette, March 18, p. 6.
  Review of Open House. Roethke is in no sense a provincial poet in "substance or technique," but the Michigan landscape and "the spirit of Michigan's people" are in this book. "Highway: Michigan" and "Night Journey" are discussed as poems from the native consciousness. "Mr. Roethke's voice is so quiet, his rhythms are so far from the merely obvious that his book may have a hard

1941

time making his way in World war time, when ordinarily
nothing less than a shout can be heard."

34    _____. "A Real Loss to Writer's Art:  A Michigan Poet." The
Bay City (Mich.) Times, March 23, p. 6.
Review of Open House.  Reprint of 1941.B33.

35    "N. B. C." "Poet Puts His Eye to Proper Use." Kansas City
Star, May 3, p. 14.
Review of Open House.  Roethke's choice of the eye over
the other senses "is the right choice, for his is the poet's
eye, which sees the world with freshness and depth."  The
reviewer sees kinship with seventeenth century lyrists and
Emily Dickinson, but Roethke is unmistakeably modern.

36    STULL, CHRISTOPHER. "The New Poetry in Review." San Francisco Chronicle, April 27, "This World" Section, p. 13.
Review of Open House.  Entire review:  "Occasionally a
book appears by a poet who lifts the lyric out of the
trough of banality and makes language vital again.  Open
House is one of them.  Not all the poems included are up
to Mr. Roethke's highest standard but the general level is
high and several of the poems are superb."

37    SWEENY, JOHN L. "New Poetry." Yale Review, XXX (June),
817-818.
Review of Open House.  Roethke's first book yields
"honest evidence of purpose and promise," as the poet
chooses the intense area of inner experience, "reducing
it to simple but skilful poetic forms."

38    WALTON, EDA LOU. "Bridges of Iron Lace." New York Herald
Tribune Book Review, August 10, p. 4.
Review of Open House.  Roethke's form is traditional,
his language simple, and his vision fresh; "a blend of
humor, irony and gentle affection for the familiar."  The
metaphysical poets and the "Byronic Auden" are close behind some of the poems, though not the best.  He is cogni-
zant of the limits of his technical equipment and never
strains for effect.

39    WEST, MAXINE. "Poet-In-Residence." Headlight on Books at
Penn State, X (May), 2.
Review of Open House.  A technical evaluation of poems
that go beyond technique, this review stresses Roethke's
sensitive eye and intense lyricism.

40   WHITTAKER, BETTY A.   "Roethke on Review."   Portfolio (Penn
        State University), III:2 (December), 2, 8.
            The author surveys the more significant reviews of
        Roethke's Open House, concluding that, as a group, they
        do justice to the work.  Few, however, get beyond their
        own critical jargon.  Page eight includes a "Bibliography
        of Reviews."

41   WINTERS, YVOR.   "The Poems of Theodore Roethke."   Kenyon
        Review, III (Autumn), 514-516.
            Review of Open House.  There are some good poems, in the
        manner of Bridges, with emphasis on clarity and precision.
        Roethke is occasionally brilliantly descriptive.


1942 A BOOKS - NONE

1942 B SHORTER WRITINGS

1    ANON.   "'Ted' Roethke Chosen Lecturer at Harvard."   Centre
        Daily Times (State College, Pa.), February 27, p. 4.
            Roethke will be Morris Gray lecturer at Harvard in the
        spring.

2    ANON.   "M.(ineral) I.(ndustries) Art Gallery Formally Opened."
        Centre Daily Times (State College, Pa.), April 13, pp. 1,
        6.
            Roethke read his "Dedicatory Poem," reprinted here, for
        the occasion.

3    ANON.   "M.(ineral) I.(ndustries) Art Gallery Formally Opened
        on April 11th."   Mineral Industries (Penn State University),
        XI:8 (May), 1, 3.
            Roethke read his "Dedicatory Poem," reprinted here, for
        the occasion.

4    ANON.   "The Daily Half Colyum."   Centre Daily Times (State
        College, Pa.), June 12, p. 4.   Signed A. R. W.
            Though cited by McLeod in Theodore Roethke:  A Bibliog-
        raphy (B 61, p. 134), there is no reference here to
        Roethke.

5    ANON.   "Poet-Coach Again Breaks into Print."   The Daily Col-
        legian (Penn State University), November 18, p. 2.
            A drawing of Roethke by M. Kunkel is accompanied by a
        caption that mentions Roethke's poem "The Minimal" in the
        current issue of Harper's Bazaar.

1942

6    BAILY, BEN. "Tennis Situation Presents Problem." The Daily
Collegian (Penn State University), April 11, p. 3.
    As coach, Roethke has faced numerous problems with the
weather and practice facilities in the preparation of his
team. His players refer to him as "MacArthur" for his
various strategies, including midnight drills.

7    "P. M. J." "Michigan Poets." New York Times Book Review,
January 4, p. 5.
    Review of New Michigan Verse, edited by Carl Edwin
Burklund. "Perhaps the only verses to give a sharp focus
to the scene are those by Theodore Roethke: it is not that
he writes more about Michigan, but he writes better, and
one can then add Michigan to his poems of the seasons."

1943 A BOOKS - NONE

1943 B SHORTER WRITINGS

1    ANON. "Roethke, Lion Tennis Coach Leaves College; Dickinson
New Mentor." Centre Daily Times (State College, Pa.),
March 31, p. 2.
    Roethke will take a leave of absence to teach at Ben-
nington, Vermont. His four-year record is 29 wins and 21
losses. Roethke's efforts will be missed, "and no one
will ever be able to take the place in State College life
formerly occupied by the big 'Bear.'"

2    ANON. "To Theodore Roethke." Portfolio (Penn State University), V:3 (April), 10.
    This issue of the magazine is dedicated to Roethke, "a
fine teacher and a grand fellow."

3    ANON. "Old Main Columns." Penn State Alumni News, XXIX
(May), 12.
    Roethke has left Penn State for a one-year leave of
absence. He has presented the library with the original
Open House manuscript.

4    DOLINGER, MILTON [signed "Cassius"]. "A Lean and Hungry Look."
The Daily Collegian (Penn State University), March 24, p. 2.
    Roethke, soon to leave Penn State, is having trouble
getting books he has loaned to students returned.

5    _____. [signed "Cassius"]. "A Lean and Hungry Look: Pot-
pourri." The Daily Collegian (Penn State University),
April 7, p. 2.
    Roethke has published "Germinal" in the New Yorker.

6   MILLER, ART.  "Collegian Sports."  The Daily Collegian (Penn
        State University), March 25, p. 3.
            Roethke will soon leave Penn State for a leave of ab-
        sence to teach at Bennington College.  The author sketches
        some interesting experiences in Roethke's life, dwelling
        on his achievement as a tennis coach.

7   WERNER, W. L.  "The Bookworm."  Centre Daily Times (State
        College, Pa.), March 24, p. 4.  Article unsigned.
            Roethke will leave Penn State for a two semester leave
        of absence to teach at Bennington College.  His many pub-
        lications are mentioned as well as his success as a tennis
        coach.

8   WINTERS, YVOR.  "Post Scripta."  The Anatomy of Nonsense.
        Norfolk, Conn.:  New Directions, pp. 247, 250.
            Winters comments on the "highest achievement" by
        Roethke to this date, the poems "The Adamant" and "Reply
        to Censure."  Also, Roethke is linked with other "profes-
        sional scholars and teachers," such as Van Doren, Tate,
        Ransom, etc. with "a good deal of maturity, not only of
        style but of mind."


1945 A BOOKS - NONE

1945 B SHORTER WRITINGS

1   ANON.  "Academic Procession:  Fellowship."  Penn State Alumni
        News, XXXI (May), 15.
            Roethke has been awarded a $2500 Guggenheim fellowship
        for work on his second volume of poetry.


1946 A BOOKS - NONE

1946 B SHORTER WRITINGS

1   LERMAN, LEO.  "The Shoutings About--At Bennington."  Junior
        Bazaar, October, p. 223.
            "About poet Roethke, a member of the Bennington faculty
        now on a Guggenheim:  'He'd break his neck for talent.
        He's the best teacher we ever had.  He takes more time and
        trouble than anyone we know.'"  Roethke's poem "Academic"
        is reprinted on page 224.

2   WERNER, W. L.  "The Bookworm."  Centre Daily Times (State
        College, Pa.), February 12, p. 4.  Article unsigned.

1946

> Roethke has contributed "Old Florist" to Harper's
> Magazine.

1947 A BOOKS - NONE

1947 B SHORTER WRITINGS

1   WINTERS, YVOR.  "Post Scripta," in In Defense of Reason.
       Denver:  University of Denver Press, pp. 571, 574.
       Reprint of 1943.B8.

1948 A BOOKS - NONE

1948 B SHORTER WRITINGS

1   ANON.   Review of The Lost Son.  Kirkus Reviews, XVI
       (February 1), 78.
          The present poems, as a group, "lack body and substance,"
       though they possess grace and precision.  "A minor voice,
       which does not seem to gain stature with the years."

2   ANON.   "In Verse."  Washington (D.C.) Star, March 28, page
       unknown (from the Roethke collection, University of
       Washington).
          Review of The Lost Son.  Roethke's short poems state a
       child's experience of the country; while the longer ones
       symbolize the individual's development "through confused
       darkness and into the brilliancy of light."

3   ANON.   "Native Saginaw Poet Listed for State Talk."  The
       Saginaw News, March 28, p. 27.
          Roethke will speak in Ann Arbor, but the occasion is not
       given.  His publications are cited, as well as critical
       commentary by Auden and Bogan.  There is also a brief
       biographical sketch.

4   ANON.   "University Poet Writes 'More for Ear Than Eye.'"
       Seattle Times Magazine, April 4, p. 19.
          On the occasion of the publication of The Lost Son, this
       article gives biographical information on Roethke, a
       Seattle newcomer.  It says little about the book itself
       except that the words flow easily and the lines "flash
       out like pictures on a darkened screen."  Roethke is said
       to be writing a libretto for a children's operetta based
       on "Cinderella."

1948

5    ANON.   Title unknown.   Record (Chelsea, Mass.), May 15, page
        unknown (from the Roethke collection, University of
        Washington).
            Little more than an announcement of publication of The
        Lost Son.

6    ANON.   Review of The Lost Son and Other Poems.   The Tiger's
        Eye, IV (June), 112.
            "Some of Mr. Roethke's writing is wordy, prose-explicit"
        and sounds like Pound, Cummings, or Eliot.  But the good
        poems "are organized for the imagination as well as for
        eye and mind."

7    ANON.   Review of The Lost Son.   The Argus (Seattle), June 5,
        p. 5.
            Roethke's quality of personal speech "is both unique and
        charming"; he succeeds with direct, simple imagery.  "The
        poet's disenchanted recollections of enchantment (without
        the moralistic drive for redemption) make for some of the
        most refreshing and sensitive verse to be read today."

8    ANON.   "Youthful American Poets Show Ability."   Los Angeles
        Times, July 4, Part III, p. 6.
            Review of The Lost Son.  Reviewed in one paragraph with
        Randall Jarrell, Roethke earns this comment:  "Theodore
        Roethke is less explosive, but he writes with uncommon
        sensibility and economy."

9    ANON.   "Professor Buys Poetry Volumes."   University of Wash-
        ington Daily, September 30, p. 1.
            Roethke has bought about fifty volumes of poetry and
        criticism, while shopping in New York, and donated them
        to the library.

10   BADER, A. L.   "The Lost Son and Other Poems."   Michigan
        Alumnus Quarterly Review, LIV (Summer), 367-368.
            Roethke has gained maturity and power, without eccen-
        tricity and without being derivative.  The first section
        contains poems reminiscent of early imagist poetry, in
        which a mood of nostalgia is quickly sensed.  "But what
        gives the poems significance is the successful depiction
        of a child's world, a child's world seen objectively with
        the emphasis on the seeing rather than upon the nostalgic
        emotion."  Objectivity is seen again in the pervasive
        nature theme.  The Freudian "Lost Son" sequence is Roethke's
        "most original" work, but not to the reviewer's taste.

1948

11   BOGAN, LOUISE. "Verse." New Yorker, XXIV (May 15), 118-119.
       Review of The Lost Son and Other Poems. Roethke
       doesn't describe, he "relives." His pattern is "light-
       found-after-darkness." He and Jarrell are two worth read-
       ing together.

12   DAVIDSON, EUGENE. "Poet's Shelf." Yale Review, XXXVII
       (June), 747.
       Review of The Lost Son and Other Poems. Roethke's
       method is expansive, symbolic. He works "the turbulent
       anxieties of a young man and the return of a hard-won
       equilibrium with many lines of considerable talent."

13   DAVIDSON, GUSTAV. "Original Talent." Hartford (Conn.)
       Courant, August 29, page unknown (from the Roethke col-
       lection, University of Washington).
       Review of The Lost Son. Roethke says the "many-said"
       thing freshly, and without acrobatics. A favorable review
       that includes the entire "Cuttings (Later)" and general
       commentary on the "Lost Son" sequence.

14   DERLETH, AUGUST, ed. "Books of Today." Madison (Wisc.)
       Capital Times, April 6, page unknown (from the Roethke
       collection, University of Washington).
       Review of The Lost Son. This book justifies the praise
       for Open House. The author finds a "genius sense of lyric
       style, the same telling wit, the recognizable feeling for
       the little things in life...."

15   DEUTSCH, BABETTE. "Fusing Word with Image." New York Herald
       Tribune Book Review, July 25, p. 4.
       Review of The Lost Son and Other Poems. Deutsch cites
       Eliot's discussion of the "auditory imagination" to talk
       of the title poem. Roethke is not an Eliot imitator. He
       has turned to his own uses, sometimes painfully private,
       lessons learned from his masters. The shorter lyrics have
       "delicate music" and a "rare" tenderness, "clean of
       sentimentality."

16   FERRIL, THOMAS H. Review of The Lost Son and Other Poems.
       San Francisco Chronicle Magazine, June 13, p. 18.
       Roethke "gets cosmic implications out of protozoan
       sludges, yet never in the romantic sense--no literary
       eternities cramped into grains of sand." Tending toward
       "pure poetry," his work becomes disjointed. But he attains
       a "spiritual certainty," this "wise and ancient young man."

17   FLINT, F. CUDWORTH. "Nearing the Hour of the Phoenix."
     Virginia Quarterly Review, XXIV (Summer), 476-477.
          Roethke's book is disconcerting, moving from simple to
     "what?" "The dark night of the soul" suggests itself as a
     parallel, yet "the universe he arrives at is the universe
     he set out from."

18   GIBB, HUGH. "Symbols of Spiritual Growth." New York Times
     Book Review, August 1, p. 14.
          Review of The Lost Son. Roethke's poems never remain
     merely brilliant descriptions. Here is "the eternal pro-
     cession of nature to which all life conforms, including
     the spiritual life of man." He has a finely honed imagina-
     tion and, with the greenhouse images and the "rapidly
     altering rhythms," the major poems become illuminating
     spiritual experiences.

19   GRIFFIN, HOWARD. "Exciting Low Voices." Saturday Review of
     Literature, XXXI (July 10), 21, 26.
          Review of The Lost Son. "Because of the delicacy of
     touch and breadth of implication," the shorter poems are
     best. Though speaking in low tones for the most part,
     Roethke somehow "manages to see far into the life of lit-
     tle things."

20   HALL, JAMES. "Between Two Worlds." Voices, CXXXIV (Summer),
     57-58.
          Review of The Lost Son. Roethke sometimes is derivative,
     but in a few longer poems between "more direct imitators
     of the new and angrier defenders of the old," his indi-
     vidual accent can be heard. "Roethke's most effective
     theme is the cycle of life--its renewal and attrition.
     But his special talent as a poet is for imposing upon the
     associative pattern of the symbolist some of the energy
     and tension of the neo-romantic." Not in the short,
     descriptive poems, "But in the longer poems Roethke faces
     the major task of integrating his rhythms and symbols to
     express the complexity of a personal emotion. He gains
     his real force only when he has room to combine, to jux-
     tapose, and to score by multiplicity rather than by expan-
     sion of the single image."

21   HANLON, FRANK. "The Ivory Tower: The Lost Son and Other
     Poems." Sunday Bulletin Book Review (Philadelphia, Pa.),
     April 18, page unknown (from the Roethke collection,
     University of Washington).
          As a whole, Roethke's book "fails to stir the emotions
     or propel the imagination." It is difficult to determine
     if this material is prose or poetry.

1948

22   HINES, MARILYN. "Roethke Acting, Poetic Reading Charm Audi-
        ence." Detroit Collegian (Wayne State University),
        March 17, p. 2.
           Roethke read from his own work and commented on the
        poetry of Kunitz, Auden, Bogan and Hopkins. "Characteriz-
        ing both Kunitz and Bogan as two contemporary poets who
        'have an ear for the language,' He declared: 'Poetry
        should be approached primarily as an auditory experience.
        Too much late poetry has been directed to the eye. It's
        become an elaborated game not played too well by many of
        the boys.'"

23   "L. M." "Poetry in the Spring." Kansas City Star, March 27,
        page unknown (from the Roethke collection, University of
        Washington).
           Review of The Lost Son. Roethke's strength is original-
        ity. The editor of the poetry page of the newspaper would
        like to send a copy of The Lost Son rather than rejection
        slips, as an example for young poets.

24   "L. S." "'Lost Son', Other Roethke Roems." Star-News
        (Pasadena, Calif.), April 25, page unknown (from the
        Roethke collection, University of Washington).
           By singing of drab and commonplace subjects, Roethke
        can be compared to Sandburg and Lindsay.

25   MARTIN, SUZANNE. "Counterpoint." Seattle Post-Intelligencer
        Magazine, August 15, unpaginated, inside back cover.
           When Louise Bogan visited the University of Washington,
        the author interviewed her briefly, asking especially if
        she could clarify some of the obscurity in Roethke's new
        book, The Lost Son. For the author, Roethke failed to
        communicate clearly.
           "'Communicate!' snapped Miss Bogan. 'Communication has
        become one of those cliches.
        'Why all to (sic) many things communicate.
        'Someone has to keep the complicated line going.'"

26   MORGAN, FREDERICK. "Recent Verse." Hudson Review, I (Summer),
        261-262.
           Review of The Lost Son and Other Poems. Roethke's
        stripped-down images, functioning almost as concrete ob-
        jects, are stressed. This involves a sacrifice of scope.
        He solves this problem with the long poems, masterly com-
        binations of style and metrics, "held in excellent order
        by the framework of meditation and dialogue."

27   MOWRER, DEANE. "Reviews of Some Current Poetry." New Mexico
        Quarterly, XVIII (Summer), 255-256.

1948

Review of The Lost Son and Other Poems. Roethke's work
shows true originality, not just artful difference. His
"poems are vigorous and alive, syntheses of experiences
sensuous as well as cerebral.... Here indeed is a poet
who can sharpen perception with the techniques of nonsense
and nursery rhyme, and from the mind's midden of humiliation and desire, from sensual empathy in sap-filled roots
and dung-fed growth, make poetry to illuminate life's
darker levels."

28    PARSONS, EUGENE O. "Exciting Poet of a Refreshing Type."
Worcester (Mass.) Telegram, July 4, page unknown (from the
Roethke collection, University of Washington). Review of
The Lost Son.
"These are several good jobs of horticultural-poetical
reporting which gardeners especially should enjoy." The
reviewer says little more about the poetry, but suggests
that Roethke is an "exciting author to watch out for in
the future."

29    PARSONS, MARGARET. "MacDonalds, MacInnesses and Other Seattle
Authors." Worcester (Mass.) Telegram, May 23, p. 4C.
A review of The Lost Son as well as an account of a
personal visit with Roethke. New in Washington, he speaks
of the "defensive" nature of its inhabitants who try to
"sell" their state to visitors. There is nothing conventional about Roethke, as teacher or poet, and, "big-built
man," he meets life with "gusto." The sequence of poems
in The Lost Son develops its theme in a "spiral manner"
suggestive of music, and shows the stylistic influence of
Mother Goose.

30    PERRY, RALPH. "Professor's Career Moves From Athletics to
Verse." University of Washington Daily, February 3,
pp. 1, 6.
Roethke's career is one of contradictions. He began as
a "prose writer" and tennis coach, and has come to be
"hailed by many in top literary circles as America's poet
of the year." Some excerpts from reviews of Open House
are re-printed and some of Roethke's interesting earlier
jobs are listed.

31    ____. "New Professor of Poetry Publishes Second Volume."
University of Washington Daily, March 10, p. 1.
Although the author remarks briefly on The Lost Son
(stressing Roethke's "quality of personality" in his work),
he also devotes some space to Roethke's teaching techniques,
the way student writers ought to search for the rhythm in
all things, and learn "something about the use of words."

1948

32  RODMAN, SELDEN. "Second Phase: The Forties." 100 American
    Poems: Masterpieces of Lyric, Epic and Ballad from Colo-
    nial Times to the Present. New York: Mentor, The New
    American Library.
        Roethke is seen as deriving his style from William
    Carlos Williams. He is one of the few poets in the 1940's
    trying to write more than mood poetry.

33  VIERECK, PETER. "Five Good Poets in a Bad Year." Atlantic
    Monthly, CLXXXII (November), 95.
        Review of The Lost Son and Other Poems. The poems are
    too obscure, but "Roethke's original imagery and stark
    emotion-charged vocabulary outweigh all objections." His
    work suggests Hart Crane's in some ways.

34  ZILLMAN, LAWRENCE. Review of The Lost Son and Other Poems.
    Seattle Post-Intelligencer, July 18, unnumbered page,
    "Bookman's Gallery" Column in Pictorial Review Section.
        In the best sense of the word "modern," Roethke's "idiom
    communicates with freshness the drama of the natural
    world touching a nascent spirit. And though the later
    portion of the book becomes more private, as the personal-
    ity matures, Roethke's book is distinguished poetry."


1949 A BOOKS - NONE

1949 B SHORTER WRITINGS

1   ANDERSON, D. M. "An Important Poet." Southland Times,
    December 3, page unknown (from the Roethke collection,
    University of Washington).
        Review of The Lost Son. Favorable review that places
    Roethke in Wordsworth's tradition.

2   ANON. Review of The Lost Son and Other Poems. U.S. Quarterly
    Book List, V (March), 29.
        Roethke has loosened his style from Open House. There
    are echoes of Blake's "Songs." "Perhaps the clearest
    articulation intended is the surrender to organic will."

3   ANON. "The Listener's Book Chronicle." The Listener,
    September 29. p. 545.
        Auden is invoked as a judge of Roethke's poetry who
    would be pleased with the "gay, child-like jingles" of
    this book, but the reviewer finds more to admire. The
    long poems are "rather too fragmentary," though frequently
    fine. Roethke is best in the "short, vivid poems...full

of sap, of a deep and clear-eyed passion for growing
things."

4    ANON.    "Theodore Roethke's Poetic Works."  Rhodesian Herald,
        September 30, page unknown (from the Roethke collection,
        University of Washington).
            Review of The Lost Son.  The author would be benevolent
        and understanding considering the changes in poetic taste,
        "But with all allowances it is scarcely possible to accept
        more than one-tenth of the lines in this collection of
        Roethke's."

5    ANON.    Title unknown.  South Wales Argus, October 10, page
        unknown (from the Roethke collection, University of
        Washington).
            Review of The Lost Son.  The reviewer finds "nightmarish
        incoherence" and too personal symbolism that result in
        obscurity.  The "inspired observation" of the garden poems
        offers something worth saving.

6    ANON.    Title unknown.  Sydney (Australia) Sun, October 29,
        page unknown (from the Roethke collection, University of
        Washington).
            Review of The Lost Son.  A favorable review that sees
        Roethke as a competent poet, but bemoans his lack of joy.

7    FITZGERALD, ROBERT.  "Patter, Distraction, and Poetry."  New
        Republic, CXXI (August 8), 17-18.
            Review of The Lost Son and Other Poems.  Roethke's
        unique sensibility combines the intuitions of the dead,
        children, farmers and green-house keepers.  The title
        poem is "a skeletal evocation of the mystery and wild fear
        in a real experience of that earth which is 'a filth a
        fairing' behind every life.  The handling of rhythms is
        original and sure, the form abstractly or dreamily dra-
        matic, with choral jingles and sharp, eery backchat in an
        earth-tongue of Elizabethan energy."

8    "F. MacM."  Title unknown.  Irish Press, October 13, page
        unknown (from the Roethke collection, University of
        Washington).
            Review of The Lost Son.  Roethke's "now old-fashioned
        surrealist cataloguing of objects" is boring.  He is
        variously characterized as dryly astringent and reaction-
        ary; a poet who cannot get beyond his feeling of being a
        misfit.  "His poems are notes, as it were, for his case-
        history.  His split heart cannot make him sing, for it
        seems he is afraid to sing."

1949

9    FRASER, G. S.  "The Riddling Style."  <u>New Statesman and Nation</u>,
      XXXVIII (September 24), 335-336.
         Review of <u>The Lost Son and Other Poems</u>.  Roethke's
      longer, more ambitious poems ask riddles.  Yet largely
      impenetrable as they are, these later poems "have a queer
      air...of belonging, under their disguises, to a familiar
      tradition; they are involute allegories about the progress
      of the soul."  With the shorter poems ("anybody's meat"),
      "the whole book has a flavour about it, rather lacking in
      contemporary British poetry, of the pressure and shabbiness
      of life as it is ordinarily lived."

10   JUMP, J. D.  "Collected Poems."  <u>Manchester Guardian</u>,
      October 4, p. 4.
         Review of <u>The Lost Son</u>.  With "superb vitality...,
      Roethke expresses a robust yet tender sympathy with life
      in all its manifestations....  His sure and flexible
      rhythms control the reader's attention" with economy on
      each precisely observed detail.  "Richness and vividness
      of imagery, vigour of language, and a humorous personal
      quality show these to be the poems of an original and
      talented writer."

11   _____.  "Collected Poems."  <u>Manchester Guardian Weekly</u>,
      October 13, page unknown (from the Roethke collection,
      University of Washington).
         Review of <u>The Lost Son</u>.  Reprint of 1949.B10.

12   KUNITZ, STANLEY.  "News of the Root."  <u>Poetry</u>, LXXIII
      (January), 222-225.
         Review of <u>The Lost Son and Other Poems</u>.  The greenhouse
      world is a place to come from and return to; not all good
      by any means.  These are powerful poems, as good as those
      of any of Roethke's contemporaries.  The poet has a fero-
      cious imagination and a murderous wit.  Living is painful.

13   NICHOLSON, NORMAN.  "Poetry Today."  <u>Time and Tide</u> (England),
      XXX (October 29), 1087.
         Review of <u>The Lost Son</u>.  Roethke handles the traditional
      "theme of the organic cycle of birth and death," but he
      does so in a surprising and new way.  The precision of the
      greenhouse poems may have been learned from William Carlos
      Williams.  But the shorter poems do not seem completely
      worked out, neither their significance nor their shape.

14   "P. H."  Title unknown.  <u>Bolton Evening News</u> (England),
      September 17, page unknown (from the Roethke collection,
      University of Washington).

Review of The Lost Son. In his greenhouse poems Roethke
is revealed "as a writer who has mastered the craft of
poetry." However, in "the field of human emotions, his
touch is not so sure, being essentially cold and lacking
in passion." The book appeals "purely to the mind and not
at all to the senses."

## 1950 A BOOKS - NONE

## 1950 B SHORTER WRITINGS

1  ANON.  Title unknown.  Christchurch (N.Z.) Press, January 28,
    page unknown (from the Roethke collection, University of
    Washington).
    Review of The Lost Son. Out of a romantic vision,
    Roethke shows a wide range of sensibility and expression.
    The greenhouse poems are of high quality, but in the later
    "vignettes of American experience" there is a pervasive
    tone of "compassionate blending of comedy and anguish."
    "His real absorption is a metaphysical one: the enigma of
    consciousness in a blank universe of physical laws which
    impinges on the mind as beauty. This enigma and its
    accompanying ecstasy Mr. Roethke expresses passionately
    but without nonsense."

2  ANON.  "Two American Poets." London Times Literary Supplement,
    2507 (February 17), p. 107.
    Review of The Lost Son and Other Poems. "The value of
    Mr. Roethke lies in his sincerity and his ability to unite
    the words he is saying with a gift for natural cadence."
    This plus atmosphere, the ability to create chiaroscuro,
    stand between the poet and mediocrity.

3  ANON.  "Poets Turn from Obscurity." Cape Argus, February 18,
    page unknown (from the Roethke collection, University of
    Washington).
    Review of The Lost Son. Roethke writes of everyday
    things, but "with a profound sense of symbolism shot
    through with irony that makes him as genuine and original
    a poet as any alive."

4  ANON.  "Roethke's Work Included in American Poetry Book."
    Seattle Times, June 18, p. 14.
    Roethke's work is included in Mid-Century American Poets,
    edited by John Ciardi. He has recently received a Guggen-
    heim Fellowship and an invitation to Yaddo. Johy Berryman
    is teaching Roethke's courses at the University of Wash-
    ington during his absence.

1950


5    ANON.   "Roethke Represents West Coast Poets."  University of
          Washington Daily, November 9, p. 4.
              Roethke will speak at the Poetry Center in New York as
          part of a series of lectures sponsored by the Young Men's
          Hebrew Association.

6    BAYLISS, JOHN.  "Americana."  The Poetry Review, XLI
          (September/October), 281.
              Review of The Lost Son.  Tennis metaphors assist the
          reviewer in saying, in one short paragraph, that Roethke
          is "instantly recognisable" as a bad poet.

7    BURKE, KENNETH.  "The Vegetal Radicalism of Theodore Roethke."
          Sewanee Review, LVIII (January - March), 68-108.
              Examination of The Lost Son and Other Poems in an attempt
          to define Roethke's ars poetica.  The method discovered is
          one of regression, adopting the vocabulary and psychology
          of adolescence and pre-adolescence, a language of "sheer
          'intuition.'"  In his confrontation with the social hier-
          archy, Roethke always gives the sense of being on the edge
          of Revelation.  See also 1966.B22 and 1971.B7.

8    FLINT, R. W.  "Ten Poets."  Kenyon Review, XII (Autumn),
          707-708.
              Review of The Lost Son and Other Poems.  "Mr. Roethke's
          gift is a small one in the total perspective of the lan-
          guage but it looms large in the world he inhabits.  Along
          with the discretion he has a mind curious, adventurous,
          craftsmanlike, cautious, down-to-earth.  His poetry might
          be described in the bulk as a cross between William Carlos
          Williams and Dylan Thomas (with affinities to Elizabeth
          Bishop) but more traditionally declarative and with less
          experimental élan."

9    GENÊT.  "Letter from Rome."  New Yorker, XXVI:3 (March 11),
          57-58.
              In looking at the contents of the fourth number of
          Botteghe Oscure, the author says this:  "...and a grand,
          impudent apostrophe to Death, a rare thing among the wor-
          ried poets of today, called 'Praise to the End!,' by the
          American Theodore Roethke, a professor of Old English at
          the University of Washington."

10   PARKINSON, THOMAS.  "Some Recent Pacific Coast Poetry."
          Pacific Spectator, IV (Summer), 302-303.
              A favorable look at The Lost Son and Other Poems.
          Roethke's "is surely one of the most remarkable poetic
          talents in the country at present."  "Dolor" and "Weed

Puller" are quoted to demonstrate the antithesis between
sadness and the fertility of growth always present in
Roethke's work.

11    SPENDER, STEPHEN. "Rhythms That Ring in American Verse."
      New York Times Book Review, September 3, p. 3.
          An account of a meeting of poets sponsored by the Harvard
      University Summer School.  After generalizing about other
      poets, the author finds Roethke "the one most difficult to
      fit into my general picture of the scene."  Roethke paints
      vivid pictures spontaneously, but pictures deeply moving
      from "an innocent, rather clumsy personality.... Roethke
      has the limitations of someone very tied up in his own
      problems, but he is to me one of the most sympathetic of
      the American poets."

12    THWAITES, MICHAEL.  Title unknown.  The Age (Melbourne,
      Australia), June 29, page unknown (from the Roethke col-
      lection, University of Washington).
          Review of The Lost Son.  Roethke is at the center of the
      author's discussion of the distinction between poetry and
      prose.  His poems are "distinctive and authentic," except
      for occasional lapses.

13    WERNER, W. L.  "Bookworm."  Centre Daily Times (State College,
      Pa.), May 31, p. 5.  Article unsigned.
          Roethke has recorded two poems, "The Long Alley" and
      "The Shape of the Fire," for Harvard Vocarium records.


1951 A BOOKS - NONE

1951 B SHORTER WRITINGS

1    ANON.  "American Poetry Today."  London Times Literary Supple-
     ment, January 19, pp. 29-31.
          Review article of John Ciardi's Mid-Century American
     Poets, 1950.  The review gives careful attention to the
     definition of New Criticism and looks closely at the works
     of each poet included.  Of Roethke, the reviewer says:
     "He is a poet who gives the impression of being dominated--
     almost stifled--by childhood memories which he is both
     trying to recover and recover from....  He is perhaps the
     writer in America nearest to those characteristic English
     poets who express an absorption in dream-like childhood
     memories."

1951

2 ANON. "Works of Roethke in Poetry Article by London Times."
   <u>University of Washington Daily</u>, February 15, p. 1.
      Roethke's work is discussed in an article, "American
   Poetry Today."

3 ANON. "Roethke Leaves for N.Y. Lecture." <u>University of
   Washington Daily</u>, March 8, p. 1.
      Roethke will lecture on "Trends in Contemporary Poetry"
   at the Poetry Center.

4 ANON. Review of <u>Praise to the End!</u> <u>Virginia Kirkus Service</u>,
   XIX (September 1), 523.
      "The fluid verse form, the tangible richness of words
   and images in this poem of spiritual growth from prenatal
   existence to fulfillment, flood the receptive reader with
   a heady insistence, but although the goal of full understanding is a rewarding one, only the brave will make the
   effort."

5 ANON. Review of <u>Praise to the End!</u> <u>Orlando</u> (Florida) <u>Star</u>,
   December 10, page unknown (from the Roethke collection,
   University of Washington).
      "In brilliant and original verse, an introspective his-
   tory of spiritual growth by one of the few top-ranking
   poets of America."

6 EBERHART, RICHARD. "Deep Lyrical Feelings." <u>New York Times
   Book Review</u>, December 16, p. 4.
      Review of <u>Praise to the End!</u> "Theodore Roethke joins
   the ranks of the pure poets.... His verse is pure. It
   is totally sensuous, totally personal, and his vision is
   totally contained." The verse is an incantation, often
   playful; an interior monologue of obscure childhood or
   complex maturity; full of penetrating, gnomic flashes.
   But there is a strict sense of economy and control.

7 "H. A. W." "The Poetry of Roethke." <u>Trenton</u> (N.J.) <u>Times</u>,
   December 23, page unknown (from the Roethke collection,
   University of Washington).
      Review of <u>Praise to the End!</u> A favorable review in
   which Roethke is seen as more than a "modern" poet.

8 LAWRENCE, WES. "The Breakfast Commentator." <u>Cleveland Plain
   Dealer</u>, November 9, page unknown (from the Roethke
   collection, University of Washington).
      Review of <u>Praise to the End!</u> Roethke's book leads the
   reviewer through a discussion of obscurity in poetry.

9   MERRICK, REBECCA. "Praise to the End!" Seattle Post-
      Intelligencer, November 17, p. 16.
      A favorable review in which the reader is cautioned to
      take Roethke's poetry slowly. His child protagonist some-
      times seems more frog than child, but Roethke's vitality
      emerges from the dense muck and so do the poems.

10  RODMAN, SELDEN. "Intuitive Poet." New York Herald Tribune
      Book Review, December 2, p. 32.
      Review of Praise to the End! "The finished product,
      bearing certain resemblences to Mother Goose, Finnegans
      Wake, and the flower poems of D. H. Lawrence, is a wholly
      original and beautiful evocation of the sexual awakening
      of an unhappy child." This intuitive verse does not make
      "sense" except as "suggestive incantation."

11  SAMPLEY, ARTHUR. "Five Poets Find Voice in Authentic Imagery."
      Dallas Morning News, December 9, Part VI, p. 9.
      Review of Praise to the End! Though Roethke is less
      than successful writing poems of the complexity of adult-
      hood, those of the experience of childhood are totally
      successful. His poetic gifts are not to be doubted.

12  SITWELL, EDITH. "Preface." The American Genius. London:
      John Lehmann, p. xxv.
      "I read Mr. Roethke's poems for the first time three
      months ago. It is not yet the time, therefore, for me to
      write about them. I could say only that to my mind they
      are amongst the most remarkable and original poems written
      by any young poet, American or English, in our age."

13  VIERECK, PETER. "Pure Poetry, Impure Politics, and Ezra Pound."
      Commentary, April, p. 342.
      Roethke is mentioned in a group favored over the "sti-
      fling Pound-Eliot cult" for its "more sensuous lyricism."

14  WERNER, W. L. "Bookworm." Centre Daily Times (State College,
      Pa.), November 6, p. 4.
      Roethke has won the $200 Levinson Award from Poetry
      magazine. He also has been mentioned in a recent (London)
      Times Literary Supplement article.

15  WILLIAMS, WILLIAM CARLOS. The Autobiography of William Carlos
      Williams. New York: Random House, pp. 310, 370.
      Accounts of two brief meetings with Roethke.


1952 A BOOKS - NONE

# Theodore Roethke's Career: An Annotated Bibliography

1952

## 1952 B SHORTER WRITINGS

1   ANON.   "Advance Guard Poetry." Nashville Tennessean,
        January 27, page unknown (from the Roethke collection,
        University of Washington).
            Review of Praise to the End! What at first reading
        sounds like absurdity "Flowers into uncommon beauty with
        a chaste, sometimes witty, symmetry."

2   ANON.   Review of Praise to the End! St. Louis Globe-Democrat,
        February 3, page unknown (from the Roethke collection,
        University of Washington).
            Roethke's "is an original talent, modern as tomorrow,
        with a sure sense of poetic values, a nice eye for imagery
        and symbolism transformed by his own feelings, and a nice
        ear for the music inherent in the language."

3   ANON.   "Teaching Poets." Time, LIX (February 25), 46, 49.
            Brief summary of Roethke's article in Poetry, "The
        Teaching Poet."

4   ANON.   "Time Quotes Prof Roethke." University of Washington
        Daily, February 27, p. 1.
            And this article quotes Time on the education of poets.

5   ANON.   "Roethke Gets Recognition in Journal." University of
        Washington Daily, February 28, p. 2.
            Poetry has published Roethke's article, "The Teaching
        Poet."

6   ANON.   "U.W. Teacher, Ten Student Poets Honored." Seattle
        Times, February 28, p. 5.
            Announcement of Roethke's article "The Teaching Poet" in
        Poetry, and the names of University of Washington students
        included.

7   ANON.   Review of Praise to the End! Cincinnati Guidepost,
        March, page unknown (from the Roethke collection, Univer-
        sity of Washington).
            "Not everybody's meat."

8   ANON.   "From a Librarian's Notebook." Seattle Times Sunday
        Magazine, March 9, p. 15.
            Mention of Roethke's article "The Teaching Poet" in
        Poetry; work of his students, one piece from an examina-
        tion consisting of eight nouns, eight verbs and eight
        adjectives from which students had to choose five and
        write.

9    ANON.   "Theodore Roethke." Seattle Times, March 9, p. 15.
       Mention of Roethke's article, "The Teaching Poet," in
       Poetry, and the accompanying student work.

10   ANON.   "Two Profs Win Grants." University of Washington
       Daily, April 1, p. 1.
       Roethke has won a Ford Foundation grant.

11   ANON.   "15 Awards Given by Arts Institute." New York Times,
       May 15, p. 29.
          Notice of $1000 prize given by the National Institute of
       Arts and Letters.

12   ANON.   "Arts and Letters Grant Won by UW Professor." Seattle
       Times, May 15, p. 48.
          Roethke has won a $1,000 grant awarded by the National
       Institute of Arts and Letters and a one-year Ford Founda-
       tion Fellowship.

13   ANON.   "Arts & Science:  Awards." Facts on File, XII (May
       16-22), 163.
          Roethke has won $1000 award from the National Institute
       of Arts and Letters.

14   ANON.   "Roethke Wins $1,000 Grant." University of Washington
       Daily, May 23, p. 4.
       The award comes from the National Institute of Arts and
       Letters.

15   ANON.   "High Honors Accruing to Ex-Saginaw Poet." The
       Saginaw News, June 1, p. 25.
          Roethke has recently received a grant of $1000 from the
       National Institute of Arts and Letters; a Ford Foundation
       Fellowship; and the Levinson Prize from Poetry magazine.

16   ANON.   "The American Workshop." The Time Literary Supplement
       (London), August 29, Special Issue, "Fresh Minds at Work,"
       p. xxvi.
          "Of all the younger generation of American poets only
       Mr. Jarrell and Mr. Roethke (when his true brilliance
       overcomes his occasional banality) seem capable of con-
       sistent universality of diction, and there is in this a
       further paradox, for both of them, and Mr. Roethke pre-
       eminently, are egocentric poets."

17   ARMSTRONG, MARTIN.   "The Spoken Word." The Listener,
       October 16, p. 655.
          Review of Dylan Thomas' reading of Roethke's poems over
       BBC, October 8, 1952.  Entire review:  "Theodore Roethke's

1952

poetry cannot be fully appreciated at a single hearing,
but, judging by the many striking and beautiful details
scattered by the way, I take him to be a considerable
poet. Dylan Thomas' reading of the three poems was impres-
sive, although I noticed, as I have noticed before, that I
missed a word here and there. Whether this is Mr. Thomas'
fault--some peculiarity of articulation perhaps--or the
fault of the not-yet-faultless radio, I cannot say."

18  ARROWSMITH, WILLIAM. "Five Poets." Hudson Review, IV
(Winter), 619-620.
   Review of Praise to the End! These poems are sometimes
too close to cuteness, or too close to W. C. Williams.
For "small" poetry, Roethke is better than M. Moore,
mainly because of his spirit and music. There are too
many "things" present that may be only tonal décor.

19  BOGAN, LOUISE. "Verse." New Yorker, XXVII (February 16),
108.
   Review of Praise to the End! (Reprinted as "The Minor
Shudder," in Selected Criticism: Poetry and Prose. New
York: The Noonday Press, 1965. Pp. 383-384.)
   Roethke's control of even nonsense and gibberish helps
him examine the sub- or pre-conscious worlds. "Roethke
has invented a symbolism, in his searching out of these
terrors, marginal to our consciousness, that is quite his
own."

20  BRANTLEY, FREDERICK. "Poets and Their Worlds." Yale Review,
XLI (Spring), 476-477.
   Review of Praise to the End! "By the controlled restric-
tion of his theme, the intense hyperbolical sexual wit,
the almost perceptual level of his language, Roethke asks
of us the most delicate reading even for sympathetic appreciation, let alone an evaluation. He has launched a brilliant, and to a large degree victorious, assault upon
deadening abstractions in poetry."

21  BRUNCKEN, HERBERT. "Poetry and Meaning." Milwaukee Journal,
January 6, page unknown (from the Roethke collection,
University of Washington).
   Review of Praise to the End! "It is evident that Roethke
is sensitive to the values from which poetry occasionally
emerges, but until readers are permitted to share, without
undue labor, his 'deep and private feelings' or to establish some identification with his personal symbolism and
mythology, his verse can evoke only restricted interest."

22    CALAHAN, MARGARET B.   "Seattle's Surrealist Poet."  Seattle
      Times Sunday Magazine, March 16, p. 7
           The impressionistic results of an interview held after
      a Roethke class at the University of Washington.

23    CHANG, DIANA.  "The Modern Idiom"  Voices, CXLVIII (May/
      August), 42-43.
           Review of Praise to the End!  "Theodore Roethke's
      poetry requires adjustment to an alphabet of imagery which
      is entirely his own.  In Praise to the End, he traces by
      a sequence of poems the personal growth of a man's soul,
      and delves into his own subconscious, coming up with only
      half-realized symbols netted by words which perforce are
      on the conscious level."

24    "C. M. R."  "Poetry."  Boston Traveler, January 17, page
      unknown (from the Roethke collection, University of
      Washington).
           Review of Praise to the End!  "Granting a continued
      wealth of brilliant and sophisticated imagrey (sic), and
      the chaotic outcires (sic) that are so nervously invigora-
      tion (sic), the theme is too deeply buried in obscurities
      for the ordinary reader to follow."

25    FRANKENBERG, LLOYD.  "The Year in Poetry."  Harper's Magazine,
      CCV (October), 106.
           Review of Praise to the End!  Roethke's three books show
      "an extraordinarily dramatic line of development."  Open.
      House is "polished, perceptive, occasionally wry, always
      distinguished."  The Lost Son, with the tone changed,
      gives us "poems unfurling, (that) literally blossom."
      "Praise to the End! is a triumph; a true greening of the
      'private substance.'"

26    HOLLEY, FRED.  "Young Poets Show Zest."  Norfolk (Va.)
      Virginian-Pilot, January 20, page unknown (from the
      Roethke collection, University of Washington).
           Review of Praise to the End!  "The poems contain almost
      a minimum of direct communication and will be appreciated
      more for occasional striking lines than as aesthetic
      wholes."

27    HUMPHRIES, ROLFE.  "Verse Chronicle."  Nation, CLXXIV
      (March 22), 284.
           Review of Praise to the End!  Roethke has established
      "avenues of communication to his own unconsciousness."
      His direct images, metaphors and even rhythms seem ob-
      sessed and are very easy to imitate.

1952

28  JOHNSON, DONALD B. "Vague Verse Has Distinctive Flavor."
    <u>Worcester</u> (Mass.) <u>Telegram</u>, February 24, page unknown
    (from the Roethke collection, University of Washington).
        Review of <u>Praise to the End!</u> In a discussion of poetic
    factions, Roethke is linked with the obscurantists; but
    his work seems genuine communication.

29  "L. F." "Among the New Books." <u>San Francisco Chronicle</u>,
    January 20, p. 11.
        Review of <u>Praise to the End!</u> Roethke's book, in "lean,
    unlovely English," is a sequence of long poems worth
    appreciating; "a monologue of self in the natural world...;
    the voice of a Joycean baby...; a child talking to itself
    and to nature in that identification with river and tree...
    which...may haunt us all our lives; the full voice of a
    man standing up, speaking affirmatively."

30  SAWYER, KENNETH B. "Praises and Crutches." <u>Hopkins Review</u>,
    V (Summer), 131-132.
        Review of <u>Praise to the End!</u> Roethke is a myth-maker,
    dealing with the continuum of human existence. But he is
    not only a "mythological monster dear to the hearts of
    vestigial Romantics--the poet of pure intuition." Instead,
    he is much more complex and perhaps a crucial influence on
    English poetry.

31  SHAPIRO, HARVEY. Review of <u>Praise to the End!</u> <u>Furioso</u>, VII
    (Fall), 56-58.
        Unlike Wordsworth in his descent into the self, Roethke
    relinquishes adult logic, adopts childish gibber. "I
    suppose Roethke in his titles to be greeting literary
    fathers" (Smart, Blake). Movement is toward light, "the
    possible peace of childhood, the intimation of father."
    There is an ecstasy in the final poems that is never
    clearly earned, but somehow justifiable in terms of pre-
    identity, experience without a shape.

32  S(HAPIRO), K(ARL). "Editorial Note." <u>Poetry</u>, LXXIX
    (February), 249.
        Introduction to "Washington Workshop," which contains
    Roethke's essay "The Teaching Poet" and poems by his
    students.

33  VAZAKAS, BYRON. "Eleven Contemporary Poets." <u>New Mexico</u>
    <u>Quarterly</u>, XXII (Summer), 224-225.
        Review of <u>Praise to the End!</u> Roethke's book "sometimes
    seems fragmentary and incoherent, even arbitrary and capri-
    cious, if not just plain self-indulgent." He leans

"heavily on Rimbaud's requirement that the poet be halu-
cinated. The result is occasional phrases of 'pure poetry'
uttered in climaxes, evocative as the French Symbolists
and, when successful, a poetry of sensation."

34   VIERICK, PETER. "Techniques and Inspiration." Atlantic
     Monthly, CLXXXIX (January), 81.
        Review of Praise to the End! Roethke "exalts and ex-
     ults," and thereby transcends obscurity. "To convey
     ecstasy, not by explicit denotation but by rhythm and
     connotation, has a lucidity all its own, a meta-
     communication...."

35   WERNER, W. L. "The Bookworm." Centre Daily Times (State
     College, Pa.), January 15, p. 5. Article unsigned.
        Mentioning Praise to the End!, the author says: "As
     Selden Rodman said, it is difficult to know whether
     Roethke is writing automatically and intuitively or is
     making an elaborate imitation of such writing. Anyway he
     achieves a mellifluous incomprehensibility that pleases
     the critics."

36   _____. "The Bookworm." Centre Daily Times (State College,
     Pa.), November 24, p. 4. Article unsigned.
        Roethke contributed a poem to Poetry magazine's
     fortieth anniversary issue.


1953 A BOOKS - NONE

1953 B SHORTER WRITINGS

1    ANON. "Wild & Lively." New Hope (Pennsylvania) Gazette,
     January 29, p. 3.
        Earl Mohn, Gazette literary editor, in promoting a
     Roethke reading, says that "'He's wild and lively--the
     only new thing in poetry we have aside from Dylan Thomas....
     He has the gift of gab.'"

2    ANON. "Theodore Roethke to Present 1st Current Simmons
     Lecture." Centre Daily Times (State College, Pa.),
     February 13, p. 5.
        Roethke will read at Penn State. A biographical sketch
     is included.

3    ANON. "Noted Poet to Present Readings." The Daily Collegian
     (Penn State University), February 17, p. 1.
        Roethke will read at Penn State. A biographical sketch
     is included.

1953

*4 ANON. "Saginawia." The Saginaw News, May 5, 1953, page
unknown. Unlocatable, cited in McLeod, Theodore Roethke:
A Bibliography (1953.B97).

5 ANON. "The Waking." Virginia Kirkus Service, XXI (July 15),
464.
"If there is obscurity in Roethke's poetry, this is
offset by a frequent depth, urgency, breathlessness, even
a kind of ecstasy which marks a real poetic talent." Having already dealt with childhood in earlier work, Roethke
here "has achieved expression of more mature feelings."

6 ANON. Review of The Waking. Booklist, L (October 15), 74.
An autobiography in verse. "Readers of modern poetry
will appreciate his (Roethke's) precise observation, his
controlled exuberance, and the clarity with which he con-
veys his homely wisdom."

*7 ANON. "Ex-Saginawian's Poems Collected in Book Form." The
Saginaw News, December 22, page unknown. Unable to locate
on this date; as cited by McLeod, Theodore Roethke: A
Bibliography (1953.B99).

8 BOGAN, LOUISE. "Verse." New Yorker, XXIX (October 24),
158-159.
Review of The Waking. "Amid the dreary and abstract
poetry of Roethke's generation, it is a pleasure to come
upon such well-made, humane, and wise lyrics."

9 BURKE, KENNETH. "Post-Roethkian Translation." Hopkins Review,
VI (Winter), 6-7.
A poem in tribute to Roethke.

10 CARRUTH, HAYDEN. "The Idiom Is Personal." New York Times Book
Review, September 13, p. 14.
Review of The Waking. Roethke's experimentation and
originality are praised, not as discrete acts of craft,
but as direction forced upon the poet by his subject matter, i.e., childhood in the greenhouse among the "groping
roots." His poems written in the child's voice are of our
"fearful and murderous heritage."

11 CIARDI, JOHN. "Poets of the Inner Landscape." Nation,
CLXXVII (November 14), 410.
Review of The Waking. Roethke is the "medicine man" of
the psyche. He finds his emotional equivalents to his
inner self in "the physical impact of things." His poetry
is one of therapy, from madness to reflective calm. "His

style seems most nearly founded on Christopher Smart, Blake, the Elizabethan rant, and the backwoods brag, all scattering free, but always with a sense of breaking through a tremendous formal control."

12   DEMPSEY, DAVID. "In and Out of Books: Program Notes." New York Times Book Review, February 8, p. 8.
    An account of a Roethke reading in which he was "accompanied by two trombonists, a cornetist, accordianist and a lady tuba player. There was also a clarinetist who sat behind a pillar probably hiding out from James Petrillo." Roethke put on a good show with his audience always "in a state of expectancy." "In addition to your correspondent, the event was covered by a crime reporter for the New York Daily News. The program came to an end with the ensemble playing 'On Wisconsin.'"

13   DEUTSCH, BABETTE. "Poetry Chronicle." Yale Review, XLIII (December), 280-281.
    Review of The Waking. Some deletions from earlier books are to be lamented. "Some of the most memorable poems are the familiar ones that evoke childhood memories with a sensitive and significant realism."

14   FRAME, MARALLYN. "Work of English Prof. Gets Praise of Critic." University of Washington Daily, October 21, p. 1.
    Hayden Carruth's remarks on The Waking are quoted from the New York Times. An account of Roethke's book is given, as well as some of his recent activities, such as guest editor for New World Writing, reading for the BBC, and traveling for the "Fund for the Advancement of Education." Some of Roethke's poems have lately been translated for several foreign journals.

15   HALL, DONALD. "American Poets Since the War." World Review, NS XLVII (January), 48-49.
    "Another older poet, but one whose career changed so abruptly that we may put a 'II' after his name and consider him a new poet, is Theodore Roethke. Roethke published a book called Open House in 1941; it was a good book of verse written expertly in neat stanzas, and received the favourable attention it merited. But when The Lost Son was published in 1948...the adept builder of quatrains has (sic) been replaced by Roethke II. Now his poems had the initial appearance of brilliant fragments, but the best of them showed a genius and intelligence anything but fragmentary." The poems also showed a "close, needle-like quality" of imagery. The long poems were best; and showed "no hint of

1953

> dimunition in quality. Roethke's language combines
> accuracy and hallucinatory force. After a close descrip-
> tion of whatever, his diction raises itself to a pitch of
> controlled hysteria...."

16  KOHLER, DAYTON. "A Poet Arrives: Roethke's Work of 20 Years
Is Significant Achievement." Richmond News Leader,
December 14, p. 11.
Review of The Waking. A favorable review that looks
forward to Roethke's future accomplishments. His individual books are examined in order to establish the progression of the poet's talent and personality.

17  REISS, EDMUND. "Roethke Poems Delight Audience." The Daily
Collegian (Penn State University), February 19, p. 2.
Roethke read as part of the Simmons Series at Penn State.


1954 A BOOKS - NONE

1954 B SHORTER WRITINGS

1  ANON. "Notes on the Margin." San Francisco Chronicle
February 21, This World supplement, p. 18.
Roethke's reading at San Francisco State College will,
it is hoped, "help stimulate interest in the project for
a poetry center."

2  ANON. Review of The Waking. U.S. Quarterly Book Review, X
(March), 55.
This collection shows striking stylistic development by
Roethke. The poet has become more concerned with inner
conflict. There is, though, a lack of sustained strength.

3  ANON. "Pulitzer Poetry Prize Won by UW Professor." Seattle
Post-Intelligencer, May 4, p. 1.
Roethke received news that The Waking had won the award
calmly after being summoned from his classroom. He then
drove to Bellevue High School to inform his wife, who
taught there. The only statement by Roethke included here
is: "I try to write poetry that people can read and
understand."

4  ANON. "Pulitzer Awards." London Times, May 4, p. 6.
Merely announced.

5  ANON. "Roethke Wins 1954 Pulitzer Poetry Prize." Centre
Daily Times (State College, Pa.), May 4, pp. 1, 10.
Roethke received the award for The Waking.

6    ANON.   "U.W. Poet Wears Honors Modestly." Seattle Times,
         May 4, p. 9.
            Review of The Waking. Roethke has won the Pulitzer
         Prize for this volume. It is discussed briefly.

7    ANON.   "Pulitzer Poetry Prize Won by UW Professor." Seattle
         Times, May 4, p. 5.
            Roethke wins the Pulitzer Prize for The Waking. The
         article recounts his calm reception of the news and con-
         gratulations by colleagues. He drove to tell his wife
         and that evening spent a quiet time in his "far from pre-
         tentious" Lake Washington home.

8    ANON.   "Ex-Saginawian Wins Coveted Pulitzer Prize." The
         Saginaw News, May 4, p. 1.
            Roethke has won the award for The Waking. His poems'
         "authenticity" comes from their setting, "the greenhouse
         operated here by Prof. Roethke's grandfather." Some of
         Roethke's previous prizes are listed and biographical
         material relevant to the Saginaw area.

9    ANON.   "University Poet, Roethke, Given Pulitzer Prize."
         University of Washington Daily, May 4, pp. 1, 2.
            Roethke won the prize for The Waking. Numerous other
         awards and honors are listed. Roethke comments specif-
         ically on his difficulty in writing poetry, aiming at a
         particular effect; the variety of modern poetry; society's
         faults regarding poetry; the University of Washington
         poetry program; and how American "'public poetry,' written
         to be heard, is gaining popularity internationally."

10   ANON.   "Pulitzer Prize Awards for 1953; Who's Who on Winners:
         Theodore Roethke." St. Louis Post-Dispatch, May 4,
         Part III, pp. 1, 5.
            Roethke won the poetry award for The Waking. A picture
         is included, one of his worst. The final biographical
         sketch is Roethke's, all alone on page 5.

11   ANON.   "Columbia Names Seven Pulitzer Prize Winners." The
         Daily Collegian (Penn State University), May 4, p. 3.
            Roethke received the poetry award for The Waking.

12   ANON.   "Pulitzer Prize Awards." Natal Mercury (Durban, South
         Africa), May 5, page unknown (from the Roethke collection,
         University of Washington).
            An announcement that Roethke has won for The Waking.

1954

13　ANON.　"Pulitzer Award Winners." South China Morning Post
　　　(Hong Kong), May 5, page unknown (from the Roethke col-
　　　lection, University of Washington).
　　　　Roethke has won the award for The Waking.

14　ANON.　"Reason to Be Proud of State University." Seattle
　　　Times, May 17, p. 6.
　　　　Roethke is recognized in an editorial for winning the
　　　Pulitzer Prize.

15　ANON.　"Poetic Background: A Period of Consolidation." The
　　　Times Literary Supplement (London), September 17, Special
　　　Number, "American Writing To-Day," p. ii.
　　　　"All is not completely standardized, however. Theodore
　　　Roethke...has recognized that power can be released by an
　　　effort to make contact with subconscious processes: and
　　　Roethke and others have recently attempted to express the
　　　vulgarity and violence usual in modern life--which cannot
　　　be approached or utilized in literature except in the
　　　simplest and sincerest terms."

16　ANON.　"The Three Realms of the Young Poet." The Times
　　　Literary Supplement (London), September 17, Special Number,
　　　"American Writing To-Day," p. iv.
　　　　Roethke is stuck in the realm of marriage between poetry
　　　and American universities.

17　ANON.　"Expressive Voices: The Emergence of a National Style."
　　　The Times Literary Supplement (London), September 17,
　　　Special Number, "American Writing To-Day," p. xii.
　　　　The questions raised are: If there is an American
　　　national style, what is it like? and where does it come
　　　from? Roethke is linked with his contemporaries "who,
　　　with an inevitable clue from Auden and a large conscious-
　　　ness of European experiment, have tried to assimilate all
　　　they learned from Eliot, Pound, and the stylistic radicals
　　　to new modes of personal sincerity and realism."

18　BEAHAN, PADDY.　"Former Prof Wins Prize for Poetry." The Daily
　　　Collegian (Penn State University), May 6, p. 8.
　　　　Roethke has won the Pulitzer Prize for The Waking.　A
　　　brief biographical sketch is included.

19　BELL, LOU.　"Once Over Lightly." Centre Daily Times (State
　　　College, Pa.), May 7, p. 4.
　　　　Announcing that Roethke has won the Pulitzer Prize, the
　　　author reminisces about his "old and erratic opponent at
　　　squash." Before meeting Roethke, the author had read one

of his poems, "about a water fowl," and, confused by it,
sought advice from a faculty friend. The latter explained
at length the poem's symbolism and complexities. When the
author met Roethke and asked for further commentary on the
poem, Roethke said simply: "'Oh, nuts! All I did was
paint a word picture of a bird.'"

20 BENNETT, JOSEPH. "Recent Verse." Hudson Review, VII (Summer),
304-305.
Review of The Waking. "In Mr. Roethke's most successful
poems, the quality is daft and apt: surrealism and dis-
continuousness combine to provide a divisionist effect."
He disregards traditional verse, displaying a narrow range
of style. There is eccentricity at the heart of the verse,
sometimes coy, with too much word-play."

21 BREIT, HARVEY. "Pulitzer Poet." New York Times Book Review,
May 16, p. 8.
Barely an announcement of the Pulitzer Prize for The
Waking, the writer quotes liberally from Roethke's com-
ments in another source to give some insight into the
character of the man writing the poems.

22 CANTY, DAVE. "London Times Lauds Professors for Outstanding
Literary Feats." University of Washington Daily,
October 22, p. 1.
The article quotes from the Times and mentions Dylan
Thomas' view that Roethke is "one of the most remarkable
and original" of contemporary poets.

23 COLE, THOMAS. "The Poetry of Theodore Roethke." Voices,
No. 155 (September/December), pp. 37-39.
Review of The Waking. Roethke progresses through each
of his books to a position "among our most important American poets." In Open House, "What clarity prevails, what
unity!" The Lost Son shows "easily perceived formal qualities subtly undergoing a change" until, in Praise to the
End!, "The clarity and intelligible sequence of incidence
(sic) disappears and substituted is a rather intuitive,
stream-of-consciousness recollection of childhood in which
inanimate objects take on the qualities of animation and
together with the animate things cavort and speak throughout the poems." Some of these longer poems seem only
"brilliant experiments" that point toward a kind of poetry
not yet realized. The later poems too are experimentations
that fail to assimilate the style of Yeats.

1954

24    FAUCHALD, NILS. "Theodore Roethke, Pulitzer Winner, Explains
Value of Modern Poetry." Bellevue High School (Bellevue,
Wash.) Barque, May 7, page unknown (from the Roethke
collection, University of Washington).
      Brief account of The Waking and Roethke's views on
writing. Roethke read "Night Journey" to the author over
a chocolate malt.

25    HUSBAND, JOHN DILLON. "Some Readings in Recent Poetry." New
Mexico Quarterly, XXIV (Winter), 446-447.
      Review of The Waking. Roethke's craft and idiom were
almost immediately individual. His substance was known
early too, "the matter-of-fact moving of earth's substance
into earth's shapes." His mastery of craft and the limitations of his materials "were a trap into which Roethke is
too astute a poet to let himself fall." Following too
far the "experimental, exploratory idiom and manner" might
result in a too private poetry.

26    KRAMER, HILTON. "The Poetry of Theodore Roethke." Western
Review, XVIII (Winter), 131-146.
      Roethke's poetry departs from a firm American tradition
in its concentration on the pre-rational of pre-history.
It also leaves Wordsworth behind as it examines "the
spirit's education in the world of nature, and the recovery
of human feelings." The author's main interest centers on
the poems of Praise to the End! in which he sees the following general development: "the first-person protagonist,
frequently speaking out in anguished exclamations, nonsense
songs, frenzied invocations, and even moments of contemplation, begins in a situation of death and desolation, under-
goes the agony of coming alive again and of perceiving the
world anew, and then ends with what is, however minimal
and primitive, a vision of the triumph of life...: these
poems constitute the action of a soul undergoing its night-
journey." The journey is not toward an intellectual light,
but rather toward "a stage which celebrates la condition
botanique as an ideal, if only by default, salvaging from
Romanticism a certain kind of melancholy and nostalgia for
the pre-rational." Roethke's poetry is primitive, but of
a most abstract kind.

27    "L. F." "Recent Poetry in Review." San Francisco Chronicle,
January 10, p. 17.
      Review of The Waking. Roethke chose a suitable title
as the poet gradually wakens to himself and his poetic
powers increase. Despite a possible charge of regression
there is an ever-increasing sentience. The reviewer hears

a voice much like that of Stephen Dedalus in Joyce's <u>A Portrait of the Artist as a Young Man</u>.

28  MEYER, GERALD PREVIN. "Logic of the North." <u>Saturday Review</u>, XXXVII (January 16), 18-19.
       Review of <u>The Waking</u>. A joyousness fills Roethke's work, from a closeness to his northern (Michigan) roots. "It is as if the Wasteland never was."

29  MEYERS, LAURA SCOTT. "Pulitzer Prize Winners." <u>Herald-Post</u> (El Paso, Tex.), May 8, page unknown (from the Roethke collection, University of Washington).
       Roethke is a "poet's poet" and his award comes at a time when there is "a distinct dearth" of poetry.

30  NEMEROV, HOWARD. "Three In One." <u>The Kenyon Review</u>, XVI (Winter), 144-154.
       Review of <u>The Waking</u>. Although Roethke restricts himself to "archaic" and limited subject matter, his work is not primitive. Rather, there is a suggestion of great verbal sophistication. The impulsive energy of the early poems is disturbed by the conventional stanza and syntax of the later. The author looks forward to a new stage. <u>See also</u> 1963.B54.

31  PATRICK, JOHN. "Sketches of Pulitzer Prize Winners in Journalism, Letters and Music for 1954." <u>New York Times</u>, May 4, p. 26.
       Biographical sketch delineates Roethke's education, teaching and publishing careers, as well as listing several literary prizes and awards. The Associated Press photograph of Roethke does nothing for the dignity of the award.

32  SCOTT, WINFIELD TOWNLEY. "Makers of Stone Axes." <u>Virginia Quarterly Review</u>, XXX (Autumn), 621.
       Review of <u>The Waking</u>. Roethke's work has come "momentarily to rest on a meditative sort of poem heightened... in emotion and intellect." Hard to define, the poems are very powerful.

33  SEYMOUR-SMITH, MARTIN. "Where is Mr. Roethke?" <u>Black Mountain Review</u>, I (Spring), 40-47.
       Review of <u>The Waking</u> and over-all look at Roethke's writing. Roethke "is the Kafka of modern poetry.... His poems at their best are a description of a state of black melancholic horror...." Metrically he is an uneasy apologist for traditional verse. There is little originality and no profundity to substitute. Instead of exploring the

1954

"pathological sense of some kind of damnation inside life itself," Roethke stands back and says "Boo!" at it.

34  SITWELL, EDITH. "The Rising Generation." London Times Literary Supplement, September 17, p. i of Special Section, "American Writing To-day."
    "Almost the last time I saw Dylan Thomas he told me he regarded Mr. Roethke as one of the most remarkable and original of the younger poets writing in America or England in our time. And I agree. His poems are strange, and have an entirely original physical beauty."

35  TRAFFORD, JACQUIE. "Poet Reads, Reels to Own Ribald Rhyme." The Ubyssey, (University of British Columbia) March 5, p. 1.
    In his reading at the University of British Columbia, Roethke looked "like a man practising in front of a mirror." He claimed he has tended toward the "ribald" in poetry and "explained the rhymes by saying he has always been a 'Mother Goose Man.'" In praising Louise Bogan, Roethke called her a "'female commando' because she always wrote straight from the shoulder."

36  VIERECK, PETER. "The Last Decade in Poetry: New Dilemmas and New Solutions," in Literature in the Modern World. Nashville, Tenn.: George Peabody College for Teachers, pp. 38-39.
    Similar to the remarks on Roethke and Richard Wilbur in the New Republic, February 21, 1955, p. 17, 1955.B9.

37  WERNER, W. L. "The Bookworm." Centre Daily Times (State College, Pa.), September 28, p. 4. Article unsigned.
    Roethke received much attention in a recent issue on American Literature of the (London) Times Literary Supplement.


1955 A BOOKS - NONE

1955 B SHORTER WRITINGS

1   ANON. "Wins Pulitzer Prize." Florists' Telegram Delivery News, July, pp. 69-70.
    "Old Florist" is reprinted in this brief article that attempts to justify the presence of the many "vivid floral images that crowd" Roethke's poems by recounting his history in and around the greenhouses in Saginaw, Michigan.

2   ANON.   "Roethke, Theodore."   The Americana Annual:  An Ency-
       clopedia of the Events of 1954.  Edited by Lavinia P.
       Dudley and John J. Smith.  New York, Chicago, Washington,
       D.C.:  Americana Corporation, p. 636.
          Roethke won the 1954 Pulitzer Prize in poetry for The
       Waking.  A brief biographical sketch follows.

3   ANON.   "Roethke, Theodore."   Concise Dictionary of American
       Literature.  Edited by Robert Fulton Richards.  New York:
       Philosophical Library, p. 194.
          After brief mention of Roethke's teaching career and his
       first three books, the author closes with:  "He writes
       about ordinary life in ordinary language.  His subject
       might be the pickle factory where he once worked or the
       scenes of a greenhouse.  But his imagery and his coupling
       of ordinary words is extraordinary."

4   BRINNAN, JOHN MALCOLM.  Dylan Thomas in America:  An Intimate
       Journal.  Boston, Toronto:  Atlantic-Little, Brown, p. 8.
          Upon his arrival in America and after meeting with the
       author, the first American writer Thomas asked about was
       Roethke.  Because of their knowledge of and shared respect
       for Roethke's poetry, Thomas and Brinnan were more easily
       able to establish mutual confidence.

5   HALL, DONALD.  "The New Poetry:  Notes on the Past Fifteen
       Years in America."  New World Writing, 7th Mentor Selec-
       tion.  New York:  New American Library, pp. 236-237.
          Roethke moved from "precise statements" in Open House to
       the "sensuous wilderness" of Praise to the End!  His most
       recent poetry shows a "wild precision."  In his "free
       verse" there is no "hint of the arbitrary; every line is
       glued in place, as fixed as in his regular forms."

6   KUNITZ, STANLEY, ed.  Twentieth Century Authors:  First Supple-
       ment.  New York:  H. W. Wilson, pp. 837, 838.
          Roethke's own words on his life and poetry; and those
       who helped him early in his career.  The editor finishes
       the biographical sketch.

7   MURPHY, RICHARD.  "Three Modern Poets."  The Listener,
       September 8, p. 374.
          "Roethke seems unconcerned with things as they are, but
       very much concerned with the new universe of feeling he
       can create with words....  He deliberately does not de-
       scribe things.  He does not tell us who is talking to whom.
       Words take place.  We feel either free or lost in his com-
       pany."  Roethke cares little for precision; he uses words

1955

"emotionally." He has to combine speech and music; "but it is more important to have meaningful words than meaningful music."

8   PEARCE, DONALD. "The Waking." Michigan Alumnus, LXI (May 21), 273-275.
    "The surprising thing is the freshness. After that, the music, alert and clear to the last studied lines. After that, the spectacle of growth--what Collected Poems since Yeats's displays a comparable personal development?" Poetry for generations has elegized the lack of Belief, the wasteland. In Roethke, however, "Instead of the arid tumuli of the Cactus Land (however projected symbolically) we have poems full of wet, growing things," root cellars, greenhouses, "and everywhere the felt assurance of dark waters underground feeding growing things, making all things flourish, as primevally scheduled." It is the child mind, never static, that matures to a waking. "The break--the Waking--occurs at the end of the volume with the last five poems, and is achieved by frank adoption of the deep, rocky voice of the later Yeats. It is quite a sight, the old, sure hand of the Irish poet guiding the younger, tumultuous American toward the desolation of reality; and out of it comes one of the finest, simple lines in English, good enough to rest the whole busy volume on, but at the same time an annunciation: 'I learn by going where I have to go.' At this point the entire work makes explicit multiple contact with the Eliotic wasteland, accepts it, makes its peace, and prepares to go on through."

9   VIERECK, PETER. "The Younger Poets and Conformity." New Republic, CXXXII:8 (February 21), 17.
    A comparative discussion of two of the most original voices among "younger" American poets, the Dionysian of Roethke and the Apollonian Richard Wilbur.

10  WERNER, W. L. "Bookworm: Fire Professor to Get Funds for Lecture." Centre Daily Times (State College, Pa.), April 26, p. 4. Article unsigned.
    Roethke is represented by a few poems in the latest Untermeyer anthology of American and British poetry.


1956 A BOOKS - NONE

1956 B SHORTER WRITINGS

1   ANON. "Institute of Arts Adds 13 Members." New York Times, February 7, p. 38.

1956

Roethke joined the National Institute of Arts and
Letters.

2   ANON.   "Ex-Saginaw Poet Wins High Honor."  The Saginaw News,
        February 28, p. 17.
            Roethke is cited in the 1956-1957 volume of Who's Who
        in America.  A few paragraphs summarize his awards.

3   ANON.   "U Poet Winner of Yale Award."  University of Washington
        Daily, May 18, p. 8.
            James Wright gives credit for much of his success in
        winning the Yale Series of Younger Poets award to Roethke.

4   ANON.   "Two Arts Groups Make 24 Awards."  New York Times,
        May 24, p. 25.
            Roethke is inducted as new National Institute of Arts
        and Letters member.

5   FRANKENBERG, LLOYD.  Invitation to Poetry:  A Round of Poems
        From John Skelton to Dylan Thomas Arrranged with Comments.
        Garden City, New York:  Doubleday & Co., p. 255.
            The author comments briefly on the nature of the speaking
        voice in Roethke's poem, "Big Wind."

6   KIZER, CAROLYN.  "Poetry:  School of the Pacific Northwest."
        New Republic, CXXXV (July 16), 18-19.  Reprinted:  Con-
        gressional Record, July 12, 1956, Sect. A., p. 5490.
            Roethke influences his students toward the expression of
        their own individuality, with a high level of aural sen-
        sibility.  He, along with Stanley Kunitz, abhors "cosy"
        writing, that stands in fear of displaying emotion, or
        striving for emotional sophistication even at the cost of a lie.
        The author has much to say about the environment for poetry
        at the University of Washington, the gifted students, and
        especially Roethke's importance to the whole affair.

7   WERNER, W. L.  "Bookworm:  Patent Could Save Wear on Legis-
        lators."  Centre Daily Times (State College, Pa.),
        March 27, p. 4.  Article unsigned.
            Roethke was elected recently to membership in the
        National Institute of Arts and Letters.

8   _____.  "Bookworm:  Correction, Japan Works, Air Conditioning."
        Centre Daily Times (State College, Pa.), July 3, p. 4.
        Article unsigned.
            A recent issue of the New York Herald Tribune mentions
        Roethke's course in Modern American Poetry at the Univer-
        sity of Florence, Italy.

# Theodore Roethke's Career: An Annotated Bibliography

1957

1957 A BOOKS - NONE

1957 B SHORTER WRITINGS

1    ANON. "U. to Get Annual Prize for Poetry." Seattle Times, April 11, p. 25.
      A $100 yearly prize from the Academy of American Poets will be offered to a University of Washington student, according to Robert Heilman, primarily because of the work of Roethke.

2    ARNETT, CARROLL. "Minimal to Maximal: Theodore Roethke's Dialectic." College English, XVIII (May), 414-416.
      Each of Roethke's volumes is seen as a step in the process of self-knowledge. "He finds his answer in the hope, almost conviction, that 'the spring and rush of the child' is knowable as a necessary term in an organic dialectic; that the existence of order and harmony implied through the creative act of composition is evidence of a universal order inacessible to man, but one whence orderly change and harmonious growth are derived."

3    PEARCE, ROY HARVEY. "On the Continuity of American Poetry." Hudson Review, X (Winter 1957/1958), 538.
      Roethke's poetry is seen as falling into line with that of "the imposing self" from the nineteenth century.

4    PHILLIPS, DOUGLAS. "Over the Imagination's Far Frontier." Western Mail (Cardiff), December 14, page unknown (from University of Washington Roethke Collection).
      Review of Words for the Wind. Roethke's poetry trembles "on the brink of greatness." The poems exhibit a completeness of vision and perfectly controlled technique. Roethke travels to the far frontiers of the imagination in these days of "the back-garden poet."

5    WILLIAMS, WILLIAM CARLOS. Letter to Kathleen Hoagland, July 26, 1950. The Selected Letters of William Carlos Williams. New York: McDowell, Oblensky, p. 291.
      Roethke is one of Williams' favorites at Yaddo Colony in Saratoga Springs, N.Y.

1958 A BOOKS

1    MATHESON, WILLIAM. Theodore Roethke: A Bibliography. University of Washington Master's Thesis.
      Includes a Preface discussing the difficulties of the bibliographer; an Introduction; Works by Roethke; Works about Roethke; and an Index of first lines to the poems.

## 1958 B SHORTER WRITINGS

1   ALVAREZ, A.  "Art and Isolation."  Stewards of Excellence.
    New York:  Charles Scribner's Sons, pp. 186-188.
       Discussion of The Lost Son and Praise to the End!  Com-
    bination of material previously published, but not located,
    in the Listener and London Times Literary Supplement.

2   _____.  "Art and Isolation."  The Shaping Spirit:  Studies in
    Modern English and American Poets.  London:  Chatto and
    Windus, pp. 186-191.
       Roethke has talent but it is essentially unfulfilled.
    He does not serve his material, he exploits it.  "There
    is an air of coy exhibitionism to it all."

3   _____.  "To Be or Not to Be a Poet."  The Observer (London),
    January 5, p. 12.
       Review of Words for the Wind.  Roethke is a poet who has
    suffered and recovered from the importance placed by con-
    temporary tastes on going "through a poetic act--the more
    shocking and extreme the better--" rather than writing
    poetry.  "What he says is less important than his technical
    innovation in saying it."  Roethke's work shows three
    stages:  a peculiar innocence in the plant poems; the
    exploitation of the source of his poetry, for display, in
    the psychic poems; and the lucidity of the late poems in
    which he shows "extraordinary awareness of the edges of
    experience, no longer a matter for tricks and conceit."

4   ANON.  "Poetry Society Honors Book by Professor."  University
    of Washington Daily, January 8, p. 1.
       Words for the Wind has been chosen by the London Poetry
    Book Society as one of the four best books published in
    England in 1957.  Roethke describes his divisions of the
    book.

5   ANON.  "Points of Origin."  London Times Literary Supplement,
    February 7, p. 72.
       Review of Words for the Wind.  Roethke is obsessed by
    childhood, his own and "archetypal resemblances between
    it and any other experience of newness, of freshness, of
    beginning to become."  He particularly limits his scope
    (an "ascetic honesty") because he knows his conceptual
    limitations.  Not lack of consistency, but imitative
    styles, changed frequently, are his weakness.

6   ANON.  "Many Like His Poems--And You?"  Manchester Evening
    News, February 21, page unknown (from the Roethke collec-
    tion, University of Washington).

1958

>      Review of Words for the Wind. Roethke is hereby estab-
>      lished as a major American poet.

7    ANON.   Review of Words for the Wind. The Listener,
>           February 27, p. 375.
>           Roethke displays here "the steady development of an
>      entirely original writer." His language is simple, with-
>      out jargon; his rhythm is delicate like that of Emily
>      Dickinson. "Mr. Roethke is deeply mystically concerned
>      with man's affinity to nature--particularly to plant life
>      and the life of small creatures..." but without moral over-
>      tones of Wordsworth. His poems defy analysis. "Like
>      Walter de la Mare he is a unique phenomenon; he will found
>      no school, he can have no imitators."

8    ANON.   "A Modern Poet." Madras (India) Mail, March 15, page
>           unknown (from University of Washington Roethke Collection).
>           Review of Words for the Wind. Of Roethke's progress as
>      a modern poet, the reviewer says: "1941 is at worst
>      straightforward, 1948 is becoming deliberately precious,
>      1951 has become as deliberately eccentric." Or, Roethke's
>      career could be that of "a man through a dangerous illness."
>      The problem is that all readers cannot be initiates. Much
>      is hysterical and, even, derivative (Dylan Thomas and the
>      Chinese of Arthur Waley).

9    ANON.   portrait. "Five Music Men of Words." Newsweek, LI
>           (March 17), 110.
>           Brief biographical sketch of Roethke in which it is
>      stated that he "is known for a comic spirit both subtle
>      and blunderbuss."

10   ANON.   "Magazine Cites Poet Ex-Prof." The Daily Collegian
>           (Penn State University), March 22, p. 2.
>           Newsweek has cited Roethke as being one of the "'five
>      music men of words'" in America. Professor of American
>      Literature William L. Werner's comments are included.

11   ANON.   "Literature: Amateurs and Pros." Calcutta (India)
>           Statesman, March 30, page unknown (from University of
>           Washington Roethke Collection).
>           Review of Words for the Wind. Roethke receives a
>      favorable paragraph that closes with: "His poetry is very
>      much sui generis, startling and unexpected, highly civi-
>      lized in the best sense...."

12   ANON.   "Three Modern Poets." Church Times (London), May 16,
>           page unknown (from the Roethke collection, University of
>           Washington).

Review of Words for the Wind. Roethke is refreshingly
un-academic. Despite his over-confidence, he is one of
the most original of American poets.

13  ANON.  "Words for the Wind." Virginia Kirkus Service, XXVI
(June 1), 402.
"This book demonstrates the development of this poet--
from the early, concrete lyrics of 1941--hardly more than
obscure poetic annotations--these poems increase in scope,
depth, substance and skill as they approach the middle
'50's."

14  ANON.  "A Lyricist on Life." Albany (Ore.) Democrat Herald,
November 8, page unknown (from the Roethke collection,
University of Washington).
Review of Words for the Wind. Favorable brief review.

15  ANON.  "Two Authors Offer Fine Books of Verse." Miami
(Florida) News, November 23, page unknown (from the
Roethke collection, University of Washington).
Review of Words for the Wind. Roethke does not attain
the stature of the major poets of the 20's, but his poems
"compel an excited interest." He traces, "altogether
unabstractly, the progress from preconscious to conscious,
irrational to rational, infantile to adult...."

16  ANON.  Review of Words for the Wind. Denver Post, November 30,
page unknown (from the Roethke collection, University of
Washington).
Little critical commentary.

17  ANON.  "Kin to the Bat." Time, LXXII (December 29), 55.
Review of Words for the Wind. Roethke "writes poetry in
which the meaning is just below the surface.... (He) has
restored simplicity to the tortured, packed lines of U.S.
moderns. He has brought back melody." Roethke's new book
includes love poems "reminiscent in their intensity, in
their bemused exploration of the interplay of passion and
spiritual love, of the poems of John Donne." Though always
promising revelation, there is no resolution in Roethke's
poems, no "coherent whole," perhaps because there is none
in him.

18  BELLMAN, SAMUEL.  "Riding the Literary Circuit." Fresno
(Calif.) Guide, December 11, p. 23.
Review of Words for the Wind. "Nature, the aging process,
and love are among his major themes, but he does not text-
book-treat them, nor scalpel their flesh. He takes them

1958

into his mist-world of half meanings, fractional feelings,
and quasi-impulses, remolding them startlingly."

19    CONQUEST, ROBERT. "The Language of Men." <u>Spectator</u>,
February 14, pp. 210-211.
    Review of <u>Words for the Wind</u>. Roethke's method "is to
make a poem out of a series of sentences each perfectly
clear and meaningful in itself but not logically connected
with its successors." His best subject is "a numinous and
empirical treatment of love." "Roethke in many ways re-
sembles a Yeats with a blunter cutting edge and a less
strongly organized mind."

20    DEUTSCH, BABETTE. "Roethke's Clear Signature." <u>New York
Herald Tribune Book Review</u>, December 7, p. 3.
    Review of <u>Words for the Wind</u>. Lavish praise is given
this volume, including "a group of new poems as moving as
any written in our time." Roethke is praised for his
honesty, his progress in making the "earthly concrete"
yield a "meaningful symbolism," his successful confronta-
tion against cruelty and sordidness, his risks that make
the almost-common fresh and his ability to identify with
a great range of things and individuals. But most of all,
his own touch emerges clear.

21    EBERHART, RICHARD. "Creative Splendor." <u>New York Times Book
Review</u>, November 9, p. 34.
    Review of <u>Words for the Wind</u>. Roethke's book is "a
major achievement in the Romantic tradition of American
poetry." Roethke's early work was his "worm period," not
quite whole in conception. He later took Yeats as a model
and broadened his poems to a level both "intuitive and
cognitive." Maturity necessitated meditation. All his
work possesses "direct personal-lyrical utterance of force,
a strong sense of the paradoxical, a repeated belief in
madness as insight, a sense of alienation provoking
authoritarian attitudes, and a brooding sympathy and
sensitivity."

22    "E. J. D." "Roethke Verse Wins High Praise." <u>Standard-Times</u>
(New Bedford, Mass.), November 23, page unknown (from the
Roethke collection, University of Washington).
    Review of <u>Words for the Wind</u>. Favorable review in which
Roethke is seen as having earned all his honors.

23    ENGLE, PAUL. "Poetry: Humblest of All the Arts." <u>Chicago
Tribune</u>, December 14, "Magazine of Books," Part 4, p. 5.
    Review of <u>Words for the Wind</u>. Theodore Roethke is "one
of the country's most insightful and furious poets,

speaking against the 'stupor of knowledge lacking inward-
ness.' Out of the scraps of his childhood around his
father's plants and flowers, out of the exploding sky
behind his eyes, out of the rage and rant of these dirty
times, he has come to honest wisdom: 'What's hell but a
cold heart?' The United States is lucky to have poets like
this one."

24 EVANS, SIR IFOR. "Some Contemporary Poets." Birmingham
(England) Post, May 13, page unknown (from the Roethke
collection, University of Washington).
Review of Words for the Wind. Words for the Wind is
mistakenly referred to as Roethke's second volume, that
possesses "that intense cerebration which accompanies so
much American verse and a tightness in composition which
leaves no room for a lazy reader. What it all amounts to
is a little difficult to say."

25 HOBSON, WILDER. "Men at Work." Newsweek, LI (March 17),
108-110.
An attempt to answer the thorny question of "What is
contemporary poetry?" Roethke's The Waking is cited as
an example of the "buoyantly lyrical."

26 "J.S." Untitled review of Words for the Wind. Punch (London),
CCXXXIV (February 26), 303.
Though showing British influence (Yeats, Graves, Auden),
Roethke is "strongly American." His style moves from
deliberately "country bumpkinish, to smoother rhythms that
offer outlets for his natural romanticism without any loss
in characteristic sharp observation." He has gained richness, while losing nothing important. Roethke's humor is
American too, "quite deplorably unfunny." The love poems
and those about Yeats show his real gift.

27 KIZER, CAROLYN. "Poetry of the 'Fifties: In America."
International Literary Annual No. 1. Edited by John Wain.
London: John Calder, pp. 65, 68, 78, 83-85, 88-89, 90, 94.
Roethke's presence dominates the author's discussion of
the decade of American poetry under the headings: "Elders
and Betters," "Brothers and Sisters," and "Two Worlds and
Their Ways." His language and technique is called upon to
clarify and evaluate the language and techniques of others,
including Archibald MacLeish, Phelps Putnam, Elizabeth
Bishop, Jean Garrigue, William Carlos Williams, Stanley
Kunitz, Robert Lowell and Richard Wilbur. In addition to
establishing this astonishing poetic presence, the author
discusses at length (pp. 83-85) Roethke's Words for the

1958

Wind (printed in England the previous year, but not yet published in the United States). "My own opinion...is that Roethke has made the most significant contribution to the form and content of poetic language since Yeats and Joyce." But he has pushed beyond Yeats "to pioneer and lay claim to areas of sensibility unexplored by previous poets." Roethke's love poetry is his supreme accomplishment, and "Words for the Wind," the poem, "is the finest love poem written in the twentieth century."

28  McGAFFIN, AUDREY R. "Moving Experience in Modern Poetry." Baltimore Sun, December 28, page unknown (from the Roethke collection, University of Washington).
      Review of Words for the Wind. Stressing the accomplishment of the newer poems, in Part Two, the reviewer closes with this praise: "To read 'Words for the Wind' is to share in some of the most lyrical and moving experiences of modern poetry."

29  MEACHAM, HARRY M. "Roethke's Verse Collection Shows Rate of Growth." Richmond (Va.) News Leader, December 17, page unknown (from the Roethke collection, University of Washington).
      Review of Words for the Wind. This book reflects "the inevitable changes in style and technique through which all good writers pass on the road to mastery."

30  MILLS, RALPH J., JR. "Towards a Condition of Joy." Tri-Quarterly, I (Fall), 25-29.
      More so than his contemporaries (Lowell, Jarrell, and Eberhart), Roethke has shown "an exploratory spirit, a continual plumbing of new areas of experience and an ability to alter and develop his style in accord with this. Coupled with his fine lyric gift, this progression has a cumulative effect, for each successive stage of his work grows naturally out of the former.... There is gradually built up by means of this organic scheme a body of meaning and value, a universe of discourse in which the poems themselves fit and are comprehended." The author then examines Open House, The Lost Son and The Waking in more detail. (See also 1966.B68 and 1967.B57)

31  MUIR, EDWIN. "New Verse." New Statesman, January 18, pp. 76-77.
      Review of Words for the Wind. "Mr. Roethke is a poet of the native American tradition," of the same family as Frost, Ransom, Moore, Elizabeth Bishop and Dickinson. "His poetry reads like whimsy even when it is most serious; this is

1958

because things are deceptive and have two or more sides;
turn them over and they have quite a different look. This
awareness results in a sense of balance, or a sequence of
canny qualifications," with nothing like it in contemporary, and little like it in traditional, English poetry.
The American poet inquires, "his mind is not compromised
but quite free, but is particularly attracted by the
enigmatic, the two- or many-sided." In some of his poems,
Roethke "is like a piece of nature observing nature."

32    "N. J." "Parade of Books: Seattle Genius." Seattle Post-
      Intelligencer, December 6, p. 13.
          Review of Words for the Wind. The author includes many
      of Roethke's own words in this favorable review. He thinks
      that Roethke will be established as a leading American
      writer by the book and that it will "bring him the popular
      fame which has brushed him too lightly in passing by."

33    "P. B." "Both Free and Formal." Christian Science Monitor,
      December 24, p. 7.
          Review of Words for the Wind. Favorable review stres-
      sing the great variety of Roethke's collected verse, both
      stylistic and thematic.

34    POST, KIRBY. "Strange Poems by 'Individual.'" Austin-
      American Statesman, November 9, page unknown (from the
      Roethke collection, University of Washington).
          Review of Words for the Wind. Favorable review that
      stresses Roethke's "refreshing difference."

35    RALEIGH, SALLY. "Home Career Is Possible: Take Children,
      Creative Work, Stir Well, All Happy." Seattle Post-
      Intelligencer, February 2, p. 2 (numbered page 2, but it
      and succeeding pages are placed after pages 1-40, numbered
      consecutively).
          This article is about Carolyn Kizer Bullit, homemaker
      and poet. She incidently mentions her debt to Roethke,
      as both poet and teacher.

36    ROSS, ALAN. Review of Words for the Wind. The London Magazine,
      V (March), 75, 77-79.
          Roethke's poems have their roots in the soil, or blood,
      and stay there, never blooming into a social response. "I
      do not see, as some have suggested, that Mr. Roethke is a
      major American poet, for Cummings liberated form for him,
      and it is the small, perfect likenesses that one prizes,
      rather than the anarchy, beguiling as it is, of the longer
      pieces in Praise to the End!"

1958

37   SEYMOUR-SMITH, MARTIN.  "Form and Substance."  Time and Tide
        (England), XXXIX (February 8), 167.
          Review of Words for the Wind (mistakenly called Words
        on the Wind).  In his use of strict poetic forms Roethke
        is "loud-mouthed and loose."  His latest style, consciously
        Yeatsian, in "the imitative richness of its surface, which
        is not far from parody, conceals the same confused aim-
        lessness."  The reviewer's original evaluation remains
        unchanged:  "given the explosive psychological situation
        which it so frequently suggests, it is a pity he can only
        say 'Boo!' at it like this."

38   SKELTON, ROBIN.  "Poets' Ways of Speech."  Manchester Guardian,
        February 4, p. 4.
          Review of Words for the Wind.  Roethke's "moods and modes
        are various, his technical range considerable, and his
        sensuous delight in the minutiae of existence, which in
        its wayward clarity sometimes approaches the whimsical,
        is appealing.  His work tends to be affectionate rather
        than passionate...however, the attack is in terms of the
        addition of perception to perception rather than by way of
        a thorough exploration of one over-riding concept or image."

39   WAIN, JOHN.  "Half-way to Greatness."  Encounter, X (April),
        82, 84.
          Review of Words for the Wind.  "Mr. Roethke is an
        enjoyable poet," but, he "has all the attributes of a
        major poet except the one that really matters..., an un-
        mistakeable identity."  He has two voices:  the poems of
        the last ten years, with "many a quaintly attractive
        phrase" that he doesn't know how to organize; and the
        "ventriloquist" poems that imitate Yeats.

40   WERNER, W. L.  "Bookworm:  Library Week with a Bang!"  Centre
        Daily Times (State College, Pa.), March 25, p. 4.  Article
        unsigned.
          Roethke is praised as one of America's four outstanding
        poets in a recent issue of Newsweek.

41   _____.  "Bookworm."  Centre Daily Times (State College, Pa.),
        November 11, p. 4.  Article unsigned.
          Richard Eberhart's review (1958.B21) of Roethke's Words
        for the Wind is summarized from the New York Times Book
        Review.

42   WITT-DIAMANT, RUTH.  "The Poems of a Singular Poet."  San
        Francisco Examiner, November 28, "Highlight" Section, p. 30.
          Review of Words for the Wind, called here Collected
        Verse of Theodore Roethke.  Roethke's early poems show the

"terrifying reality of the child's unconscious life."
The "New Poems" offer "the joy and anguish of adult
life"--"tender and voluptuous" love poems, "nightmare
dreams of self-doubt and the terrors of annihilation,"
and "deep ribald laughter"--all with a music that "has
the quality of the thing itself."

1959 A BOOKS - NONE

1959 B SHORTER WRITINGS

1    ANON.   "Awarded Yale's Bollingen Prize."  New York Herald
        Tribune, January 12, Sect. I, p. 11.
            Announcement of $1000 prize for Words for the Wind.

2    ANON.   "Yale's Bollingen Prize Won by Professor-Poet."  New
        York Times, January 12, p. 13.
            Notice that Roethke had won the $1000 prize for Words
        for the Wind.  The Associated Press picture, often re-
        printed, is not at all complimentary.

3    ANON.   "UW Professor Awarded Top Poetry Prize."  Seattle
        Post-Intelligencer, January 12, p. 9.
            Roethke has won the Bollingen Prize of $1,000 for Words
        for the Wind.

4    ANON.   "Prof. Roethke Wins Top Yale Poetry Award."  University
        of Washington Daily, January 13, p. 1.
            Roethke has won the Bollingen Award for Words for the
        Wind.

5    ANON.   "Roethke Gets $1,000 Prize for Poetry."  Centre Daily
        Times (State College, Pa.), January 14, p. 11.
            Roethke has won the Bollingen Prize for Words for the
        Wind.

6    ANON.   "Roethke Wins Poetry Prize."  Faculty Bulletin (Penn
        State University), XLVI: 16 (January 16), 3.
            Roethke has won the Bollingen Prize for Words for the
        Wind.

7    ANON.   "U.W. Poet Gets Second Major Award."  Seattle Times,
        January 23, p. 19.
            Roethke received the Edna St. Vincent Millay Memorial
        Award for Words for the Wind.

1959

8    ANON.   "Prof. Roethke Wins Second Major Award."  University
of Washington Daily, January 27, p. 3.
     Roethke has won the Edna St. Vincent Millay Award, from
the Poetry Society of America, for Words for the Wind.

9    ANON.   "Prize Winner."  Seattle Post-Intelligencer,
January 30, p. 12.
     Roethke has won the Bollingen prize for Words for the
Wind.

10   ANON.   "Roethke Wins Two National Awards for Latest Poetry
Book."  University Record (Seattle), I (January/February), 6.
     Words for the Wind has won for Roethke the Bollingen
Prize ("considered to be the most important single poetry
prize an American poet can win") and the Edna St. Vincent
Millay Memorial Award.  Roethke, 50, "is the youngest poet
ever to be given the Yale-Bollingen Prize."

11   ANON.   "Former Professor Gets Bollington (sic) Poetry Award."
The Daily Collegian (Penn State University), February 5, p. 8.
     Roethke won the $1,000 award for Words for the Wind.

12   ANON.   "Two-Year Award for UW Poet:  Foundation Honors
Theodore Roethke."  Seattle Post-Intelligencer,
February 15, Sect. IV, p. 18.
     Roethke has received a Ford grant and says he will "spend
one year writing a series of serious poems dealing with
this country's historical mistakes....  He said he will
devote the other year to helping with translations of
English writing into German, French and Italian."

13   ANON.   Title unknown.  Albany Times-Union, February 15, page
unknown (from the Roethke collection, University of
Washington).
     Review of Words for the Wind.  Favorable review that
stresses Roethke's variety of poetic form and expression.

14   ANON.   "Bollingen Poetry Prize."  Library Journal, LXXXIV
(February 15), 574.
     Announcement of $1000 prize to Roethke, the youngest
recipient since the prize was instituted at Yale University
in 1948.  He was selected for Words for the Wind.

15   ANON.   "Ford Fund Gives Writers $150,000."  New York Times,
February 16, p. 31.
     The amount of Roethke's grant is not given.  Among other
recipients are James Baldwin, Saul Bellow, E. E. Cummings,
Stanley Kunitz, Bernard Malamud, Flannery O'Connor, and
Katherine Anne Porter.

1959

16    ANON.    $150,000 for U.S. Writers." London Times,
          February 16, p. 8d.
          Announcement of Ford Foundation grants.

17    ANON.    "Roethke Wins Grant From Ford Foundation." Seattle
          Times, February 16, p. 11.
          Roethke is one of eleven to share in $150,000 in grant
          funds, allotment to be determined by individual need.

18    ANON.    Review of Words for the Wind. Wisconsin Library Bul-
          letin, LV (March), 193.
          Entire review: "Poems that have won the poet many
          prizes are included in this National Book Award title
          with poems that have not appeared in book form. Universal
          experiences are described in vigorous imagery."

19    ANON.    Review of Words for the Wind. Bookmark (Idaho State
          Library), XVIII (March), 148.
          The new poems and their themes in this collection in-
          clude "animals, nature, love and death, expressed with
          originality and technical grace."

20    ANON.    "Compton Solicits Writers' Visions." New York Times,
          March 4, p. 23.
          Account of the National Book Award ceremony.  Roethke
          received $1000 for Words for the Wind.

21    ANON.    "Saginaw-Born Poet Adds Another Literary Honor." The
          Saginaw News, March 4, Section B, p. 1.
          Roethke has won the National Book Award for Words for
          the Wind.  Some remarks regarding Roethke are excerpted
          from the citation of award.  Other winners, the nature of
          the award, and previous Roethke prizes are mentioned.

22    ANON.    "Former Faculty Member Wins Award for Poetry." Penn
          State Alumni News, XLV:  16 (April), 13.
          Roethke has won the Bollingen Prize for Words for the
          Wind.

23    ANON.    "In The Argus-Eyes." The Argus (Seattle), LXVI
          (April 3), 1.
          Recognition of Roethke for his many awards, especially
          those most recently given for Words for the Wind.  "An
          effort to name Prof. Roethke poet laureate of the State of
          Washington failed during the 1959 Legislature."

24    ANON.    "Miscellaneous." Facts on File, XIX (April 9-15), 123.
          Roethke won the National Book Award for Words for the
          Wind.

1959

25  ANON.  "Miscellaneous."  Facts on File, XIX (April 9-15), 124.
        Roethke won the Bollingen Prize for Words for the Wind.

26  ANON.  "Bentley Terms University 'Trail Blazer' in Poetry."
        University of Washington Daily, May 29, p. 3.
            Roethke, "'the most brilliant poet in America today,'"
        is directly responsible for the University of Washington's
        prominence as a center for poetry.

27  ANON.  "Literary News:  This Is the Poet Today." Newsweek,
        LIII (June 15), 110.
            Roethke "deserves to be called the prizewinning poet of
        the year....  He is thus not only a superb modern master
        of English verse...but a fantastic financial performer in
        the exceedingly limited poetic sweepstakes."  An excerpt
        from "A Walk in Late Summer" is reprinted on page 106.

28  ANON.  "Theodore, Roethke, Famed Poet, Reads His New Works
        Today, Tonight Here and at Poetry Center." Golden Gater
        (San Francisco State College, now California State Univer-
        sity at San Francisco), July 3, p. 1.
            Announcement of reading, accompanied by brief biography.

29  ANON.  "Pulitzer Poet to Give 2 Readings." The San Francisco
        Chronicle, July 8, p. 36.
            Announcement of Roethke readings at San Francisco State
        College and the San Francisco State Downtown Center.

30  ANON.  "U.W. Professor Wins Northwest Writers' Award."
        Seattle Times, August 3, p. 9.
            Words for the Wind received the first Pacific Northwest
        Writers' Award offered jointly by the Seattle Municipal
        Art Commission and the Pacific Northwest International
        Writers' Conference.

31  ANON.  "Writers' Award Won by Roethke." University of
        Washington Daily, August 6, p. 2.
            Roethke won the Pacific Northwest Writers' Award for
        Words for the Wind.

32  ANON.  "Taking Stock:  A Scattered Abundance of Creative
        Richness." London Times Literary Supplement, November 6,
        p. xii of "The American Imagination," Special Section.
            Roethke mentioned with Lowell, Shapiro and Kunitz as
        generally some of the best writers in America at the time.

33  ANON.  "Roethke, Pulitzer Winner, Has New Book of Poems Out."
        Seattle Times Magazine, November 30, p. 23.

Review of Words for the Wind. An indefinite evaluation
of Roethke's book and his accomplishment. Though finding
dignity and beauty, the anonymous reviewer admits to frequent bewilderment.

34    ASHTON, DORE. "Forward." Poets and the Past. New York:
      Andre Emmerich Gallery, p. 10.
          "Sometimes love itself is the theme embodied in tender,
      universal imagery. Theodore Roethke's hallucinatory image
      of love, its surface roiled but its depth silvered with
      silence, can find its counterpart in an Aztec love poem
      or a lovingly fashioned Mayan sculpture of a serene young
      woman." These comments are directed toward Roethke's poem,
      "The Swan."

35    BERRYMAN, JOHN. "From the Middle and Senior Generations."
      American Scholar, XXVIII (Summer), 384-385.
          Review of Words for the Wind. Roethke and Robert Lowell,
      the two poets who "possess the most powerful and original
      talents that have emerged during the last fifteen years,"
      are briefly compared. "Lowell is a poet of completed
      states, Roethke a poet of process." Roethke has mastered
      his images, rhythms and psychology, but he has perhaps
      submitted too "gleefully" to his influences, Yeats and
      Eliot.

36    BODE, CARL. "The Poems Across the Way." Time and Tide
      (England), XL (August 29), 933.
          Roethke is linked with Wilbur, Lowell and Jarrell. Two
      versions of "Cuttings" are examined to illustrate the
      heightened tension ("a poetry which has that intellectu-
      ality tightened into obscurity") that makes Roethke's
      better poems. See also 1965.B21.

37    BOGAN, LOUISE. "Verse." New Yorker, XXXV (October 24),
      195-196.
          Review of Words for the Wind. No rhetoric in these
      poems. Roethke gives a forthright treatment of terror on
      all levels of consciousness and unconsciousness.

38    BRYSON, ARTEMISIA B. "'Words for the Wind' Has Lines for
      Remembering." Fort Worth Star-Telegram, January 11,
      Sunday Book Page number unknown (from the Roethke collec-
      tion, University of Washington).
          Roethke's poetry is memorable. Little more of a critical
      nature is contained in this article.

1959

39    CIARDI, JOHN. <u>How Does a Poem Mean</u>?  Cambridge, Mass.:  The
          Riverside Press, pp. 1003-1004.
             Roethke's poem, "My Papa's Waltz," is nearly constant
          in metrics, pace, diction, imagery and grammatical struc-
          ture.  What Ciardi calls the <u>fulcrum</u> occurs after the last
          line, in silence.

40    COBLENTZ, STANTON A.  "The Reviewer's Quill."  <u>Wings</u>, XIV
          (Spring), 23-24.
             Review of <u>Words for the Wind</u>.  Roethke manages in the
          more traditional forms of verse "artless simplicity,"
          "tenderness," and an occasional "lyric turn."  Yet some of
          the poems in more open forms are "monstrosities."

41    DeYONGE, JACK.  "Roethke Gives Warm, Informal Reading."
          <u>Seattle Times</u>, August 21, p. 27.
             Roethke's reading was a performance.  "What made this
          reading last night so strong was the feeling that with his
          humor Roethke maintains an objectivity which edges his
          jokes about himself and which, in his poems, manifests
          itself in form and irony."

42    FASEL, IDA.  "Lyrical Poems Always Creative."  <u>Wichita Falls
          Times</u>, February 1, page unknown (from the Roethke collection,
          University of Washington).
             Review of <u>Words for the Wind</u>.  A general discussion
          that praises Roethke's wry humor and earnestness of feeling.

43    FLINT, F. CUDWORTH.  "Seeing, Thinking, Saying, Singing."
          <u>Virginia Quarterly Review</u>, XXXV (Spring), 313.
             Review of <u>Words for the Wind</u>.  "Roethke would evoke, out
          of the half-conscious wishes, the hop-skip-and-jump
          unreasonings, the unaimed energies, the undefined fears
          of childhood, through the visions and frustrations of
          adolescence, the adult self accepting with happiness its
          station in its world."

44    FULLER, JOHN G.  "Trade Winds."  <u>Saturday Review</u>, XLII
          (March 7), 10-11.
             An appreciative look at Roethke, the author's former
          teacher, who is being considered for the National Book
          Award for <u>Words for the Wind</u>.  "He was a teacher who
          never taught--he breathed his knowledge, and it came
          through by osmosis."

45    GUNN, THOM.  "Poets English and American."  <u>Yale Review</u>,
          XLVIII (June), 623-625.
             Review of <u>Words for the Wind</u>.  Roethke's collected poems
          exhibit three distinct styles and attitudes:  traditional,

as of Bogan and Winters; nonsense, and not too good; and the poems of a pernicious influence of Yeats. The early poems are better. Yet the three voices have distinct power.

46   HALL, DONALD. "Words for the Wind." Michigan Alumnus
     Quarterly Review, LXV (May), 270-271.
        The new poems contain some of Roethke's best writing; and among these, the love poems are finest. Those older poems carried forward, especially lyrics such as "My Papa's Waltz" and "Dolor," "retain their quality. The achievement of Roethke's long autobiographical sequence, Praise to the End!, seems to me definite, though it takes time to appreciate its particular quality. It is his best sustained work, and a modern poem which will survive modernity."

47   HOLZHAUER, ROBERT A. "'Hard Views, Tender Truths.'"
     Milwaukee Journal, April 12, page unknown (from the Roethke collection, University of Washington).
        Review of Words for the Wind. The reviewer generalizes about Roethke's philosophical and formal links with Williams, Stevens, Stein, Joyce and Yeats.

48   HUFF, ROBERT. "Spring Run." Colonel Johnson's Ride. Detroit:
     Wayne State University Press.
        A poem in tribute to Roethke. See also 1967.B43.

49   KAHN, HANNAH. "Roethke's Simple Poetry Speaks Wisely." Miami
     (Fla.) Herald, February 1, page unknown (from the Roethke collection, University of Washington).
        Review of Words for the Wind. Roethke's book shows wide range and depth; it contains poetry that is "profound and meaningful without being involved or difficult."

50   KEMP, ROY Z. "Poetry by Roethke." Greensboro (N.C.) News,
     February 22, page unknown (from the Roethke collection, University of Washington).
        Review of Words for the Wind. Favorable review in which Roethke's ability to see beneath both the beautiful and ugly is discussed. The reviewer seizes the opportunity to remark on modern poetry and obscurity while praising Roethke's efforts.

51   KOHLER, DAYTON. "A Cross Section of the Big Crop of Poetry."
     Courier-Journal (Louisville, Ky.), January 25, page unknown (from the Roethke collection, University of Washington).
        Review of Words for the Wind. "...plants, animals and the nonintellectual impressions of a child's world were

not enough" for Roethke. He was led to Freud, Yeats and the meditative lyric.

52   LETENDRE, DONALD H. "Poetry Reaches a Stalemate." Worcester
     (Mass.) Telegram, March 1, page unknown (from the Roethke
     collection, University of Washington).
         Review of Words for the Wind. "Largely romantic in tone,
     the writing reveals precise observation and disastrous use
     of language. In content and form, the verses are intensely
     personal, often erratic, at times erotic. Frequently they
     lapse into monotony, and mannerism. Muted exclamations
     and rhetorical questions abound."

53   MacGILLIVRAY, ARTHUR, S. J.  Review of Words for the Wind.
     Best Sellers, XVIII (February 1), 422-423.
         "Despite the lack of universal overtones in his (Roethke's)
     poetry, one can still delight in the artistry of his craft
     and the pleasure of recognition in the minuteness of his
     observation. He is a welcome member in the company of
     true poets."

54   McPHERSON, HUGO. "In a Greenhouse the Poet Found Images of
     Love." Toronto Daily Star, February 7, p. 30.
         Review of Words for the Wind. Roethke now deserves
     public acclaim, more than the "amorous advances of the
     critics." Words for the Wind is a lyric volume that, the
     author hopes, will be followed by a work of greater magni-
     tude. Roethke's understanding of nature and human nature
     is broad enough that he can be expected to "make the sky
     his limit." "She (I think the dead are tender)" is re-
     printed here.

55   MILLS, RALPH J., JR. "Keeping the Spirit Spare." Chicago
     Review, XIII (Winter), 114-122.
         Review of Words for the Wind. Roethke comes to terms
     with life in the act of writing about it. Mills traces
     the evidence for this statement through poems from each
     of the earlier volumes. He discusses stylistic changes
     in the manner of Joyce or Woolf and relates them to the
     already mentioned confrontation with life. Love poetry
     is commented on at some length. He concludes with opin-
     ions as to why Roethke is not a mere imitator of such
     poets as Yeats and Eliot.

56   RICHARDSON, MARY and COURTNEY JOHNSTON. "Roethke Rates Local
     Writers Among Nation's Top Young Poets." University of
     Washington Daily, June 3, p. 1.

Roethke comments on the "Beat" movement to show the contrast with Northwest poets. Much of the article consists of direct quotation.

57  ROSENTHAL, M. L. "Closing in on the Self." Nation, CLXXXVIII (March 21), 258-259.
   Review of Words for the Wind. Roethke is at his best when he displays his "stunning mishmash of agonized gibber," where he "throws all kinds of dissimilar effects into the great, ceaseless mixer of his sensibility, stirring together notes of driving misery and hysterical ecstacy, of Rabelaisian sensuality and warm, wet regressiveness." A "projection without comment of opposed psychological states is characteristic of Roethke's most interesting work," all taking place in a subjective universe. His attempts to conceptualize, "give his poems a further implication of victory over the frenzy through a Freudian rebirth of the Self," are not very convincing.

58  ROSS, ALAN. "Foreward." London Magazine, VI (December), 9.
   "The liberation of form, evident in such American poets as Marianne Moore and Theodore Roethke, is novel only in so far as it is based on personal re-discovery. The original experiment is all but half a century old."

59  RYAN, DENNIS. "Poetess Moore to Read: Gives Advice to Anagramists." University of Washington Daily, October 9, p. 7.
   Miss Moore "praised Roethke for his insight into life and his skill as a craftsman."

60  SCHWARTZ, DELMORE. "The Cunning and the Craft of the Unconscious and the Preconscious." Poetry, XCIV (June), 203-205.
   Roethke's power is beneath the surface, the unconscious brought out by his craft. He uses the phrasing and cadence of Yeats' mature work, not as an imitation, but for advancement to avoid self-imitation. Roethke is important enough to be compared with Yeats. See also 1970.B19 and 1971.B40.

61  SCOTT, WINFIELD TOWNLEY. "Has Anyone Seen a Trend?" Saturday Review, XLII (January 3), 13.
   Review of Words for the Wind. Roethke causes some uneasiness. His greenhouse poems are freshest and most beautiful. Yet he is unlike anyone else.

62  SNODGRASS, W. D. "Spring Verse Chronicle." Hudson Review, XII (Spring), 114-117.

1959

<u>Review of Words for the Wind</u>. "The stylistic progress of <u>Words for the Wind</u> is like a history of twentieth-century American verse in miniature." The author follows Roethke's work from its "romantic lyricism," to "marked prosiness," to the experimental poems, and finally to the more recent poems owing debts to Yeats and Eliot. He finds the prose/poems the most satisfying.

63　SPENDER, STEPHEN. "Words for the Wind." <u>New Republic</u>, CXLI (August 10), 21-22.
　　"Self-bound, sense-bound poets do have a particular kind of moral limitation. They inhabit purgatory." "Voices characterized by passionate yearning to reach out to some beyond--not the poet himself: the characteristic of this Otherness being its very strong resemblence to the poet himself, who finds the universe a mirror in which he meets his own features." These generalizations introduce Roethke, whose best poetry "is tragic in feeling and beautiful in operation." His nostalgia entails a "passionate regret that the desires of maturity cannot be fused with the beauty and innocence of youth." His poetry is perhaps best when both centrifugal and centripetal at once, when "the images remain the same but the thought becomes salvationist and abstract."

64　TAYLOR, GEORGE W. "Books and Readers." <u>The Argus</u> (Seattle), LXVI (September 11), 5.
　　An account of a recent Roethke reading that was so rewarding it was worth sitting on a cold floor. He warmed everything with his various poetry, never strained for effect, always honest and from the heart. "Seattle needs you" Mr. Roethke.

65　THORP, BERENICE. "Prize Poetry: Roethke's Exciting Verse." <u>University of Washington Daily</u>, January 15, pp. 4, 6.
　　Review of <u>Words for the Wind</u>. Favorable review that draws upon Roethke's comments in John Ciardi's <u>Mid-Century American Poets</u>.

66　WATSON, EMMETT. "This Our City." <u>Seattle Post-Intelligencer</u>, August 31, p. 11.
　　Regarding a recent poetry reading by Roethke: "'He was wonderful!' gushed a listener. 'He's a combination of Mort Sahl and Jack Paar.'"

67　WEIL, JAMES L. "Worthwhile Reading." <u>American Weave</u>, Spring, pp. 35-36.
　　Taking issue with another reviewer's belief that Roethke's poems show no resolution, this writer excerpts some of

Roethke's remarks on his poetic method from the Poetry Book Society Bulletin of 1957. In "Forcing House" the writer finds a faithful example of Roethke's poetic "telescoping." He concludes: "But the very nature of an 'actuality' created through immediate language is to defy mediation or judgement by its maker. We must see this as a Vision and hear what it will reveal for us.

"After the way saints know shall they know who devote themselves to these poems."

68   WERNER, W. L. "Bookworm." Penn State Alumni News, XLV:14 (January), 5.
     Roethke has recently published Words for the Wind. It exhibits his evolution from "conventional verse through an introspective phase, then a Yeats-like period, to his mature reflective poems of today."

69   _____. "Bookworm: Run, Don't Walk for Report." Centre Daily Times (State College, Pa.), January 27, p. 4.
     Entire quote--"And poor Ted Roethke won the $200 Edna Millay prize from the Poetry Society of America last week, while a volume of his poems, 'The Lost Son,' was remaindered by Marboro at three for a dollar."

70   _____. "Bookworm: Familiar Names in the News." Centre Daily Times (State College, Pa.), February 24, p. 4.
     The author mentions Roethke's sharing in a recent Ford Foundation grant of $150,000. Also mentioned is a recent publication by Roethke's student, David Wagoner.

71   _____. "Bookworm: Anecdote, Poem and Letters." Centre Daily Times (State College, Pa.), April 7, p. 4.
     The author excerpts remarks of John G. Fuller from the Saturday Review on Roethke as a teacher. He then recalls Roethke at Penn State, his success as teacher, poet and disciple-maker, and questions if Roethke would pass the "Good Teacher Personality Rating" test.

1960 A BOOKS - NONE

1960 B SHORTER WRITINGS

1   ANON. "In the Argus Eyes of 1959." The Argus (Seattle), LXVII (January 1), 5. (Incorrectly cited as volume LXVIII in Theodore Roethke: A Bibliography, by James McLeod.)
     No text, only a picture of Roethke with the caption: "UW professor and winner of many poetry prizes."

1960

2    ANON.   "English Prof. Wins National Poetry Award."   University of Washington Daily, January 20, p. 8.
    Roethke has won the Longview Award of $300 for work written in 1958.

3    ANON.   "Ten Americans to Watch in 1960:  Literature."
    Pageant Magazine, February, p. 27.
    These comments from James Costigan are quoted:  "'I choose Theodore Roethke because he is one of the finest poets this century has produced and has been shamefully neglected in his own country.  I wish some of the millions who sit night after night ingesting television's large proportion of illiterate drivel might turn their attention to the beautiful accomplishments of men like Roethke."

4    ANON.   "Lecture Tour Takes Prof to Eastern US."   University of Washington Daily, March 30, p. 1.
    Roethke, among other things, will deliver the Hopwood Lecture at the University of Michigan.  A European tour will follow.

5    ANON.   "Roethke Poems Sung."   Seattle Times, April 4, p. 34.
    An announcement of the Alice Esty program at Carnegie Recital Hall which included eight of Roethke's poems, set to music by Ned Rorem.   Excerpts from the New York Times and New York Herald Tribune reviews are quoted.

6    ANON.   "Morris Gray Poetry Reading."   Harvard University Gazette, April 23, p. 179.  (As cited in Theodore Roethke: A Bibliography, by James McLeod).
    Brief announcement of Roethke's April 27 reading.

7    ANON.   "Roethke Gives Poetry Reading."   Wellesley College News (Wellesley, Mass), April 28, pp. 1, 4.
    Account of a Roethke reading, with brief biography.  His reading style receives more comment than his works.  At one point, when his audience laughed at his antics, Roethke said:  "'Don't; you'll get me to singing.  No, I won't do my song about Nixon'!"

8    ANON.   "Arthur Hill Honors Prize-Winning Poet."   The Saginaw News, May 24, Section B, p. 1.
    Roethke was honored as the high school's "Distinguished Alumnus."  Listing his many awards, the article states that Open House appeared "in the early 1930's," and the second book, The Lost Son, "appeared in 1949."  Critical comments by Stephen Spender, Carolyn Kizer and The Listener are reprinted.

9    ANON.    "Theodore Roethke '25, 10th Honor Alumnus." The
        Arthur Hill News, May 25, pp. 1, 5.
            Roethke is praised for his talents as writer and teacher,
        his many prizes are enumerated, and his influence at an
        important center of American poetry is emphasized.

10   ANON.    "Famed Poet Greets Hill Students." The Saginaw News,
        May 25, Section B, p. 9.
            Roethke was named Arthur Hill High School's "10th annual
        Honor Alumnus." His award-filled career is mentioned, then.
            But he wore his greatness with a disarming charm
        that made him appear the friendly, warm person he is.
        He delighted the present generation of Arthur Hill
        pupils with a few wise cracks, but when he started
        reading his poetry the jammed auditorium was quiet.
        Roethke bears a resemblance to Charles Laughton,
        and he reads beautifully. He let his poetry speak
        for him, and in it came his thanks to his school
        for the honor it gave him...He finished to a tre-
        mendous ovation that only befitted the talent he
        has developed.

11   ANON.    "U.W. Professor Receives Award." Seattle Times,
        May 27, p. 11.
            Roethke received the "honor alumnus" award from Arthur
        Hill High School of Saginaw, Michigan.

12   ANON.    "Poet Honored at Home Town Commencement." University
        of Washington Daily, June 1, p. 1.
            Roethke was honored as Arthur Hill High School's Honor
        Alumnus of 1960 in Saginaw, Michigan. "His first published
        poem on record was an ode entitled 'Goofy Gardenias,' in
        the humor section of the high school yearbook. Roethke
        was also credited with starting a striped-socks fad in
        the school."

13   ARDOIN, JOHN  "Alice Esty.......Soprano." Musical America,
        LXXX (May), 41.
            Review of Ned Rorem's "Eight Poems by Theodore Roethke."
        "To one accustomed to Mr. Rorem's usual freshness, these
        new songs came as a disappointment. They seemed contrived
        and each seemed to harp too much on one persistent idea."

14   BENTLEY, NELSON. "U Workshops Pave Way for Neo-American
        Poetry." University of Washington Daily, June 1, p. 2.
            Roethke, "now recognized as the greatest poet writing in
        the U.S.," was the nucleus around which the new poetry was
        built. "The result is a highly versatile Northwest poetry,
        made up of a well-balanced variety of schools, romantic

and classicist, incantational and restrained, intellectu-
ally complex and passionately primitive, ironic and devo-
tional, autobiographical and satirical."

15  BYRON, STUART. "Poetry Review: Poetic Greats." The
    Wesleyan Argus (Middletown, Conn.), May 20, p. 2.
        The author comments on Roethke's place in American poetry
    and how distinguished he is in his style. But he concludes
    that perhaps Stanley Kunitz, who read his work at Wesleyan
    at the same time as Roethke, and who writes in a more
    typical style, may be the more lasting poet.

16  GUZZO, LOUIS R. "Words and Music: Roethke Chooses Remote
    Irish Isle for Poetry Premiere." Seattle Times,
    September 6, p. 29.
        An account of the "world premiere" of Roethke's book of
    poems I Am! Says the Lamb (not yet published) at Day's
    Hotel, Inishbofin, Ireland. Roethke read and sang his
    poems, and coaxed a group of children to sing them too.
    On a Ford Foundation Grant, Roethke stopped off to visit
    with Irish poet Richard Murphy. Announced here too is
    that I Am! will contain musical settings along with the
    poems. Roethke is also working on another volume to be
    illustrated by Seattle artist Richard Gilhey.

17  JACOBS, MARY JANE. "notes...and...notables." Seattle Times,
    March 27, Section IV, p. 4.
        Mr. and Mrs. Roethke's itinerary for much of 1960, in-
    cluding readings and lectures in the United States, as
    well as foreign travel on a Ford Foundation Grant.

18  "J. B." "Alice Esty Is Heard in Program of Song." New York
    Times, April 3, p. 38.
        Review of Ned Rorem's setting of eight Roethke poems,
    at Carnegie Recital Hall on April 2. "Mr. Rorem's songs
    exhibited great intensity, although his music and
    Mr. Roethke's texts often seemed to be at cross-purposes."

19  OPPENHEIM, JUDITH. "Poet Bogan Called Lyric by Roethke."
    Michigan Daily (U. of Michigan), May 20, p. 1.
        Roethke was at the University of Michigan for the presen-
    tation of the Hopwood awards in creative writing. Bogan
    writes in the "'severest lyrical tradition in English,'"
    that of Campion and Jonson. She will not be popular, but
    should be a model for the young.

20  PELTO, DICK. "Roethke: Area Prodigy." University of Wash-
    ington Daily, June 1, pp. 3, 5.

1960

The standard Roethke biography is repeated here while
the author praises Roethke for his position at the center
of influence in Pacific Northwest poetry.

21  PERKINS, FRANCIS D.  "Alice Esty in Song Program at Carnegie
    Recital Hall."  New York Herald Tribune, April 4, p. 10.
       Favorable review of Ned Rorem's musical setting of eight
    of Roethke's poems included in Miss Esty's program.

22  ROSENTHAL, M. L.  The Modern Poets.  New York:  Oxford Univer-
    sity Press, pp. 240-244.
       Roethke, unlike so many of the so-called "confessional"
    poets, manages a "total concentration on the Self."  As
    hypnotic as his poems can be, their resolution usually
    does not live up to their initial demands.  The author
    concludes:  "Although I do not believe the special variety
    of Romanticism he represents permits of consistent control,
    his gift for release among the gaudy Walpurgisnacht images
    of the tormented subconscious life is unrivaled."

23  SLOTE, BERNICE.  "The Whitman Tradition."  Start with the Sun:
    Studies in Cosmic Poetry.  Edited by James E. Miller, Jr.,
    Karl Shapiro and Bernice Slote.  Lincoln:  University of
    Nebraska Press, p. 4.
       Roethke is "perhaps" one of the strongest figures in the
    Whitman tradition.

24  SOUTHWORTH, JAMES G.  "The Poetry of Theodore Roethke."
    College English, XXI (March), 326-338.
       Following Roethke's poetry chronologically reveals the
    poet's maturation from guarded individuality and frustra-
    tion in the early work to the deeper and freer, though
    more obscure, later work.  Movement is important and it is
    toward an affirming confidence and universality.

25  VORHEES, JOHN.  "Roger Wagner Chorale Work Not as Good as Last
    Season's:  New Composition."  Seattle Post-Intelligencer,
    March 14, p. 6.
       This article includes an announcement that Roethke's
    poetry will be set to music and performed by Ned Rorem at
    Carnegie Hall.

26  WATSON, EMMETT.  "This Our City:  Blue Monday Memos."  Seattle
    Post-Intelligencer, January 25, p. 9.
       Recognition of Roethke's election as one of "10 Americans
    to Watch in 1960" in Pageant Magazine.

1960

27   WERNER, W. L.  "Bookworm:  Giving the Replies Instead of
     Exams."  Centre Daily Times (State College, Pa.),
     February 2, p. 6.
         Roethke was chosen as one of "Ten Americans to Watch in
     1960" by Pageant Magazine.

28   ____.  "Bookworm:  Need for Libraries Stressed in County."
     Centre Daily Times (State College, Pa.), March 15, p. 2.
         The author comments on an article on Roethke in College
     English by saying "Pretty skimpy except for the inevitable
     greenhouse."

29   WRIGHT, FERGUS.  "Suddenly, Inishbofin Becomes a Fashion."
     Sunday Independent (Ireland), August 28, p. 13.
         A sketchy account of the meeting of Roethke, Thomas
     Kinsella and Richard Murphy at this retreat.  Little is
     said of Roethke.


1961 A BOOKS - NONE

1961 B SHORTER WRITINGS

1    "A. C. B."  "A Joyous Collection of Nonsense Poetry."  Newport
     News (Va.) Daily Press, July 30, page unknown (from the
     Roethke collection, University of Washington).
         Review of I Am! Says the Lamb.  Favorable brief review.

2    "A. C. H."  "Nonsense Verses."  Savannah (Ga.) News, July 30,
     page unknown (from the Roethke collection, University of
     Washington).
         Review of I Am! Says the Lamb.  Favorable brief review.

3    "A. F. W."  Review of I Am! Says the Lamb.  Columbus (Ohio)
     Dispatch, August 20, page unknown (from the Roethke col-
     lection, University of Washington).
         Favorable brief review.

4    ANON.  "Oxford Diary:  Poet's Visit."  Oxford Mail,
     February 16, page unknown (from the Roethke collection,
     University of Washington).
         Roethke will give a reading to the Oxford University
     Poetry Society.

5    ANON.  "Pulitzer Poet Roethke Reads Works, Comments on Life,
     Love, Literature."  The Williams Record, March 10, p. 11.
         An extensive account of a Roethke reading at Williams
     College (Massachusetts), filled with "humorous anecdotes,
     reminiscences..., and some wry remarks."  Roethke's

commentary that accompanied many of the poems is reprinted, including that for "Cuttings," "My Papa's Waltz," "I Need, I Need," and "The Lady and the Bear."

6    ANON.    "Roethke to Recite Poetry at Trinity." The Hartford (Conn.) Times, March 16, p. 41.
     Announcement of Roethke's reading and the several days he will spend at Trinity College discussing poetry and creative writing with students. Some of Roethke's prizes and awards are listed.

7    ANON.    "Roethke to Give 'Journeys' as Feature of Arts Festi- val." The DePauw (Greencastle, Indiana), May 1, p. 2.
     Announcement of Roethke reading, with a brief biography and closing lines of 'Journeys,' a poem commissioned for the festival. W. H. Auden and Richard Wilbur had previ- ously presented commissioned poems.

8    ANON.    "Roethke Punctures Facade of Beatniks." The DePauw (Greencastle, Indiana), May 3, pp. 1, 2.
     Remarks made by Roethke during reading at DePauw Univer- sity. "Behind the 'beats' attitude lies a profound thing, but as writers they just never bothered to learn how to write. I suspect that they aren't really honest with themselves." Behind the Zen Buddhist philosophy, to which many of them adhere, "is a flimsy facade of half-baked ideas. They are all timid Coleridges." Roethke also speaks on the definition of poetry (Auden's 'memorable speech') and the poet's place in the disorderly world of the twentieth century.

9    ANON.    "Poetry." Saturday Review, XLIV:28 (July 15), 23.
     Review of Words for the Wind.
     "There's nothing of spilling-over in these poems; they are cool, precise, and occasionally overwhelmingly tender...."

10   ANON.    "Rhymes by Roethke." Christian Science Monitor, LIII (August 3), 7.
     Review of I Am! Says the Lamb. "It's a delight to wel- come Theodore Roethke, one of America's most thoughtful poets, to the realm of wise foolishness." A favorable review that even goes so far as to reproduce two of Robert Leydenfrost's drawings.

11   ANON.    "Old Greenhouse No Longer Exists." The Saginaw News, August 3, Section B, p. 5.
     This article accompanies James W. Henderson's review of I Am! Says the Lamb. The greenhouse has "been torn down

1961

to accomodate a real estate development." Roethke, the author reveals, was editor of the Arthur Hill High School _Criterion_. A brief biographical sketch follows.

12 ANON. "Terse Verse." _Cedar Rapids_ (Ia.) _Gazette_, August 6, page unknown (from the Roethke collection, University of Washington).
Review of _I Am! Says the Lamb_. "...one couldn't do better...."

13 ANON. "Serious Poet Turns Frivolous." _Springfield_ (Mo.) _News & Leader_, August 6, page unknown (from the Roethke collection, University of Washington).
Review of _I Am! Says the Lamb_. A "sprightly little collection."

14 ANON. "Roethke Surprises Admirers With Book of Nonsense Poems." _Seattle Times Magazine_, August 6, p. 22.
Review of _I Am! Says the Lamb_. Quoted excerpts from the book as "jingly as anything A. A. Milne or Lewis Carroll ever produced." And this from the poet "who had led readers through the murky depths and mazelike ways of ultramodern verse."

15 ANON. "Roethke Named for Award." _Seattle Times_, August 10, p. 25.
An announcement that Roethke will receive the "Golden Plate Award" at the first annual banquet of the Academy of Achievement in Monterey, California. Among others receiving awards are Dr. Charles Mayo, Dr. Werner Von Braun, and Edward Teller.

16 ANON. Title unknown. _Wilmington_ (Del.) _News_, August 14, page unknown (from the Roethke collection, University of Washington).
Review of _I Am! Says the Lamb_. Favorable brief review.

17 ANON. Title unknown. _Kansas City Star_, August 19, page unknown (from the Roethke collection, University of Washington).
Review of _I Am! Says the Lamb_. Juxtaposition of the two halves of this book causes strain.

18 ANON. "Modern Poet." _Hartford_ (Conn.) _Courant_, August 20, page unknown (from the Roethke collection, University of Washington).
Review of _I Am! Says the Lamb_. "The nonsense poems are written archly but without any particular point, so that their mild absurdity of wording is not particularly funny."

19    ANON.    Review of I Am! Says the Lamb. Wichita (Ks.) Eagle,
      August 27, page unknown (from the Roethke collection,
      University of Washington).
         Favorable brief review.

20    ANON.    "Some Poems." Sacramento Union, September 10, page
      unknown (from the Roethke collection, University of
      Washington).
         Review of I Am! Says the Lamb. "The nonsense poems are
      made up of wonderfully wild rhythms and rich exuberance,
      while the latter are delicately-crafted pearls of thought
      on nature inside a glass world."

21    ANON.    Title unknown. Tacoma (Wash.) News-Tribune,
      September 24, page unknown (from the Roethke collection,
      University of Washington).
         Review of I Am! Says the Lamb. Favorable brief review.

22    ANON.    "The Reading Lamp." South Bend (Ind.) Tribune,
      September 24, page unknown (from the Roethke collection,
      University of Washington).
         Review of I Am! Says the Lamb. "...a delightful compan-
      ion to Carroll, Milne and Ogden Nash."

23    ANON.    Review of I Am! Says the Lamb. New Orleans Picayune,
      October 15, page unknown (from the Roethke collection,
      University of Washington).
         Favorable brief review.

24    ANON.    "Here's Poetry for Children, and for Adults as Well."
      Denver Post, November 12, page unknown (from the Roethke
      collection, University of Washington).
         Review of I Am! Says the Lamb. Favorable brief review.

25    ANON.    Title unknown. Washington (D.C.) Star, December 10,
      page unknown (from the Roethke collection, University of
      Washington).
         Review of I Am! Says the Lamb. Favorable brief review.

26    "A. V. S." "Pulitzer Prize-Winning Poet Also Writes Fine
      Nonsense Verse." New Haven (Conn.) Register, July 30,
      page unknown (from the Roethke collection, University of
      Washington).
         Review of I Am! Says the Lamb. Favorable review with
      little critical commentary.

27    BOWEN, MARY ULA. "Joyous Book Offers Verse, Nonsense."
      Columbia Missourian, November 14, page unknown (from the
      Roethke collection, University of Washington).

1961

> Review of _I Am! Says the Lamb_. Favorable review with little critical commentary.

28   CHAMBERS, PETER. "Poets Without Appointments: Professor: Journey." _Daily Express_ (London), January 28, page unknown (from the Roethke collection, University of Washington).
> Roethke tells the author how well he lives as a poet and teacher in America.

29   COOLEY, FRANKLIN D. Title unknown. _Richmond_ (Va.) _News Leader_ July 30, page unknown (from the Roethke collection, University of Washington).
> Review of _I Am! Says the Lamb_. Nonsense poems are hard to evaluate, but book seems successful.

30   DeLANCEY, ROSE MARY. "Poet Roethke Prize Book Re-printed." _Fort Wayne News-Sentinel_, May 27, page unknown (from the Roethke collection, University of Washington).
> The Doubleday edition of _Words for the Wind_ (1958) has been re-printed by Indiana University Press. Some of Roethke's poems in Part I are too "avantgarde." The poems of Part II are what make Roethke a good poet.

31   _____. "'I Am' Poems by Roethke Delightful." _Fort Wayne_ (Ind.) _News Sentinel_, July 29, page unknown (from the Roethke collection, University of Washington).
> Favorable brief review.

32   DEUTSCH, BABETTE. "The Poet and His Critics: A Symposium Edited by Anthony Ostroff." "Babette Deutsch: Essay." _New World Writing, Number 19_. Philadelphia: J. B. Lippincott, pp. 201–206.
> Roethke fights for identity and his poem purges the self clear. His voice is one among many in Western tradition. He alludes to others and their common stock of symbols as his being emerges through a tightly controlled madness.

33   DICKEY, JAMES. "Correspondences and Essences." _Virginia Quarterly Review_, XXXVII (Autumn), 640.
> Review of _I Am! Says the Lamb_ and _Words for the Wind_. "Roethke seems to me the finest poet now writing in English..., not so much because of his beautifully personal sense of form..., but because of the way he sees and feels the aspects of life which are compelling to him." His poems come from a depth "where everything one says is the right, undreamed-of, and known-by-the-gods-all-the-time thing that should be and never is said." Reading Roethke's

poems "one feels guilty of an unjust act, of a dislocation
of nature, in referring to them as 'literature' at all."
See also 1968.B28.

34    EHRIG, VICTOR.  "Roethke's Nonsense Verse Delightfully Dif-
      ferent."  St. Louis Globe-Democrat, August 13, p. 4F.
         Review of I Am! Says the Lamb.  Favorable review, though
      its author finds it difficult to reconcile Roethke's title
      of "professor" with the nonsense poems and their vividly
      imaginative exuberance.  Also reviewed (in the next column)
      is Aneurin Bevan:  Cautious Rebel, by Mark M. Krug.  Inter-
      estingly Roethke's thoughtful picture appears above the
      name "Aneurin Bevan," while Mr. Bevan smiles devilishly
      above "Theodore Roethke."

35    "E. M. J."  "Sense, Nonsense in Poetry Book."  Lewiston-Auburn
      (Me.) Journal, October 28, page unknown (from the Roethke
      collection, University of Washington).
         Review of I Am! Says the Lamb.  Favorable brief review.

36    FERGUSON, ADELE.  "The Sun's Book Shelf."  Bremerton (Wash.)
      Sun, July 29, page unknown (from the Roethke collection,
      University of Washington).
         Review of I Am! Says the Lamb.  The greenhouse poems are
      acceptable, but some of the nonsense verse fills the re-
      viewer with "nothing."

37    FERRIS, PAUL.  "Sound Radio:  Madmen."  The Observer Weekend
      Review (London), February 12, p. 31.
         A review of a moving performance by Roethke of his poems
      when he "actually sang the last one" and shook up the woman
      announcer.

38    FRESHWATER, PHILIP C.  "Nonsense or Lyric, Poems Are Exquisite."
      Sacramento Bee, September 3, page unknown (from the
      Roethke collection, University of Washington).
         Review of I Am! Says the Lamb.  "The nonsense verses are
      witty, pomposity puncturing and agile...."  The greenhouse
      poems "are extraordinary in the cool accuracy of phrasing,
      rhythm and observation."

39    GHOSE, ZULFIKAR.  "Roethke:  I ran with the roaring boys."
      Western Daily Press (Bristol), January 18, page unknown
      (from the Roethke collection, University of Washington).
      Reprinted in The Glass House, pp. 268-270.
         From what was essentially an interview, the author draws
      Roethke as a restless man, obsessed with poetry, yet still
      having a sense of humor.  He comments on several topics,

1961

       including his college life, early influences (Bogan, Wordsworth, Blake and Herrick), and his recent shift to a more formal poetry. He stresses rhythm in poetry, but admits other approaches are possible. He does not want to make pronouncements about his contemporaries. Teaching is also discussed.

40    \_\_\_\_\_. "The World's Best--Young and Old." Western Daily Press (Bristol), June 21, page unknown (from the Roethke collection, University of Washington).
    This article deals generally with the recent work of several important American poets, including Roethke. His progress, as evidenced in Words for the Wind, is discussed, as well as his rising reputation in England and his influence on English poets.

41    GLAUBER, ROBERT H. "A Varied, Exciting Collection." Chicago Sun-Times, November 19, page unknown (from the Roethke collection, University of Washington).
    Review of New World Writing 19. The reviewer comments at some length on the symposium on Roethke's poem "In a Dark Time."

42    GOFF, RICHARD. "Humor Forced: Better Verse Is Worthwhile." Pittsburgh (Pa.) Press, August 27, page unknown (from the Roethke collection, University of Washington).
    Review of I Am! Says the Lamb. The nonsense poems lack spontaneity, are studied.

43    "H. A. K." Review of I Am! Says the Lamb. Boston Globe, July 30, page unknown (from the Roethke collection, University of Washington).
    The juxtaposition of sense and nonsense gives a not too happy result.

44    HAYES, LINDA. "Varied Verses." Chattanooga Times, November 19, page unknown (from the Roethke collection, University of Washington).
    Review of I Am! Says the Lamb. The greenhouse poems are of higher quality than the nonsense poems.

45    HENDERSON, JAMES W. "Nonsense, Nostalgia in Roethke Volume." The Saginaw News, August 3, Section B, p. 5.
    Review of I Am! Says the Lamb. This book should be subtitled as "Poems for people who think they hate poetry." It gives nonsense and mature sensitivity that "should go far to reduce their numbers."

1961

46  HOLZHAUER, ROBERT A.  "How the Wagtail Woos."  Milwaukee
    Journal,  November 12, page unknown (from the Roethke
    collection, University of Washington).
        Review of I Am! Says the Lamb.  "...the complete book
    should become a classic of masterly wild whimsey, which
    is an everlasting joy."

47  "H. T. M."  "Roethke Verse Is Bright, Light."  Boston Herald,
    July 30, page unknown (from the Roethke collection, Uni-
    versity of Washington).
        Review of I Am! Says the Lamb.  Favorable brief review.

48  JACOBSEN, JOSEPHINE.  "New Books in Review."  Baltimore Sun,
    July 28, page unknown (from the Roethke collection, Uni-
    versity of Washington).
        Review of Words for the Wind.  The reviewer sees
    Roethke's definite development, not as theorist or
    thinker, but as poet.  This is the "purest poetry," be-
    cause all else is subordinated to the poem.

49  JOHNSON, DONALD B.  "A Joyous Book of Verse."  Worcester
    (Mass.) Telegram, August 6, page unknown (from the Roethke
    collection, University of Washington).
        Review of I Am! Says the Lamb.  Favorable brief review.

50  "J. W."  Review of I Am! Says the Lamb.  Auburn (N.Y.) Citizen-
    Advertizer, July 29, page unknown (from the Roethke collec-
    tion, University of Washington).
        Favorable brief review.

51  KEELEY, CAROL.  "Roethke Reads Works in Ballroom Tonight."
    Connecticut Daily Campus, March 16, p. 1.
        An extensive biography of Roethke that includes general-
    izations about his accomplishment as a poet.

52  "K. J."  "'58 Book Award Winner Usually Shows Unexpected."
    Columbia Missourian, May 28, page unknown (from the
    Roethke collection, University of Washington).
        Review of Words for the Wind.  Roethke's shift of
    styles is here emphasized.

53  KUHAR, KYRA.  "A Full Collection of Verse by Poet Theodore
    Roethke."  Charleston (S.C.) News & Courier, August 20,
    page unknown (from the Roethke collection, University of
    Washington).
        Review of I Am! Says the Lamb.  Favorable review with
    little critical comment.

1961

54  KUNITZ, STANLEY. "The Poet and His Critics: A Symposium
    Edited by Anthony Ostroff." "Stanley Kunitz: Essay--
    The Taste of Self." New World Writing, Number 19.
    Philadelphia: J. B. Lippincott, pp. 206-214.
        Paradox is the method and substance of Roethke's poem.
    Form makes poetry of a scream, the style of "oracular
    abstraction." The question asked is: How find the Self
    among confused and divided selves? The answer is: Knowing
    he is lost, helps him find himself. See also 1964.B36.

55  LAYTON, MIKE. "UW Poet Publishes Lighthearted Verse."
    Olympian (Olympia, Wa.), August 20, page unknown (from
    the Roethke collection, University of Washington).
        Favorable brief review.

56  LOWELL, ROBERT. Interview with Frederick Seidel. Paris
    Review, VII:25 (1961-1962), 87.
        Lowell speaks of his sharing with Roethke of "the exul-
    tant moment," though he concedes mastery to Roethke in the
    "musical" poem of the ear. "He rejoices in the rhetoric
    and the metrics, but there's something very disorderly
    working there. Sometimes it will smash a poem and some-
    times it will make it." See also 1963.B52 and 1968.B53.

57  MAXWELL, EMILY. "The Smallest Giant in the World, and the
    Tallest Midget." New Yorker, XXXVII (November 18), 237.
        Review of I Am! Says the Lamb. Roethke divides his book
    into two sections, "Nonsense Poems" and "Greenhouse Poems,"
    both excellent and highly original.

58  MEACHAM, HARRY M. "Light Verse: Theodore Roethke Joins Out-
    standing Nonsense Poets." Richmond (Va.) News Leader,
    October 4, page unknown (from the Roethke collection,
    University of Washington).
        Review of I Am! Says the Lamb. Roethke's nonsense verse
    "will outlive much of the serious poetry written in the
    past 100 years."

59  NAPIER, JOHN. "Poetry in the Vernacular and Otherwise."
    Voices, CLXXVI (September/December), 54.
        Review of Words for the Wind. Roethke's later work
    abandons the relatively successful "domestic idiom" in
    favor of "elegance and brave show of philosophy." The
    "New Poems" are not convincing, whereas "Lighter Pieces
    and Poems for Children" are "embarrassingly unamusing."
    The failure of the former seems linked to Roethke's
    "intense drive toward formal perfection."

1961

60    NATHAN, NORMAN.  Judging Poetry.  New York:  G. P. Putnam's
         Sons, pp. 99-100.
           Questions for students on Roethke's poem "Epidermal
      Macabre."

61    "N. H."  "Nonsense Verse Wild, Rampart (sic)."  Los Angeles
      Herald Express, August 21, page unknown (from the Roethke
      collection, University of Washington).
           Review of I Am! Says the Lamb.  Faborable brief review.

62    OSTROFF, ANTHONY.  "The Poet and His Critics:  A Symposium
         Edited by Anthony Ostroff."  "Anthony Ostroff:  Introduc-
         tion."  New World Writing, Number 19.  Philadelphia:
         J. B. Lippincott, pp. 189-191.
           See individual commentators, Babette Deutsch (1961.B32),
      Stanley Kunitz (1961.B54), and John Crowe Ransom (1961.B66)
      for annotations.  See also 1964.B43.

63    PATTERSON, ELIZABETH.  "Theodore Roethke Writes Verse for
         Everybody."  Seattle Post-Intelligencer, July 22, p. 13.
           Review of I Am! Says the Lamb.  Roethke evokes the
      "unfathomed adult world" over which the child has no con-
      trol.  This is "a book to be enjoyed almost from the cradle
      but certainly to the grave."

64    _____.  "Letter."  Seattle Post-Intelligencer, July 30, page
      unknown (from the Roethke collection, University of
      Washington).
           The writer adds to her review (1961.B63) of I Am! Says
      the Lamb.

65    PILSK, ADELE.  "Fresh Verses Are for All."  Nashville
      Tennessean, September 10, page unknown (from the Roethke
      collection, University of Washington).
           Review of I Am! Says the Lamb.  Faborable brief review.

66    RANSOM, JOHN CROWE.  "The Poet and His Critics:  A Symposium
         Edited by Anthony Ostroff."  "John Crowe Ransom:  Essay."
         New World Writing, Number 19.  Philadelphia:  J. B.
         Lippincott, pp. 191-201.
           Roethke is a theological poet.  But in order to under-
      stand how this poem operates as a religious conversion, it
      is necessary to get an overview of Roethke's entire body
      of poetry, to grasp the evolution of his style that has
      led him to this terse confrontation with God, "In a Dark
      Time."  See also 1964.B50.

1961

67 RENDON, ARMANDO. "'Find Out How the Ceiling's Feeling.'"
Oakland Tribune, August 6, Your Town supplement (Section M),
p. 4.
Review of I Am! Says the Lamb. Favorable review in which
the author finds each section of the book, the "Greenhouse"
and "Nonsense" poems, necessary to the other, two dicho-
tomous views that are "parts of the author's singularly
persistent effort to grasp the essence of this world."

68 RIDLAND, JOHN M. "Whirlybird: Roethke Reading." Poetry
Northwest, II (Winter 1961/1962), 26. Reprinted in "A
Garland for Theodore Roethke." Michigan Quarterly Review,
VI (Fall 1967), 257-258.
A poem in tribute to Roethke.

69 SCOGGIN, MARGARET C. "I Am! Says the Lamb." Virginia Kirkus
Service, XXIX (May 1), 423.
Roethke's "nonsense" poems, by their titles alone, "would
delight children or any adult who can still think like a
child." Of the "greenhouse" poems: "Roethke has always
seemed at his best about a garden or a greenhouse, and
these poems show a fine sense of color and observation
through which graver matters are delicately transparent."

70 _____. "Outlook Tower." Horn Book, XXXVII (December), 567.
Review of I Am! Says the Lamb. "The Nonsense Poems...
have, for the most part, just the right irrational quality.
The Green House poems are rather more limited in appeal."

71 SMITH, RAY. Review of I Am! Says the Lamb. Library Journal,
LXXXVI (June 15), 2320.
"The poems are brief, sensuous, cool as the fervently
striving rootlets described empathically in their pervasive damp of earth and cellar." Bats and rats "add an
element near horror, of unbearable touch.... Most of the
poems...are instant perceptions breathing intimate
identification."

72 STANFORD, DEREK. Review of The Modern Poets: A Critical
Introduction, by M. L. Rosenthal. English (London), XIII
(Summer), 199.
Rosenthal's treatment of Roethke is mentioned several
times.

73 TERRY, J. WILLIAM. "Books and Authors." Patterson (N.J.)
Call, August 16, page unknown (from the Roethke collection,
University of Washington).
Review of I Am! Says the Lamb. "Roethke is sure to be
a likeable man. Any man is who sees things with so much

114

whimsey. It is one of those things that cannot be created
artificially."

74   VAN FLEET, VIRGINIA. "Hilarious Poems." Fort Worth Star-
        Telegram, July 30, Sunday Book Page number unknown (from
        the Roethke collection, University of Washington).
           Review of I Am! Says the Lamb. Favorable brief review.

75   WAIN, JOHN. "Farewell to the World." Spectator, January 13,
        p. 50.
           Review of Colossus, by Sylvia Plath. The reviewer sees
        a too obvious admiration for Roethke in some of Plath's
        verse.

76   WERNER, W. L. "Bookworm: Favorite Reading Was Editorial
        Page." Centre Daily Times (State College, Pa.), August 1,
        p. 3.
           Announcement of the publication of Roethke's I Am! Says
        the Lamb; and his recent return from Ireland and England.

77   WYATT, BOB. "Playful Poems, Sensitive Lyrics." Tulsa (Okla.)
        World, August 13, page unknown (from the Roethke collec-
        tion, University of Washington).
           Review of I Am! Says the Lamb. Favorable brief review.


1962 A BOOKS - NONE

1962 B SHORTER WRITINGS

1   ALLEN, MORSE. "The Moderns." Hartford (Conn.) Courant,
        August 5, p. 13.
           Review of New World Writing 19. The reviewer comments
        at some length on the symposium on Roethke's poem "In a
        Dark Time."

2   ANON. "Prof. Wins Shelly (sic) Award for Poetry." University
        of Washington Daily, January 19, p. 5.
           Roethke has won the $1280 award at the 52nd annual din-
        ner of the Poetry Society of America.

3   ANON. "People." Time, LXXIX (January 26), 40.
           An account of the 52nd anniversary dinner of the Poetry
        Society of America honoring Robert Frost. Roethke's poem
        "I like New England men," the "airy dessert," is printed
        here also.

4   ANON. "Poetry in English: 1945-62." Time, LXXIX (March 9),
        93, 95.

1962

> "In much of his poetry he (Roethke) writes like a self-
> made idiot, a regressive pioneer who chooses to explore
> the primary ground of being.... Roethke is a nature poet
> as well as a metaphysician, and the best of his poems
> celebrate the spiritual experience in a natural metaphor,
> as a sort of vegetation mystery." Roethke is condemned
> with most other contemporary poets when the author says:
> "Inevitably, most of them are scops without scope who
> write poetry about poetry and not about life."

5   ANON.   "Faculty Profile: Theodore Roethke." Washington
    Alumnus, V (Spring), 9-10, 22-23.
        An extended profile that outlines the major events of
    Roethke's life, as well as develops at length an image of
    Roethke as an important literary force in the university
    community and northwest region. Of special interest are
    the contemporary views of Roethke's physical demeanor and
    his life-style, as well as the latter's relation to his
    work. The article deals extensively too with the thematic
    development clear in the poems, and their style, conclud-
    ing that "Roethke is not a facile poet. ...he has created
    something like a new poetic image." Discussions of the
    stature of American poetry and Roethke's part in it, as
    teacher, close out the profile.

6   ANON.   "Notes on the Margin." San Francisco Chronicle,
    April 29, This World supplement, p. 38.
        Roethke's reading at San Francisco State College "will
    be a feature of the student Contemporary Arts Festival."

7   ANON.   "Poetry Reading." Daily Californian (University of
    California, Berkeley), May 7, p. 11 (as cited by McLeod
    in Theodore Roethke: A Bibliography).
        An advertisement.

8   ANON.   "UM To Honor Poet From Saginaw." Saginaw News,
    June 7, Sect. B, p. 4.
        Roethke will receive honorary Doctor of Letters degree
    from the University of Michigan. A brief biography and
    some of his prizes for his poetry are also mentioned.

9   ANON.   "Roethke to Be Honored at U. of Michigan." Seattle
    Times, June 12, p. 16.
        In recognition of his "contributions to poetry," Roethke
    will receive an honorary doctor-of-letters degree.

10  ANON.   "Michigan Fetes Roethke for Poetry Contribution."
    University of Washington Daily, June 15, p. 6.

1962

Roethke received an honorary Doctor of Letters degree
from his alma mater, the University of Michigan.

11    ANON.    "Honorary Degrees Given."  New York Times, June 17,
        Sect. I. p. 27.
        Announcement of degrees awarded by the University of
        Michigan.

12    ANON.    "Prof. Roethke, Poet, Given Honorary Title."  Seattle
        Times, June 23, p. A.
        Roethke has been named "Poet-in-Residence" at the Univer-
        sity of Washington, the first time anyone has been given
        the honorary title there.

13    ANON.    Title unknown.  Baton Rouge (La.) Advocate,
        October 7, page unknown (from the Roethke collection,
        University of Washington).  Review of I Am! Says the Lamb.
        Favorable brief review.

14    ANON.    "Prof Roethke to Read Own Works at Fair."  University
        of Washington Daily, October 12, p. 1.
        Highlight of the reading will be "The Rose," "written
        especially for this reading at the World's Fair."  Some
        remarks are made of biographical interest, including:
        "Roethke sold his first poem while he was in his early
        30's.  At this time he was working simultaneously as a
        tennis coach, a public relations councilor (sic), and a
        teacher of English."

15    ANON.    "Noted American Poet Will Read Own Works at UCR."
        Riverside Press (University of California at Riverside),
        October 22, p. 1.
        Announcement of Roethke reading, with brief biography.
        "His next work 'Dance On, Dance On, Dance On' will appear
        first in Ireland, and then in an Italian edition."

16    ANON.    "Poet Roethke Recites Selection of Own Poems."  The
        Highlander (Riverside, California), October 24, p. 1.
        Announcement of Roethke reading and brief biography.
        "His next work, to appear first in Ireland and in Italy,
        will be 'Dance On, Dance On, Dance On.'"

17    ANON.    "Famous American Poet Will Read Works at Oxy Tuesday."
        The Occidental (Los Angeles), October 26, p. 1.
        Announcement of Roethke reading, with brief biography.
        "Roethke's poetry reveals the restlessness of his spirit
        and a sense of deep emotional and philosophical anguish."
        "He has achieved an astounding versatility because of his
        belief that a poet should work on as many levels as
        possible."

1962

18    ANON.  "Pulitzer Poet at UCR Soon." Riverside Press (University of California at Riverside), October 26, p. 1.
       Announcement of Roethke reading, brief biography and estimate of his world-wide status. Mention is made of "Dance On, Dance On, Dance On," to be published in Ireland and Italy.

19    ANON.  "Noted Poet." (As cited in Theodore Roethke: A Bibliography, by James Richard McLeod.) The Occidental (Los Angeles), November 2, p. 11.
       Photograph caption in which Roethke's recent reading is mentioned.

20    ANON.  "View from Parnassus." Time, LXXX (November 9), 102.
       Excerpts from Randall Jarrell's talk at the National Poetry Festival in Washington when he said: "'Many poets are sometimes childish; Roethke, uniquely, is sometimes babyish, though he is a powerful Donatello baby who has love affairs, and whose marsh-like Unconscious is continually celebrating its marriage with the whole wet dark underside of things."

21    ANON.  "Roethke, Theodore." The Reader's Encyclopedia of American Literature. Edited by Max J. Herzberg. New York: Thomas Y. Crowell Co., 1962; 4th printing, pp. 969-970.
       Roethke's poems fall into two categories: "those written in strict forms and employing generally witty and rational modes of thought and those in free forms using irrational, sometimes surrealistic modes of thought. Among the latter are some remarkable evocations of childhood and old age.... They are strong poems, strikingly original and frequently deeply moving. Roethke...is certainly among the foremost American poets of his generation."

22    BENNETT, NANCY and BOB T. PETERSON.  "Prof Roethke Receives Title From Regents." University of Washington Daily, June 28, pp. 1, 2.
       Roethke has been honored with the title 'Poet-in-Residence' at the university. No other poet has held it. The article tells how Roethke, though to many unknown, deserves the honor. Comments from W. H. Auden and Stanley Kunitz are included.

23    BRAZIER, DOROTHY BRANT.  "Introduction to a Poet's Wife." Seattle Times, October 9, p. 19.
       A biographical sketch of Beatrice Roethke that discusses her parents, her meeting with Roethke while his student at Bennington College, and their simple life together in Seattle.

1962

24    CAMBON, GLAUCO. Recent American Poetry. University of
        Minnesota Pamphlet on American Writers Number 16.
        Minneapolis: University of Minnesota Press, p. 7.
          While dismissing Roethke as not within the scope of this
        study, the author makes the following remarks: "Theodore
        Roethke, whose 'words' are really not 'for the wind,' has
        likewise not begun his career recently enough, from our
        point of view, to justify more than a cursory mention,
        even though it was not until 1958, with the publication
        of his collected poems, that a broad view of his often
        exciting, if uneven, endeavor was possible. The 'meta-
        physical' sensibility predominant in modern American verse
        modulates with him from a Yeatsian strictness of formal
        statement all the way to a visionary rapture in the Blake
        manner, which breaks up rhythm and stanza patterns into
        seemingly loose utterances having only 'the shape of the
        fire.' The nursery rhymes Roethke includes in his canon
        are delightfully close to this earnest magic, as they were
        for Blake, and they subtly confirm his lyrical gift."

25    DONNELLY, DOROTHY. "Words for the Wind." Michigan Quarterly
        Review, I (Summer), 212.
          The traces of Roethke's many "admirations" (Dickinson,
        Blake, Whitman, Thomas) do not dim a poetry that is
        essentially of exuberance and praise, reminiscent of
        Christopher Smart. Life, breaking "through the skin of
        one's identity," is Roethke's concern. His style receives
        some mention, as well as his occasional excesses.

26    "F. S." Untitled review of I Am! Says the Lamb. New Haven
        (Conn.) Journal Courier, July 2, page unknown (from the
        Roethke collection, University of Washington).
        Favorable brief review.

27    GRAY, NANCY. "A Package of Poetry and Jazz: From T. S. Eliot
        to Vince Guaraldi at S.F. State." San Francisco Examiner,
        August 29, Highlight section, p. 12.
          Roethke, "an undisputed leader and major force among
        contemporary poets," will read as part of the Contemporary
        Arts Festival at San Francisco State College.

28    GUZZO, LOUIS R. "Roethke Wins $1,280 Shelley Award." In
        "Words and Music" Column. Seattle Times, January 9, p. 13.
          Roethke received the award in New York at the Poetry
        Society of America's 52nd annual dinner at the Astor Hotel.
        When asked to recite a short poem, he looked at Robert
        Frost, honorary president of the society and said: "I
        like New England men...."

1962

29 _____. "Words and Music:  Roethke Proves Himself an Enter-
     tainer, Too."  Seattle Times, October 15, p. 21.
         Roethke read to an overflow crowd as part of the Seattle
     World's Fair.  In writing of many topics discussed by
     Roethke, the author gives a feeling of the wide and various
     interests of the poet.  He regrets that the poet refused
     to use a microphone, allowing his "pungent commentary" to
     be lost for posterity.

30 HALL, DONALD, ed.  A Poetry Sampler.  New York:  Franklin
     Watts, pp. 71, 225-226.
         An anthology, including Roethke's poems "My Papa's
     Waltz" and "Dolor," without comment.

31 JACOBSEN, JOSEPHINE.  "Books in Review:  Three Varieties of
     Poetry."  Baltimore Sun, January 4, page unknown (from
     the Roethke collection, University of Washington).
         Review of I Am! Says the Lamb.  The greenhouse poems are
     in their sum "a special small masterpiece."  The nonsense
     poems, both excellent and poor, all have unusual
     consequence.

32 LINKLATER, CAROL.  "UW Writing Courses."  University of
     Washington Daily, November 30, pp. 7, 9.
         An attempt at explaining the nature and goals of the
     University of Washington's writing program in which
     Roethke's ideas are referred to:  "Professor Roethke
     pointed out that the beginning writer is like the begin-
     ning piano student.  Both will drudge along in a most
     uninspiring manner until for some reason a jump occurs and
     an inkling of potential is revealed.  In the case of the
     writer, a single line is pure poetry, a single idea clearly
     delineated--and one neophyte writer discovers the begin-
     nings of a creative mind within himself.  He may not pro-
     gress far beyond that beginning--few of us do--but the
     satisfaction will remain and often inspire efforts in other
     areas."

33 MILLS, RALPH J., JR.  "Roethke's Garden."  Poetry, C (April),
     54-59.
         Review of I Am! Says the Lamb.  Roethke remains as
     exuberant as ever in new "Nonsense Poems" and selections
     from earlier works in "Greenhouse Poems."  The old range
     of experience is insisted on, though he is more selective,
     "for the major theme of his poetry is the pursuit of being,
     which he conceives as a physical and spiritual harmony."

1962

34   MOSER, NORMAN C. "Roethke 'Wows Em' in World Fair's Reading."
     University of Washington Daily, October 18, p. 2.
         Roethke read at the World's Fair Playhouse. His show
     was spiced with Irish pub songs, many asides and two poems
     written especially for the occasion, "The Rose" and "With
     Odegaard as Pres..." (included here).

35   _____. (James Richard McLeod, in Theodore Roethke: A Bibli-
     ography, lists this article as anonymous--but Moser is
     listed as editor of Dimensions and a brief biography is
     given beneath the text although his name does not appear
     above. KM) "Dimensions: Poetry--North West South and
     East." University of Washington Daily, November 30, p. 7.
         Roethke is at the center of the Northwest's particular
     kind of "formalist" writing--yet he is "overflowing with
     conflicting strains," among them the "almost divinely
     pure-poet,...the 'wit,' ...the prophet in his own time."
     But he is not a "great" poet. Distinctions are made in
     the nature of Northwest poetry versus California poetry,
     the former being more 'naturalistic' and the latter more
     'symbolic.' Roethke's poem "Her Longing" is reprinted
     from the London Observer.

36   MUSSER, JEAN. "Roethke's Poetry in Mime and Song Is Love
     Feast." Seattle Post-Intelligencer, October 16, p. 26.
         A review of Roethke reading that emphasizes the motion
     and rhythm of poetry, the voice, and the "infectious joy
     and energy" of Roethke as a reader.

37   RIBNER, IRVING and HARRY MORRIS. Poetry: A Critical and His-
     torical Introduction. Chicago: Scott, Foresman, p. 405.
         Roethke is grouped with younger poets who "sharpened
     their talents in experience of war."

38   ROSENTHAL, M. L. "The American Influence on the Coots of
     Hamstead Heath." Antioch Review, XXII (Summer), 189-201.
         A very brief mention of Rotheke's influence on British
     poetry.

39   SCHEAR, BILL [printed as "Rill."] "All Alone: Roethke to
     Read Poetry." Seattle Times, October 14, p. A.
         An interview in Roethke's home prior to his reading
     that night. He speaks candidly about his nervousness
     ('If I had known what this reading would involve in terms
     of wear and tear...'); the city of Seattle; the University
     of Washington English Department; his admiration of early
     Hemingway stories, but irritation at the novelist's suicide;
     and how 'Poetry is essentially an aristocratic art.'

1962

40    SWALLOW, ALAN. "Foreward." <u>An Editor's Essays of Two Decades</u>.
       Seattle & Denver: Experiment Press, p. 9 (not marked).
       Roethke receives brief mention as one of the "most inter-
      esting talents," with Robert Penn Warren and J. V.
      Cunningham, born during the period 1905-1910.

41    "T. A." "Roethke: Voice of Balder Through the Mouth of
       Groucho." <u>The Argus</u> (Seattle), October 19, p. 8. Par-
      tially reprinted in <u>The Glass House</u>.
       Roethke "appeared on the stage waving and grinning,
      straining out of his tux like a precocious panda. For the
      next two hours he regaled a capacity audience with gags
      and asides, a juggler tossing up a dazzling repartee of
      balls and bellows and baubles.... One sensed a secret,
      cunning dialogue between the Poet and the Clown.... Like
      Crazy Jane, Roethke can be guilty of 'tremendous spiritual
      arrogance,' but like Yeats' 'other self,' Roethke, too,
      redeems himself by attacking with love. All this is done
      in the style of a tough but lovable Detroit mobster run-
      ning booze during Prohibition.... Any man who exposes
      himself that way <u>must</u> be all right.... His audience knows
      he is working, sweating, by God, doing all this for <u>them</u>.
      At least they can see why Roethke is one of America's great
      teachers, why he can whip a class into a frenzy of creative
      adoration. But how many could hear the voice behind the
      act?... Roethke baits us on laughter and hooks us on pain.
      Love or no love, that is the meaning of the silent dialogue
      between the Showman and the Poet.... The voice would grow
      quiet, controlled, reverent and poetry would happen....
      And suddenly one knew why Roethke was up there and what it
      had cost."

42    TERTE, ROBERT H. "Cherne's Bust of Frost Unveiled at Poetry
       Awards Dinner Here." <u>New York Times</u>, January 19, p. 29.
      Notice that Roethke had received the $1,280 Shelley
      Award at the Poetry Society of America dinner, for his
      total accomplishment.

43    WAIN, JOHN. "On Record: Olivier Testament." <u>Observer Week-
       end Review</u> (London), October 14, p. 23
      Review of <u>Words for the Wind</u>, Folkways Record, FL9736.
      An exuberant review that closes with: "Roethke doesn't
      just render his poetry, he celebrates it: every reading
      is an act of gratitude for the inspiration that made him
      write the poem in the first place."

44    WEGARS, DON. "Bookmarks: A Basement Publisher Helps the
       Avant Garde: Bookends." <u>San Francisco Examiner</u>,
      August 29, <u>Highlight</u> section, p. 4.

1963

Brief mention that Roethke will read at San Francisco
State College.

45    WERNER, W. L.   "Bookworm:   A New Museum and an Award for Poet."
      Centre Daily Times (State College, Pa.), January 23, p. 6.
      Roethke received a $1,280 award (the Shelley Award) from
      the Poetry Society of America.


1963 A BOOKS

1    MILLS, RALPH J., JR.   Theodore Roethke.   Minneapolis:   Univer-
     sity of Minnesota Press, (UMPAW #30.)
     Roethke shows affinities to many poets but will not con-
     veniently be classified.   His work focuses on the Self and
     its relation to the Creative Act and creation.   In its
     original stages, it becomes a spiritual journey.   To illus-
     trate this, some poems from each book are examined and
     some of the poet's biography is used in support.

2    SCHEVILL, JAMES and MARK LINENTHAL.   "The Poet."   In A Dark
     Time:   A Film About Theodore Roethke.   New York and San
     Francisco:   Contemporary Films, Inc., unpaginated pamphlet
     (second and third pages).
     Brief Roethke biography emphasizing his own views on
     rhythm and the music of poetry.   In poems of remarkable
     range the Roethke voice comes through:   "Never merely
     didactic, always inside the poem, participating joyously
     in its images and rhythms, he sang it alive."


1963 B SHORTER WRITINGS

1    ALVAREZ, A.   "Sylvia Plath."   The Review (London), No. 9
     (October), p. 21.
     Roethke's influence is seen in certain of Plath's poems.
     See also 1968.B1, 1968.B2, and 1969.B1.

2    ANON.   "Film of Roethke Shows Poet in His Classroom."   Univer-
     sity of Washington Daily, January 15, p. 1.
     Roethke is the subject of a 15 minute film financed by
     the Associated Students of San Francisco State College.
     (See 1963.A2).   It is part of a series of films on major
     American poets designed "to get people interested in
     teaching poetry in the public schools."

3    ANON.   "Prize-Winning U.W. Poet Is Movie Subject."   Seattle
     Times, January 15, p. 7.

1963

David Myers is directing a film of Roethke produced and underwritten by the Associated Students of San Francisco State College.

4    ANON.   "Roethke Says: Robert Frost--'Symbol of Courage.'" University of Washington Daily, January 30, p. 1.
Roethke comments on Frost as poet and man on the occasion of the latter's death. Nothing in the article would suggest its title.

5    ANON.   "U.S. Native Poetry Best, Roethke Says." Daily Northwestern (Northwestern University), February 12, p. 4.
While a panel member of a symposium at Northwestern University, Roethke commented on the richness and variety of American poetry, its support by those interested in "culture" (such as President Kennedy), and the fact that originality in a classical art such as poetry is not the supreme concern.

6    ANON.   "Williams' Poetry Will Endure, Says Roethke." University of Washington Daily, March 7, p. 1.
After Williams' death, Roethke is quoted as saying: "'His work will be remembered long after the work of his more literary colleagues has been forgotten.'" And later: "'Williams lived one of the great lives of our time.'"

7    ANON.   "Theodore Roethke Told Policeman of Accident." Seattle Times, April 19, p. 5.
An account of Roethke's runaway car, after he had parked it; and a burglary of his home the same day.

8    ANON.   "Dirty Dinky Bites Bard that Bore Him." Seattle Post-Intelligencer, April 20, p. 1.
An account of a burglary at Roethke's home and damage caused when his car rolled, empty, down a hill.

9    ANON.   "Roethke Finishes Poetry Volumes." University of Washington Daily, June 21, p. 10.
Roethke has completed Party at the Zoo and Sequence, Sometimes Metaphysical. "A new and larger collection to be called The Far Field will appear first in Ireland, later in the United States." Mariolina Meliado is preparing a collection for publication in Italy.

10   ANON.   Untitled paragraph. Seattle Times Charmed Land Magazine, July 28, p. 23.
Entire paragraph: "A recent survey of literary prizes and winners shows Theodore Roethke of the University of

1963

Washington faculty top winner among poets, with 12 awards
to his credit."

11    ANON.   "Theodore Roethke Dies at 55; Poet Won Pulitzer in
      '54."  New York World Telegram and Sun, August 2, p. 19.
           This obituary includes the standard biographical sketch
      of jobs, awards and publications.

12    ANON.   Obit.  "Theodore Roethke."  New York Times, August 2,
      p. 27.
           Roethke's own statements are included from John Ciardi's
      Mid-Twentieth Century Authors on his early career.  From
      the things of "primordial nature" he moved to strong, con-
      ventional Yeatsian poems "that strove for control of emo-
      tion and language."  Roethke's poetry received numerous
      awards during the 1940's and 1950's.

13    ANON.   "Professor Roethke, Acclaimed as Poet, Dies."  Seattle
      Times, August 2, p. 41.
           Recounting of the main events and honors of Roethke's
      life, with special mention of his disdain of glamour and
      his belief that he was first a teacher, then a poet.

14    ANON.   "Theodore Roethke Dies, Poet, English Professor."
      New York Herald Tribune, August 2, p. 6.
           Long obituary summarizing many of Roethke's accomplish-
      ments and quoting liberally his own words from other
      sources.

15    ANON.   Obit.  "Mr. Theodore Roethke:  Notable American Poet."
      London Times, August 3, p. 8e.
           Possibly Roethke was the most distinguished American
      poet of Auden's generation.  A brief biographical sketch
      follows.  "Roethke was a poet who praised life and nature,
      with a sharp particularity of observation akin in some
      ways to Hopkins's, but also with a cryptic dry humour that
      was very American.  He had no metaphysics, no transcen-
      dental beliefs, but his love of nature was almost mystical."

16    ANON.   "Memorial Rites for Dr. Roethke."  Seattle Times,
      August 3, p. 21.
           Memorial services were held at the Episcopal Church of
      the Epiphany and Roethke's body was cremated.

17    ANON.   "Dr. Roethke Services to Be Held Monday."  Seattle
      Post-Intelligencer, August 3, p. 31.
           Services will be held at the Episcopal Church of The
      Epiphany.

# Theodore Roethke's Career: An Annotated Bibliography

1963

18  ANON.  "Theodore Roethke." <u>Seattle Times</u>, August 5, p. 8.
     Obituary containing these words:  "The death of a great
     poet is cause for universal sadness, for it means that a
     source of true human enrichment has been lost."

19  ANON.  "Obituaries." <u>Facts on File</u>, XXIII (August 8-14), 288.
     Few details.

20  ANON.  "Milestones:  Died." <u>Time</u>, LXXXII (August 9), 58.
     Roethke "built his spare verse upon recollections of his
     hothouse childhood..., blending the imagery of orchid,
     loam and garden creature with deceptively simple singsong."

21  ANON.  "Obituary." <u>Publisher's Weekly</u>, CLXXXIV (August 12),
     40.
     Short biographical sketch covering teaching jobs, prizes
     and book publications.

22  ANON.  "Prof. Roethke Leaves Effects Worth $40,000." <u>Seattle
     Times</u>, August 22, p. 5.
     Though Roethke left no will, he "left an interest in
     books, manuscripts and insurance valued at $40,000, pre-
     liminary probate papers showed."

23  ANON.  "Theodore Roethke." <u>Wilson Library Bulletin</u>, XXXVIII
     (October), 115.
     Brief mention of Roethke's death, his works, and awards.

24  ANON.  "Roethke:  A Look in His Greenhouse." <u>University of
     Washington Daily</u>, October 10, p. 11.
     Nelson Bently, David Wagoner and Arnold Stein generalize
     as to Roethke's stature as a poet and the inability to
     define his accomplishment due to its broad range.

25  ANON.  "Kunitz to Speak on Poet Roethke." <u>University of
     Washington Daily</u>, November 22, p. 13.
     Stanley Kunitz's lecture will be entitled "Recent
     Immortals" and will include a discussion of Roethke's work.
     The second part of the program will be the Pacific North-
     west premiere of the film "In A Dark Time."

26  ANON.  "Theodore Roethke." <u>University of Washington Daily</u>,
     December 4, p. 2.
     An editorial suggesting attendance at a talk on Roethke
     by Stanley Kunitz and the premiere of the film "In A Dark
     Time."  This appeal seems prompted by the reaction of local
     media to Roethke's death when "radio announcers read the
     news with indifference.  And they mispronounced his name."

27   ANON.   "'In A Dark Time' to Open Roethke Tribute Program."
     University of Washington Daily, December 6, p. 10.
          The film will be part of a program "added to the Lecture-
     Discussion course, 'Recent Immortals.'"  Stanley Kunitz
     will speak.

28   ARNOLD, MARTIN.  "Poet Roethke, 'in First Sleep,' Mourned."
     University of Washington Daily, August 8, pp. 1-2.
          Comments by friends and associates in the University of
     Washington Department of English, culminating with the
     following information: "Last year the honorary title of
     'Poet in Residence' was bestowed upon Roethke by the Uni-
     versity.  The title was created by the Board of Regents
     in order to give public recognition to the eminence of
     Roethke."

29   BARNET, SYLVAN, MORTON BERMAN and WILLIAM BURTO.  An Introduc-
     tion to Literature:  Fiction:  Poetry:  Drama.  Second
     Edition.  Boston, Toronto:  Little, Brown, pp. 364-365.
          Questions for students on "My Papa's Waltz."

30   BENTLEY, NELSON.  "Roethke:  American Poet."  Puget Sound
     English Notes, XXVI (Fall), 3-6.
          Having the tone of a eulogy, this article briefly sur-
     veys Roethke's entire achievement, including even a short
     pre-publication review of The Far Field.  The author sees
     Roethke in the tradition of American transcendentalism, yet
     moving through a career of four distinct poetic periods:
     1.  "a brilliant technique with subtle metrics expressing
     lyrically a metaphysical power"; 2.  probing, like
     Wordsworth, "'spots of time' far back in childhood memory";
     3.  great love poems; and 4.  "The intense process of con-
     templating the eternal and ordering the soul."  Concluding
     remarks are devoted to Roethke as teacher and influence
     on northwest poets.

31   BERRYMAN, JOHN.  "A Strut for Roethke."  New York Review of
     Books, I (October 17), 22.
          A poem in tribute to Roethke.  See also 1964.B12;
     1967.B18.

32   BLUESTONE, GEORGE.  "Roethke:  Milestone of Greatness."  Argus
     (Seattle weekly), August 9, pp. 1, 3.
          Roethke's optimism was always there, but "A lifetime of
     swinging from muck to the empyrean, from lust to love,
     exacts its cost.  His joints creaked with the strain of
     it."  To understand him, one must first be able to think
     as a child.  "With Roethke teaching wasn't a way of earning

1963

a living; it was a way of life. As anyone could tell who
ever watched him ferret out the one spark in a novice's
halting try, or emerge sweating and flushed from the hour's
struggle to give himself." "He always felt the urgency
of public conjuring. He told Stanley Kunitz that he valued
the esteem of his neighbors. He wanted bartenders to
recognize him. And he went as far as a 'difficult' poet
could toward becoming a modern troubador. Because he ex-
perienced his poems as coming through him, not from him,
he talked more and more about the poet as a vehicle for
God."

33 CIARDI, JOHN. "Theodore Roethke: A Passion and a Maker."
Saturday Review, XLVI (August 31), 13.
Ciardi reminisces about Roethke the poet and the man.
Open House was "pure jewelcraft." He mistakenly calls
The Waking the "second book," saying that here "Roethke
learned how to make a grace out of what his earlier poems
refused to look at." He talks of the Roethke who took to
"both rum and the rum-runners," the middle-aged married
man and his compulsive physicality. As poet, Roethke
brought the "compulsive spirit to form without denying
the existence either of the rank root or of the flower."
His first influence was the Elizabethan "rant," in a
poetry of "therapy by incantation."

34 CONQUEST, ROBERT. "A Spectator's Notebook: A Dying Light."
The Spectator, September 6, p. 279.
A reminiscence and obituary in which the author says of
the "strong, large man" Roethke: "He is a poet who treats
of sexual love in a way that can refresh us all when we
are parched with the cant of the judicial and political
intruders into the private domain.... The delicate lyrical
rhetoric which was his best mode seems to me to be the
only genuinely new way of writing poetry which has emerged
in the past generation or two."

35 CUMMINGS, GRAY. "Divergent Views of Man's Self Merge in Panel."
Daily Northwestern (Northwestern University), February 12,
pp. 4, 8.
Roethke participated in a Symposium panel, "Perspectives
on the Personal Identity," with William Barrett, Waldo
Beach, and S. I. Hayakawa. Numerous remarks on the holi-
ness of all things, human love, and the accessibility of
God are reported here.

36 DEUTSCH, BABETTE. Poetry in Our Time: A Critical Survey of
Poetry in the English-Speaking World. Second Edition.
New York: Doubleday, pp. 197-200.

Roethke, successor to Eliot, is distinguished not by
matter nor form, but tone. The poems examined are mainly
from The Lost Son as the author speaks of their "reaching
into the subhuman depths of the psyche." She finds a
"simple diction" in touching poems of privacy. Roethke's
individual voice emerges from his devotion to Yeats.

37  DONOHOE, ED. "Tilting the Windmill: Getting to Know One."
    The Washington Teamster (Seattle, Washington), XXVI
    (August 9), 1.
       The author, on the occasion of Roethke's death, remi-
    nisces over several brief meetings with him. The last
    one finds Roethke boasting of his ability as a brawler.
    The point seems to be that the man never fits the descrip-
    tion of "Pulitzer Prize poet."

38  ELLIOT, GERALD A. "State's Greatest Poet: Too Few Knew the
    Work of Saginaw's Theodore Roethke, Dead at 55." The
    Grand Rapids Press, August 18, p. 24.
       The author traces much of Roethke's biography and quotes
    frequently from his own work and that of renowned critics,
    recognizing that not all agree on his stature. The mood
    of the article is one of genuine loss.

39  GARDNER, ISABELLA. "This Room Is Full of Clocks." Encounter,
    XXI (November), 52.
       A poem in tribute to Roethke. See also 1967.B32.

40  GRAVES, HAROLD F. "Letters to the Editor: More on Roethke."
    Centre Daily Times (State College, Pa.), August 16, p. 4.
       Part of "sick souls" controversy, See 1963.B45.

41  G(UNN), T(HOM). "Roethke, Theodore." The Concise Encyclopedia
    of English and American Poetry. Edited by Stephen Spender
    and Donald Hall. New York: Hawthorn Books, pp. 277-278.
       Brief biography with mention of Roethke's stylistic
    development, from "simple, vigorous and controlled," in
    Open House and The Lost Son, to experimentation with
    "sophisticated nonsense" in Praise to the End! His later
    poetry is more rational, under the acknowledged influence
    of Yeats. Some "find the new literary influence constrict-
    ing to his basic strength, which is the power to evoke the
    physical world."

42  HAAG, JOHN. "Letter to the Editor: Profitable Meditation."
    Centre Daily Times (State College, Pa.), August 13, p. 4.
       Part of "sick souls" controversy; See 1963.B45.

1963

43    _____. "Letter to the Editor:  More Personal." <u>Centre Daily</u>
      <u>Times</u> (State College, Pa.), August 20, p. 4.
          Part of "sick souls" controversy; <u>See</u> 1963.B45.

44    _____. "Letters to the Editor:  On Roethke Again." <u>Centre</u>
      <u>Daily Times</u> (State College, Pa.), September 4, p. 4.
          Part of "sick souls" controversy; <u>See</u> 1963.B45.

45    HENDERSON, HARRY B., JR.  "Letter to the Editor:  James'
      Meaning." <u>Centre Daily Times</u> (State College, Pa.),
      August 28, p. 4.
          The writer discusses the use of William James' term
      "sick souls" by "The Bookworm" in reference to Roethke.

46    HUDSON, ROBERT V. and IRENE HENSON CARTER, eds.  "Student
      Symposium on 'Spectrum of Perspectives.'" <u>Northwestern</u>
      <u>University Alumni News</u>, April, pp. 8-11.
          Program notes for the second annual student symposium at
      Northwestern University.  Roethke was one of thirteen dis-
      tinguished panel members participating.  Some comments by
      him are reproduced here:  "'The self evolves to something
      else, the soul, a desire to be essential.  This soul, this
      spirit, need not be sparse or naked.  It can grow grace-
      fully like a candle or a flower.  The self can be found
      in human mutual love, not in tending machines.'"

47    JARRELL, RANDALL.  "Fifty Years of American Poetry." <u>Prairie</u>
      <u>Schooner</u>, XXXVI (Spring), 1-27.
          Roethke's poems are of the self, to the exclusion of any
      overt social concern.  He has been surprisingly successful
      with many styles.  Yet the longer poems suggest "a certain
      rhetorical insincerity." <u>See also</u> 1965.B46.

48    K.(IZER), C.(AROLYN).  "For Theodore Roethke:  May, 1908--
      August, 1963." <u>Poetry Northwest</u>, IV (Summer), 3.
          A memorial for "one of the great metaphysic wits and
      mundane comedians of the age."

49    KUNITZ, STANLEY.  "Theodore Roethke." <u>New York Review of</u>
      <u>Books</u>, I (October 17), 21-22.
          A portrait/reminiscence of the personal and literary
      relationship of two poets.  Kunitz speaks with a genuine
      and lasting affection for Roethke about their first meet-
      ing, Roethke's first book, his mental breakdowns (how he
      bragged in "belonging to the brotherhood of mad poets that
      includes William Blake, John Clare and Christopher Smart"),
      his greenhouse poems and <u>The Lost Son</u>, his marriage, his
      humor, and his capacity to move an audience.  John

1963

Berryman's elegy, "A Strut for Roethke," is also included.
See also 1967.B48 and 1971.B26.

50   LEE, CHARLOTTE I.   "The Line as A Rhythmic Unit in the Poetry
        of Theodore Roethke."   Speech Monographs, XXX (March),
        15-22.
           Dealt with here, specifically, is "the contribution of
        the line as a rhythmic unit--with line length, with rela-
        tion of individual lines to adjacent lines, with the num-
        ber and the arrangement of stresses within lines, and with
        masculine or feminine quality of line termination."

51   LIPTON, LAWRENCE.   "Theodore Roethke--Hail and Farewell."   Los
        Angeles Times, September 22, Calendar supplement, pp. 1, 9.
           Roethke is here linked to the "West Coast renaissance"
        and "avant-garde" of the mid-fifties occupying a position
        in relation to the poets of that movement analogous to
        that of Emerson when Whitman made his breakthrough with
        "Leaves of Grass."   The author refers to Roethke as the
        "Sage of Seattle."   Also important in this discussion is
        the high mortality rate of avant-garde writers.   In this
        regard, Roethke is linked with Ambrose Bierce and other
        west coast poets of his generation.   Roethke, like Bierce,
        was an "organization" man, never exempt from its politics,
        even though frequently an embarassment to it.   Because of
        this, and an inability to accept his own culture, accord-
        ing to the author, Roethke was in general sympathy with
        the renaissance poets and, beyond this reaction, "withdrew
        into the Self."   The political cynicism of an Ambrose
        Bierce was no longer possible so, the author seems to sug-
        gest, Roethke's daemonic obsession with the Self, and the
        accompanying high mortality rate, were natural results.

52   LOWELL, ROBERT.   Paris Review interview.   Writers at Work:
        Second Series.   New York:   The Viking Press, p. 362.
           Reprint of 1961.B56; See also 1968.B54.

53   MURPHY, RICHARD.   "The Poet on the Island."   Sailing to an
        Island.   London:   Faber; New York:   Chilmark Press.
           A poem in tribute to Roethke.   See also 1967.B60.

54   NEMEROV, HOWARD.   "On Shapiro, Roethke, Winters."   Poetry and
        Fiction.   New Brunswick:   Rutgers University Press,
        pp. 134-142.
           Reprint of 1954.B30.

55   NICHOLS, LEWIS.   "In and Out of Books:   Numbers:   Value."
        New York Times Book Review, May 19, p. 8.

1963

A listing of some information taken from Literary and
Library Prizes, edited by Olga S. Weber, in which Roethke
is found to be top winner among poets, with twelve awards.
In his best year Roethke picked up $3,450.

56   REDDIN, JOHN J.   "Book Dedicated to Roethke's Godchild."
Seattle Times, September 6, p. A.   In "Faces of the City"
Column; with picture of "Meggie," Margaret Valerie
Walkinshaw, on page 1.
   The point that Roethke's passing was more noticed in the
east than Seattle is sorrowfully made.   And his strength
and gentleness is indicated by this passage:   "In the
Enchanted Land of fantasy, populated by small children,
Mother Goose, imaginative poets and other sensitive and
kindred souls like Lewis Carroll and Dr. Seuss, anything
is possible--even for a hulking big bear of a man to dedi-
cate a book of delightful nonsense to a 4-year-old girl
living on Capitol Hill AND to a successful playwright on
far-off Broadway."   The girl is "Meggie," the playwright
is Lillian Hellman, and the book is Party at the Zoo.

57   rice.   "Roethke--Death of a Poet."   University of Washington
Daily, August 8, p. 2.
   "This was a man ignored by most citizens in an age that
gave him only a passing glance.   In another time or even
another place, the name Roethke would mean something to
everyone.   But even here at an institution devoted to
higher learning the name was meaningful to only a few--
most of whom are concentrated in the English Department...."

58   ROETHKE, BEATRICE.   Untitled.   Encounter, XXI (December), 45.
   Comments on the nature of the "poem," "A Tirade Turning,"
published posthumously under Roethke's pseudonym, Winterset
Rothberg.

59   SKREEN, C. J.   "The Night Watch."   Seattle Times, October 23,
p. 52.
   CBS will present a program called "Tribute to Ted" which
will include readings by Robert Lowell and Stanley Kunitz,
as well as excerpts from In A Dark Time, a film about
Roethke completed only "two weeks ago."

60   _____.   "C.B.S. Offers Warm Tribute to Roethke."   Seattle
Times, October 28, p. 14.
   Announcement of the program called "A Tribute to Ted"
devoted to discussion by Stanley Kunitz and Robert Lowell
of "Roethke's stature as a poet, teacher and human being."
Excerpts from an earlier interview with David Myers, maker
of the film In A Dark Time, are also included.

61  SPILLER, ROBERT E., WILLARD THORP, THOMAS H. JOHNSON, HENRY S
    SEIDEL CANBY, and RICHARD M. LUDWIG, eds. Literary History
    of the United States, third edition (revised). New York:
    Macmillian; London:  Collier-Macmillan, pp. 1429-1430.
       Roethke is one of the most important American poets
    "since 1945." He is characterized here as a poet of
    "exciting if uneven powers." Some major critical points
    are made about each of his books.

62  TATE, ALLEN. "In Memoriam--Theodore Roethke, 1908-1963."
    Encounter, XXI (October), 68.
       A reminiscence of Tate's first meeting with Roethke and
    how he followed Roethke's rise later. Some comments on
    the poet in the university, Roethke as lyric and elegiac
    poet.

63  WATSON, EMMETT. "This Our City:  Passing of a Giant."
    Seattle Post-Intelligencer, August 6, p. 13.
       The author discusses his relationship with Roethke as
    one filled with boasting and bravado on the poet's part.
    But a feeling of genuine regret emerges because of the
    loss of "a rare and important man."

64  WERNER, W. L. "Bookworm:  Roethke a Rebel in a World He Didn't
    Conceive." Centre Daily Times (State College, Pa.),
    August 6, p. 5.
       The column includes a standard, sketchy Roethke biography.
    When commenting on Roethke's teaching at Lafayette, the
    author says that he "helped write the president's speeches."
    The article closes with a reference to William James as the
    author applies the term "sick soul" to Roethke, thus setting
    off a controversy involving several readers of this column.

65  _____. "Bookworm:  Word of Thanks, Clarification, and Litera-
    ture." Centre Daily Times (State College, Pa.),
    August 27, p. 2.
       The author comments on the recent controversy raised by
    his reference to Roethke in this column. Several readers
    had been debating the meaning of William James' term
    "sick souls" and its relation to Roethke.

66  _____. "Bookworm:  Problems, Aid and the Poets." Centre Daily
    Times (State College, Pa.), October 22, p. 2.
       Stanley Kunitz and Robert Lowell will participate in a
    memorial program to Roethke on "Camera 3."

67  _____. "Bookworm:  Milk, Medicine Not Subversive." Centre
    Daily Times (State College, Pa.), October 29, p. 9.
       Remarks on the contents of "Camera Three's TV tribute"
    to Roethke.

1964

## 1964 A BOOKS - NONE

## 1964 B SHORTER WRITINGS

1 ANON. "New Tribute to Roethke." Charmed Land Magazine
(Seattle Times), January 26, p. 19.
Review of Theodore Roethke, by Ralph J. Mills, Jr.
Summarizes Mills' views with little critical comment.

2 ANON. "Roethke Work in Steuben Collection." Seattle Post-
Intelligencer, March 1, p. 33.
A work entitled "The Victorians" based on a Roethke poem
is included in the glass collection.

3 ANON. "Roethke's Twilight Testament." Seattle Magazine, I
(April), 12-13.
Two drawings of Roethke by Laurie Olin accompany his
poem "The Far Field."

4 ANON. "British Poet to Read Here." University of Washington
Daily, April 7, p. 8.
Vernon Watkins, visiting professor teaching the late
Theodore Roethke's classes, will give a reading.

5 ANON. "Noted Poet to Present First Roethke Reading." Seattle
Times, May 21, p. 31.
John Crowe Ransom will give the first Roethke Memorial
reading in a program designed to "preserve the university
as a poetry center."

6 ANON. "Library Exhibit in Honor of Poet." University of
Washington Daily, May 28, p. 8.
Announcement of an exhibition of Roethke material on the
occasion of the First Roethke Memorial Poetry Reading.

7 ANON. "Last Poems." Time, LXXXIV (July 10), 98. Review of
The Far Field. (Ascribed to John R. Willingham in the
Index to Reviews in the Humanities, 1964.)
Roethke loved growing things and their textures. He
celebrated his love for his young wife. He feared death.
"As death approached..., his poems seem to have taken on
a new clarity of line and image, a new depth of tone."
Whitman's influence is seen in loving catalogues of ob-
jects; and Marvell's sense of time touches the conscious-
ness of Roethke, "who cannot even playfully think of love
without remembering death." The book closes with "Sequence,
Sometimes Metaphysical," in which Roethke "was on fire with
God."

1964

8   ANON.   Review of <u>Theodore Roethke</u> by Ralph J. Mills, Jr.
    <u>Choice</u>, I (September), 242.
        Favorable response to Mills' ability to read Roethke,
    including heightening of "psychological (Jungian) dimen-
    sions of the man and his work."

9   ANON.   Review of <u>The Far Field</u>. <u>Booklist</u>, LXI (September 1),
    29.
        "Roethke's art is distinguished by a masculine tender-
    ness for nature, his country, and marriage as well as by a
    contrasting sensitivity to life's ominous undertones pre-
    saging death."

10  ANON.   "Theodore Roethke's Verse--Published Posthumously."
    <u>Seattle Times Magazine</u>, September 13, p. 19.
        Review of <u>The Far Field</u>. Quotation of some excerpts
    from the poems with little critical comment.

11  ANON.   Review of <u>The Far Field</u>. <u>Choice</u>, I (October), 313.
        Favorable look at Roethke, "a master of several forms,
    a tireless prosodic experimenter, and an excellent light-
    versifier." He is linked to Yeats, Blake, Whitman, Smart,
    and Clare, all "transcendentalists."

12  BERRYMAN, JOHN.   "A Strut for Roethke." <u>77 Dream Songs</u>.
    New York:  Farrar, Straus, and Giroux, 1964.
        Reprint of 1963.B31; See also 1967.B18.

13  BOGAN, LOUISE.   "Verse." <u>New Yorker</u>, XL (November 7), 243.
        Review of <u>The Far Field</u>. "...a final, moving contribu-
    tion to the high metaphysical tradition, again in purely
    American terms."

14  BROOKS, CLEANTH, JOHN THIBAUT PURSER, and ROBERT PENN WARREN,
    eds. <u>An Approach to Literature</u>. Fourth Edition. New
    York: Appleton-Century-Crofts, p. 374.
        A brief discussion of "The Abyss," with some questions
    for students.

15  BRYANT, HILDA.   "'Man in a Dustcoat':  America's New Poet
    Laureate." <u>University of Washington Daily</u>, May 22,
    pp. 1, 5.
        John Crowe Ransom will give the first annual Theodore
    Roethke Memorial reading.

16  CARRUTH, HAYDEN.   "Requiem for God's Gardener." Nation, CXCIX
    (September 28), 168-169.
        Review of <u>The Far Field</u>. Roethke "was too unsure of
    himself, technically and emotionally, to write the handful

1964

of absolute poems that one needs to enter the first rank."
The reviewer sees three chief modes in Roethke's work:
"the song; the longer poem in loose meters devoted to
themes from nature, including human nature; and the dense
poem in end-stopped pentameters, usually rhymed and usually
philosophical in substance." All his poems are about
death, but in these it is more insistent. His statements
made to transcend poetry fail to do so. His presence is
too strong in the poems to do so.

17   COLE, JAMES. "Christmas Eve." Virginia Quarterly Review,
     XL (Winter), 62.
          A poem in tribute to Roethke. See also 1967.B23.

18   COOKSON, WILLIAM. "Roethke's Last Poems." Agenda, III
     (September), 21-27.
          "The Far Field...makes most recent poetry seem pro-
     foundly trivial." The author tries to give a feel of the
     poems by excerpts but finally admits the impossibility of
     doing so. He comments on the significance of "place" in
     the poems and the journey metaphor. "A distinction,
     though not a separation, between imagination and percep-
     tion is implicit in Roethke's work." From here the author
     comments briefly on "Love Poems" and "Mixed Sequence."
     With "Sequence, Sometimes Metaphysical," Roethke makes a
     final expression of many earlier themes never handled
     completely. The book closes with a sense of deep suffering.

19   DAVIE, DONALD. "Two Ways Out of Whitman." The Review, XIV
     (December), 18-19.
          Review of The Far Field. Whitman, "maker of catalogues,"
     is ubiquitous in Roethke's posthumous volume, yet made new,
     "at a level far below similarities of syntax or metre."
     But Roethke is sloppy and misses his target among all the
     words.

20   DEUTSCH, BABETTE. "On Theodore Roethke's 'In a Dark Time.'"
     The Contemporary Poet as Artist and Critic. Edited by
     Anthony Ostroff. Boston: Little, Brown, 1964, pp. 36-40.
          Reprint of 1961.B32.

21   _____. "Lament for the Makers: 1964." Atlantic, CCXIV
     (December), 72-73.
          Poem that includes a tribute to Roethke. See also
     1969.B15.

22   DICKEY, JAMES. "Theodore Roethke." Poetry, CV (November),
     119-122.

Review of Sequence, Sometimes Metaphysical. "What matters to me is not so much the form the poems took as the sensibility that lived in them, the superior quality of observation that made them possible, the presence of insight, of vision." See also 1968.B27.

23    DICKEY, WILLIAM. "Poetic Language." Hudson Review, XVII (Winter 1964/1965), 596.
      Review of The Far Field. This volume is the "fulfillment of his (Roethke's) very great abilities." Roethke is a poet of daring, whose poems are not "about" limited things. "...what Roethke has done is abandon abouts, and try instead to deal with central patterns and motions of human experience, patterns which recur, are relevant, in terms of religious experience or madness, but which are really larger than any one of their limited manifestations suggest."

24    ENGEL, BERNARD F. Marianne Moore. New York: Twayne Publishers, p. 40.
      Mention of Miss Moore's admiration for Roethke's teaching ability.

25    FIEDLER, LESLIE. "A Kind of Solution: The Situation of Poetry Now." Kenyon Review, XXVI (Winter), 61-64.
      Roethke represents "a return to all that is truly subversive in the line which comes down to us from Poe by way of symbolisme." Surrealism, greenhouse Gothicism, nursery rhymes are the evidence of this linkage.

26    FRIEDBERG, MARTHA. "Sharing the Joy of Being Alive." Books Today (Chicago Sunday Tribune), September 6, p. 9.
      Review of The Far Field. "The Far Field expresses the deepest feelings with an openness, a directness of content, and a simplicity of language rarely found in poetry today.... Roethke voices, as no other poet of our computerized age does, the unutterable joy of being alive." All of Roethke's poems are, in this sense, love poems.

27    GARRIGUE, JEAN. "A Mountain on the Landscape." New Leader, XLVII (December 7), 33-34.
      Review of The Far Field. Roethke made the traditional lyric forms his own and his "wild originality" was not stifled by them. His work has always changed and in the last poems this is a breakthrough, "translucence, a stripped-down shimmering clarity where being, just always this side of the abyss, plays with the meanings of the opposites, alternating between the fall and the sudden

achieved state of grace, and in between dances the taut
tight rope between vision that is its own exultance and
darkness that is its own descent."

28   GROSS, HARVEY. "Stanley Kunitz, Theodore Roethke, and Robert
Lowell." Sound and Form in Modern Poetry: A Study of
Prosody from Thomas Hardy to Robert Lowell. Ann Arbor:
University of Michigan Press, pp. 282-290.
Auden influenced Roethke in the "deceptively easy doggerel meter" of his early poems. But Roethke shows more
"purity of language and firmness of rhythm." Later discussion involves Roethke's own comments from "Some Remarks on
Rhythm" in which he talks of strong-stress nursery rhymes;
the "counterpointed iambic line" from Yeats; enumeration
and varying line length in Praise to the End!; and the
unmetered verse of the "meditations" owing a debt to Eliot.

29   HAMILTON, IAN. "Theodore Roethke." Agenda, III (April), 5-10.
The "environment" of the Michigan greenhouses change in
Roethke's work. In The Lost Son, the persona allows himself to be discovered experiencing the environment, and
allows "nature a full independent life." "As soon as
Roethke attempts to remove his plants and animals from
this environment and casts them into symbolic representa-
tions of his subconscious turmoil he begins to run into
trouble." Much of his identification with minimal life
seems "grossly sentimental and Disneyesque." When writing
about others in the 1950's Roethke employs a mask, not "in
the interests of self discovery, or even of dramatic projection, but as an evasion of the self, a retreat into
bardic artifice." His direction toward anonymity in the
later books is to be regretted.

30   HEILMAN, ROBERT. "Theodore Roethke: Personal Notes."
Shenandoah, XVI (Autumn), 55-64.
Roethke will be missed and this warm reminiscence shows
why. All the strengths and weaknesses he possessed came,
in time, to be recognized as "greatness." See also
1965.B39.

31   HISCOCK, BARBARA. "The Far Field: A Last Gift From a Great
Poet." University of Washington Daily, July 23, p. 2.
Review of The Far Field. The Roethke of this book has
mellowed since Words for the Wind. There is a progression
within the poems from looking at angry ugliness without,
to discovering understanding within. The poems have a
sense of finality, farewell, as we are left with Roethke's
achieved decisions. He has achieved the description of
the indescribable and has verbalized "wordless thoughts."

1964

32    JOHNS, GODFREY. "Poetry with an Academic Accent." Christian
      Science Monitor, September 10, p. 7.
          Review of The Far Field. Roethke is contemporary Amer-
      ica's truest "metaphysical poet " There is much of Donne
      in him. Yet it is Whitman he adopts. His words have a
33    cinematic effect, an arresting "epigrammatic insight."
      "His affection for William Blake is apparent, and he is a
      lyricist, sacramental and cerebral."

      JONES, NARD. "A View from Monday: 'The Far Field.'"
      Seattle Post-Intelligencer, June 15, p. 19.
          Favorable review that does little of a critical nature
      other than link Roethke with Blake as a poet of praise.

34    KELLEY, SALLY. "Traveling toward the Sun." Memphis (Tenn.)
      Appeal, November 15, page unknown (from the Roethke col-
      lection, University of Washington).
          Review of The Far Field. Roethke "writes with a strong
      sturdy grace of the simplest things."

35    KENNEDY, X. J. "Joys, Griefs and 'All Things Innocent, Hap-
      less, Forsaken.'" New York Times Book Review, August 23,
      p. 5.
          Review of The Far Field. The book is "many a familiar
      theme more deeply explored." Love poems, "playfully ten-
      der," and always poems of close scrutiny of growing things,
      fill the book as Roethke's "concern moves past his imme-
      diate subject...to become large." Roethke the experimenter
      has absorbed Yeats in these poems successfully.

36    KUNITZ, STANLEY. "The Taste of Self: On Theodore Roethke's
      'In a Dark Time.'" The Contemporary Poet as Artist and
      Critic. Edited by Anthony Ostroff. Boston, Little, Brown,
      pp. 41-48.
          Reprint of 1961.B54.

37    LEVI, PETER, S. J. "Theodore Roethke." Agenda, III (April),
      11-14.
          Roethke "was an extreme example of a modern metaphysical
      poet." "The movement of his poems was not slick or easy...
      but disturbed and at the same time most deeply formal."
      The author speaks of "In a Dark Time" in this connection,
      concluding: "The shadow is pinned against the sweating
      wall, but Roethke is an affirmative poet." "He seems to
      have been influenced by, but not quite to have shared, the
      working principle of Wallace Stevens that poetry and
      materia poetica are the same."

1964

38   LIEBERMAN, LAURENCE. "Poetry Chronicle: Last Poems, Frag-
     ments, and Wholes." Antioch Review, XXIV (Winter 1964/
     1965), 537.
         Review of The Far Field. Some poems read like premoni-
     tions of death. Roethke is strongest in moments of tender-
     ness, yet the meditations are the most powerful works.

39   MEREDITH, WILLIAM. "A Steady Storm of Correspondences:
     Theodore Roethke's Long Journey Out of the Self."
     Shenandoah, XVI (Autumn), 41-54.
         Roethke worked hard to see where he was going. His most
     ambitious book, at the center of his work, is Praise to
     the End! But it may be least successful. Roethke moved
     toward a goal, always "shaping" his poetry to create order.
     See also 1965.B60.

40   MILLS, RALPH J., JR. "James Wright's Poetry: Introductory
     Notes." Chicago Review, XVII:2&3, 128-143.
         Roethke, along with several others, is shown to be an
     influence on the poetry of James Wright.

41   _____. "Roethke's Last Poems." Poetry, CV (November), 122-124.
         Review of The Far Field. Roethke's reputation can only
     increase with this volume. It is the culmination of his
     varied themes--"the identity of self, its relation to the
     beloved, to nature and to God."

42   _____. "Theodore Roethke, 1908-1963: A Tribute." Tri-
     Quarterly, VI (Winter), 13-16.
         A reminiscence and general overview of Roethke's work,
     as the author attempts to re-place the poet in a higher
     (and rightful) position above his contemporaries and
     juniors.

43   OSTROFF, ANTHONY, ed. "The Poet and His Critics: A Symposium."
     The Contemporary Poet as Artist and Critic. Boston:
     Little, Brown.
         Reprint of 1961.B62.

44   PECK, VIRGINIA. "Roethke's 'I Knew a Woman.'" Explicator,
     XXII:8 (April), item 66.
         The poem presents two contrasting ways of life, the
     man's and the woman's. The dance and harvest metaphors
     develop this theme.

45   POWERS, DENNIS. "Fine Final Lines of Theodore Roethke."
     Focus (Oakland Tribune), July 16, p. 21.

1964

Review of The Far Field. The column contains Alan
Pryce-Jones's review from the New York Herald Tribune.
(1964.B46).

46 PRYCE-JONES, ALAN. "Theodore Roethke Poems: What the World
Has Lost." New York Herald Tribune, July 9, p. 19.
Review of The Far Field. Despite his traditional asso-
ciations, Roethke was a man of his times. He was a "controlled technician" whose "unborrowed language" is
"instantly recognizable as his own." He is successful,
as few are, in the longer, meditative poem. His love poems
show "ironic tenderness" and "when he turns metaphysical,
it is with a fine awareness of the natural world of creature enjoyments."

47 _____. "Roethke's Last Poems Show What World Lost." Seattle
Times, July 27, p. 23.
Review of The Far Field. Favorable review in which
Roethke is found to have considerable success without
faddishness. But "Do not be put off by these old-fashioned
overtones. Roethke was a controlled technician whose skill
Tennyson would at once have recognized." His musical range
was wide, "from the short runic statement to the long re-
laxed line." He sustains the long poem in language instantly recognizable as his own. The author quotes from
"The Long Waters" and "The Meadow Mouse."

48 RALEIGH, SALLY. "Poet's Every Word Treasured." Seattle Post-
Intelligencer, November 11, p. 18.
An account of Beatrice Roethke's collecting Roethke
material, principally letters, for use in several books to
be published. Mentioned are prose writings to be edited
by Ralph Mills, Allan Seager's biography of Roethke, and
300 notebooks. Mrs. Roethke says that her husband called
himself a "notebook poet."

49 RAMSEY, PAUL "A Weather of Heaven." Shenandoah, XVI (Autumn),
73-74.
Review of The Far Field. Roethke mostly wins and may
well deserve to be considered a major poet. "All in all,
this is a beautiful, admirable and at times heartrending
book. Great beauties justify faults...."

50 RANSOM, JOHN CROWE. "On Theodore Roethke's 'In a Dark Time.'"
The Contemporary Poet as Artist and Critic. Edited by
Anthony Ostroff. Boston: Little, Brown, pp. 26-35.
Reprint of 1961.B62.

1964

51   REXROTH, KENNETH. "There's Poetry in a Ragged Hitch-Hiker."
     New York Times Book Review, July 5, p. 5.
          Review of Sequence, Sometimes Metaphysical. Not really
     a review, more a praise and memorial. The writer empha-
     sizes the loss of joy and wisdom. The poems are graceful,
     their skillful workmanship hidden.

52   SHAPIRO, KARL. "Is Poetry an American Art?" College English,
     XXV (March), 403-404.
          "How typical it is of our poetry, even a century back,
     that it is tortured into existence.... I suffered through
     Cummings' struggle..., Jeffers' gigantic bitterness,
     Sanburg's hiding..., and Roethke's roving back and forth
     between Yeats, the New Yorker, and Leaves of Grass." See
     also 1968.B73.

53   _____. "A Malebolge of Fourteen Hundred Books." Carleton
     Miscellany, V (Summer), 92.
          Entire excerpt: "Theodore Roethke was a child of
     Rimbaud who held to poetry to the end. But as an American
     he was also a child of Modern Poetry, which is to say
     Yeats, Eliot, and the whole canon of right-thinking liter-
     ature. Roethke found a strategem for remaining a poet,
     a lucky accident: his childhood in a greenhouse in Mich-
     igan; his Germanic background in the same place. His
     poetry is a running battle between this organic mythology
     and the profession of letters. Strange and wonderful
     distortions of the poem and the man result." See also
     1968.B74.

54   SKELTON, ROBIN, ed. "Introduction." Five Poets of the Pacific
     Northwest. Seattle: University of Washington Press,
     pp. xv-xvi.
          Though he is not included in this anthology, the book is
     dedicated to Roethke and his influence as "teacher and
     visionary" on the poetic environment of the northwest. As
     craftsman, with close attention to detail, Roethke has led
     other poets, including the five here, "toward the discovery
     and exploitation" of their unique voices.

55   SMITH, WILLIAM JAY. "Verse: Two Posthumous Volumes."
     Harper's, CCXXIX (October), 133-134.
          Review of The Far Field. Roethke's musical sense and
     technical mastery have never seemed more apparent. He
     uses the short and long line, meditative and mystical
     poems, as well as songs. Nor has his work ever appeared
     more essentially American. "And in a volume so concerned
     with death, the predominant tone is one of pure joy."

56  SNODGRASS, W. D.  "The Last Poems of Theodore Roethke."  New
     York Review of Books, III (October 8), 5-6.
          Review of Sequence, Sometimes Metaphysical and The Far Field.
     Though not Roethke's best work, these poems are important
     for what they tell of his impending death, and death's pres-
     ence in his poetry. "They bear less the knowledge of pain,
     tnan the knowledge of numbness after pain," as they have
     grown looser and seem to take less hold on their object.
     The cause for this may lie in the fact that "love had per-
     haps been asked to fill an emptiness, effect a transforma-
     tion, which no love ever could." "What now appears dominant
     is a desire to escape all form and shape, to lose all awareness
     of otherness, not through entrance to woman as lover, but
     rather through a re-entrance into eternity conceived as
     womb, into water as woman, into earth as goddess-mother."
     Closing remarks are on Roethke's debt to Eliot and Yeats.

57  STAPLES, HUGH.  "Rose in the Sea-Wind: A Reading of Theodore
     Roethke's 'North American Sequence.'"  American Literature,
     XXXVI (May), 189-203.
          "Roethke, attempting to project his interior spiritual
     vicissitudes upon a screen much larger than that of private
     experience, achieves in these poems a dimension curiously
     suggestive of the epic," both temporally and spatially.
     The poems are a mystic's search for form, counterpointing
     in the manner of The Four Quartets.  After establishing
     this thesis, Staples deals in depth with the individual
     poems of the sequence.

58  STONEBURNER, TONY.  "Ardent Quest."  Christian Century, LXXXI
     (September 30), 1217-1218.
          Review of The Far Field.  "Roethke's poems express a
     search for the self out beyond itself.  Self discovers it-
     self in passive identification with mineral, vegetable and
     animal nature..." and "in passionate identification with
     the beloved and with God."  A theological reading is
     briefly given for the "North American Sequence."

59  WAIN, JOHN.  "Theodore Roethke."  Critical Quarterly, VI
     (Winter), 322-338.  Reprinted as "The Monocle of My
     Sea-Faced Uncle."
          "Roethke turned his back on the mass of customs and
     adaptations that shape a man's inner life, and wrote about
     those things that the mind apprehends only through the
     intuitions of the body." "He is an evangelical writer,"
     like Wordsworth, but with more emphasis on physical pas-
     sion.  The starting-point of his work is the impulse to
     identify with, "to participate in the naked processes of

life itself," a participation that is immediate and physical, not intellectual.  His evolution is a religious one.
There is a Paradiso and an Inferno in the poems, but no
Purgatorio that purifies and strengthens.  There is a
stylistic evolution in Roethke's work that stems from his
deep involvement with poets he admired, i.e. Yeats, Eliot,
Blake.  His own idiom overarches the echoes of other poets.
But there are limitations to Roethke's work: it is too
narrow, too repetitious, and it doesn't enter the ordinary
human world where social successes and failures have their
effect--it lacks a sense of total participation in life.
See also 1965.B87.

60   WALSH, CHAD.  "Introduction:  Cautious Generalizations."
     Today's Poets:  American and British Poetry Since the
     1930's.  New York:  Charles Scribner's Sons, pp. 31-32.
        Entire remark:  "I suspect the late Theodore Roethke,
     who was doing his best work at the time of his death, will
     loom larger than even his admirers have suspected."

61   WATKINS, VERNON.  "At Cwmrhydyceriw Quarry."  Encounter, XXII
     (February), 66.
        A poem in tribute to Roethke.

62   WHITE, G. ABBOTT.  "Books and Records in Review."  University
     of Michigan Daily, November 1, pages unknown (from the
     Roethke collection, University of Washington).
        Review of The Far Field and Sequence, Sometimes Meta-
     physical.  Roethke deals "realistically and profoundly with
     death.  Death is confronted and, rather than avoided or
     simply compartmentalized, is accepted and transcended...."
     The reviewer examines each section of the book in depth.

63   WILLINGHAM, JOHN, R.  Review of The Far Field.  Library Journal,
     LXXXIX (September 15), 3320.
        "Roethke, whose impact cannot yet be gauged adequately,
     controls expertly a lucid, yet always exciting line.  His
     imagery of 'a bleak time, when a week of rain is a year'
     plumbs the mysteries of desire under the aspects of death,
     of a body forced into ambiguous terms with soul, of being
     incessantly aware of annihilation, or of that longing 'for
     the imperishable quiet at the heart of form.'"

64   WOODS, SAMUEL H., JR.  Review of Theodore Roethke by Ralph J.
     Mills, Jr.  Midcontinent American Studies Journal, V
     (Spring), 68.
        Brief summary and a re-affirmation of Mills' ranking of
     Roethke as a major figure.

# Writings about Theodore Roethke, 1922-1973

## 1965 A BOOKS

1   COLEMAN, MRS. ALICE C.  A Class Study of Theodore Roethke's
"The Waking."  New York:  Commission on English, College
Entrance Examination Board, 14 pp.
Roethke's poem is examined in order to establish a
method for students to employ in attempting to understand
any poem, but especially those that are more difficult.
The script of this kinescope is available by writing to:
College Board Publications Order Office
Box 592
Princeton, New Jersey 08540

2   MALKOFF, KARL.  "The Poetry of Theodore Roethke:  A Critical
Study."  DA 30:1569A (Columbia University, 1965).

3   STEIN, ARNOLD, ed.  "Introduction."  Theodore Roethke:  Essays
on the Poetry.  Seattle:  University of Washington Press,
pp. ix-xx.
Stein addresses himself to the question of agreement/
disagreement among the nine critics as to whether Roethke's
work shows continuing growth.  He feels it does and in
this light discusses Roethke's idiom and rhythms.  Stein
also speaks of Roethke's psychology of writing, as a
"Perpetual beginner," never certain of the work's finish,
but certain that this uncertainty was his strength.  Personal association enters in here and allows some insightful remarks on Roethke's life, almost with a tone of
reminiscence.

## 1965 B SHORTER WRITINGS

1   ALVAREZ, A.  "New Poetry."  Observer (London), October 24,
p. 27.

2   ANON.  "Poet Lectures on Roethke."  University of Washington
Daily, February 9, p. 11.
Nelson Bently will speak on how Roethke went beyond the
"great experimenters," Eliot and Joyce.

3   ANON.  "Saginaw Native Wins Book Award."  Saginaw News,
March 10, Sect. B., p. 3.
Roethke received the National Book Award for The Far
Field.  His family and his early Saginaw years, as well
as some of his accomplishments since leaving, are mentioned.
Roethke was "a man of gentle wit, trenchant pen and poetic
spirit."

1965

4   ANON.   "Roethke Book 'The Far Field' Wins Award." University
        of Washington Daily, March 10, p. 1.
            Roethke won the National Book Award for The Far Field,
        the "final view of his affinity for natural beauty."

5   ANON.   "National Book Award Given to Roethke." Centre Daily
        Times (State College, Pa.), March 13, p. 7.
            A brief biographical sketch accompanies the announcement
        that Roethke's The Far Field has won the National Book
        Award.

6   ANON.   "Roethke honored." Faculty Bulletin (Penn State Uni-
        versity), LII (March 19), 4.
            Roethke won the National Book Award for The Far Field.

7   ANON.   "National Book Award: That Was the Week That Was."
        Publisher's Weekly, CLXXXVII (March 22), 34.
            Roethke has won the 1964 award for The Far Field.
        Stanley Kunitz accepted the award.

8   ANON.   "Arts." Facts on File, XXV (April 29–May 5), 165.
            Roethke won the National Book Award for The Far Field.

9   ANON.   "A New Honor for Roethke." Seattle Times, May 16,
        p. 19.
            The Far Field has been selected by the American Library
        Association as one of the fifty-four notable books of 1964.

10  ANON.   Review of The Far Field. Country Beautiful (Waukesha,
        Wisc.) IV:1 (August), 73.
            This book "is as fine as anything he or any poet of re-
        cent years ever wrote."

11  ANON.   "Pulitzer Poet Lauds Roethke." University of Washington
        Daily, May 26, pp. 1, 3.
            Robert Lowell characterizes Roethke as "America's Bardic
        poet." Lowell gave the second annual Roethke Memorial
        Reading.

12  ANON.   "Some Other New Volumes." National Observer,
        August 16, p. 19.
            Review of On the Poet and His Craft. Roethke, the "best
        of the university poets," has written some "salty, sensible
        essays on modern poetry and its practitioners."

13  ANON.   "The Collected Poems of Theodore Roethke." Kirkus
        Service, XXXIII (September 15), 1021.
            One can, in the Collected Poems, follow Roethke's "rare
        and at times thoroughly disturbing development, as one

senses beneath the overall musical qualities an almost
agonized personal search, a visionary descent into the
troubling biographical or mythic areas, and note how out
of so much despair (Roethke was frequently institutionalized)
and darkness, a wonderfully affirmative voice developed,
illuminating at once both the physical and spiritual
worlds. One can also note the surprisingly individual
nuances Roethke was capable of sustaining, since the poet
reacted to many influences: the quirky idiom of Lear and
Carroll, the vers libre of Eliot and Pound, the romanticism of Wordsworth and Whitman, the stanzaic virtuosity
of Auden, above all the lordly manner of Yeats. During
his middle period, we find a muddle of metaphysical and
surrealistic elements, but as we read further the obscu-
rities tend to clear and brilliantly imagistic observations
and fine correspondences forcefully, movingly relate as
the themes of love, nature and self-recovery take root."

14   ANON.   "Notes Etc. on Books Etc." Carleton Miscellany, VI
       (Fall), 92.
       Review of On the Poet and His Craft. Brief summary of
       contents without evaluation.

15   ANON.   Review of On the Poet and His Craft, edited by Ralph J.
       Mills, Jr. Choice, II (October), 485.
       Though much is padding, a few paragraphs are revealing.
       "Roethke's prose style is remarkably spare and pointed in
       these pieces." "How to Write Like Somebody Else" is
       especially helpful.

16   ANON.   Review of On the Poet and His Craft. Booklist, LXII
       (November 1), 257.
       Roethke "reveals something of his life and his attitudes
       toward the craft of poetry as practised by himself and
       others." No evaluation is made.

17   ANON.   "Poems for the Good-Hearted." London Times,
       November 4, p. 156.
       Review of The Far Field. Roethke's book is disappointing
       for "in too many of the poems, eloquent though they are,
       the bardic or the courtly manner seems at odds with the
       violent, spontaneous impulses they are often about."

18   ANON.   "Poem Awaited." London Times Educational Supplement,
       November 19, p. 1113.
       Review of The Far Field. "This new collection adds very
       little that is new in approach. But it shows a careful
       talent cultivating with the rarest precision and joy the
       further edges of the visible and possible."

1965

>Review of The Far Field. This book is not Roethke's
>crowning achievement. If his work goes behond the partic-
>ular to generalization, it is most usually a platitude.
>"No poet since Henry Vaughan has managed to be so original
>yet so full of echoes of other men. Roethke's art was a
>matter of sensibility rather than style. Even in this
>last book the style is still uncertain: sometimes insis-
>tently incantatory, sometimes fey, sometimes galumphingly
>playful."

19 BAKER, ED. "Roethke Poems Inspire 'Jazz Fantasy.'" Seattle
   Times, March 25, p. 36.
   >Announcement of an improvisational show by Stan Keen
   >using Roethke poems from I Am! Says the Lamb. The show
   >will be presented at, and as a benefit for, Cornish School.
   >Keen will play piano, accompanied by trumpet and bass.
   >Ben Bradford will narrate the poems. There will be a
   >pantomimist, Diane Adler, and objects designed by Jerrold
   >Ballaine to represent images from Roethke's poems.

20 BEATY, JEROME and WILLIAM H. MATCHETT. Poetry: From Statement
   to Meaning. New York: Oxford University Press,
   pp. 225-226.
   >Brief discussion of "My Papa's Waltz."

21 BODE, CARL. "Auditor's Report: Poetry. 1959: The Poems
   Across the Way." The Half-World of American Culture: A
   Miscellany. Carbondale: Southern Illinois University
   Press, pp. 191-192.
   >Reprint of 1959.B36.

22 BOOTH, PHILIP. "Nothing but What's Human." Christian Science
   Monitor, September 16, p. 7.
   >Review of On the Poet and His Craft. "Often ill, and
   >sometimes desperate, in his daily life Roethke wrote words
   >of intuitive health; whether miserably self-doubting or
   >possessed by a pantheistic sense of peace, he was incapa-
   >ble of pretense." This kind of devotion to art receives
   >full emphasis.

23 BROOKS, CLEANTH. Modern Poetry and the Tradition. New York:
   Oxford University Press/Galaxy, p. xxv.
   >Roethke, in his formative period, was nurtured upon the
   >poets of the 1920's. His work exhibits a range of subject
   >as well as individuality of accent. It can be argued that
   >the ability Roethke showed in his early work to handle
   >"witty, intellectual, and 'tightly' organized" material
   >made his later "irrational and sometimes surrealistic modes
   >of thought" possible.

# Writings about Theodore Roethke, 1922-1973

1965

24  CAMBON, GLAUCO. "The Tangibles of Craftsmanship." Kenyon
        Review, XXVII (Autumn), 758-762.
            Review of On the Poet and His Craft. Roethke's poetic
        and critical evolution is well captured in this book.
        The influence of such poets as Yeats and Whitman is dis-
        cussed at some length.

25  CAREY, JOHN. "Lost and Found." New Statesman, December 31,
        pp. 1032-1033.
            Review of The Far Field. Roethke is much like Words-
        worth, "but his real superiority becomes plain in the
        visionary poems," especially in his final volume. "They
        take a journey beyond the egotistical sublime...where
        Wordsworth would have felt self-conscious." Roethke learns
        not to fear infinity, seeming "to sense the approach of
        death" and "rejoice in being what he is to be."

26  DAVISON, PETER. "Madness in the New Poetry." Atlantic Monthly,
        CCXV (January), 93.
            Review of The Far Field. Roethke "may have been the
        maddest poet of his generation." Madness is accepted in
        his poems as a part of reality, then vanquished.

27  DeLANCEY, ROSE MARY. "Theodore Roethke's Work Collected."
        Fort Wayne (Ind.) News Sentinel, October 16, page unknown
        (from the Roethke collection, University of Washington).
            Review of On the Poet and His Craft, edited by Ralph J.
        Mills, Jr. Brief summary of the book's contents and
        Roethke's attitudes toward poetry.

28  DONOGHUE, DENIS. "Theodore Roethke: Toward The Far Field."
        Lugano Review, I:2, 50-72.
            Roethke's quest is a rage for order. He is, in Stevens'
        sense, a connoisseur of many intimations of chaos that
        "reach us as cries, laments, protests, intimations of
        loss." To bring it off he must often play the child, never
        quite convincingly. There is frequently "too much fanta-
        sia in Roethke's lines." Longing to affirm, he sometimes
        does so artificially. Roethke is slow to give the same
        credences to man "as he does to rudimentary plants and
        animals. Yet his aim is universality." His last poems
        are his best, "marvelously rich and humane." To arrive
        at them, Roethke's work evolved through many poets' voices,
        especially Eliot's, Hopkins', Joyce's, Stevens' and Yeats'.
        See also 1965.B29 and 1965.B30.

1965

29    \_\_\_\_\_. "Theodore Roethke." Connoisseurs of Chaos: Ideas of
       Order in Modern American Poetry. New York: MacMillan,
       Pp. 216-245.
          Reprint of 1965.B28; See also 1965.B30.

30    \_\_\_\_\_. "Roethke's Broken Music." Theodore Roethke: Essays
       on the Poetry. Edited by Arnold Stein. Seattle: Univer-
       sity of Washington Press, pp. 136-166.
          Reprint of 1965.B28; See also 1965.B29.

31 EBERHART, RICHARD. "The Birth of the Spirit (For Theodore
       Roethke, 1908-1963)." Harvard Advocate, XCIX (April), 10.
       A poem in tribute to Roethke.

32    \_\_\_\_\_. "On Theodore Roethke's Poetry." Southern Review, NS
       I (July), 612-620.
          "Roethke made a large world of the imagination in lyric
       poetry, which was at once his limitation and his strength."
       This is a reminiscence, an attempt to discover what makes
       poetry and a poet, as well as to establish how a poet
       exists in his time.

33 FIEDLER, LESLIE. "The New Mutants." Partisan Review, XXXII
       (Fall), 524.
          Roethke, with Lowell and Berryman, is invoked as an
       example of what current tastes cause us to admire in
       literature; not lucidity, "but their flirtation with in-
       coherence and disorder." See also 1971.B13.

34 FITZGIBBON, CONSTANTINE. The Life of Dylan Thomas. Boston
       and Toronto: Atlantic-Little, Brown, pp. 311-312. (James
       Richard McLeod, in Theodore Roethke: A Bibliography, in-
       dicates two other editions, London: J. M. Dent, 1965,
       pages unknown; and London: Sphere Books, Ltd., 1968,
       pages unknown.)
          "One of the many friends he made in America, and perhaps
       the one he liked most, was Theodore Roethke. Before ever
       Dylan came to America, he had expressed a desire to meet
       Roethke, for he admired his poems more than those of any
       other American poet of his generation with the possible
       exception only of Robert Lowell."

35 FULLER, JOHN G. "Trade Winds." Saturday Review, XLVIII
       (March 27), 10-11.
          A reminiscence by the author as well as select comments
       by Stanley Kunitz, accepting the National Book Award for
       The Far Field, and friend and editor Ken McCormick.

1965

36   FURBANK, P. N.   "New Poetry."   The Listener, October 21,
         p. 635.
            Review of The Far Field.  "Theodore Roethke is a poet
         who never developed much and his posthumous volume shows
         his fine talent gone a little to seed.... A tired fluency
         takes over here and there.  The book is much about finding
         an attitude towards age and approaching death; and you
         feel that, being unable to create a new kind of poetry to
         express this new matter, he is resorting desperately to
         his old vein of 'embracing the world.'  The best poems are
         the ones where he is not vociferously praising inexhaust-
         ible nature but sympathizing with the old, battered and
         scruffy."

37   GILROY, HARRY.   "'Herzog' Wins 2d National Book Award for
         Bellow."   New York Times, March 10, p. 38.
            Notice of the posthumous award to Roethke for The Far
         Field.

38   HARRISON, KEITH.   "Solstice Time."   Spectator, October 15,
         p. 490.
            Review of The Far Field.  Roethke is the chief cantor of
         the "mid-century metaphysical" mode of poetry.  His work
         shows the "pathetic fallacy gone to seed:  post-
         Wordsworthian hocus-pocus....  Fellows like Roethke, who
         delude themselves that they can commune with crabs--one
         is tempted to ask what kind of advice he gets from them--
         strike me as being a bit mad."

39   HEILMAN, ROBERT B.   "Roethke:  A Candid Reminiscence."   Seattle
         Magazine, II (June), 38-44.
            A reprint of the author's article in Shenandoah, 1964.B30.

40   HICKS, GRANVILLE.   "Meeting the Genuine Mystery."   Saturday
         Review, XLVIII (July 31), 15-16.
            Review of On the Poet and His Craft.  The reviewer
         quotes long passages from Roethke's prose as illustrations
         of his attitudes toward other poets and the age.  There is
         little explicit evaluation.

41   HINTERBERGER, JOHN.   "Jazz Comment:  Theodore Roethke's Poems
         Unify Music and Dance."   Seattle Times, April 2, p. 24.
            Favorable review of the 'jazz fantasy' created by Stan
         Keen, using poems by Roethke, a pantomimist, animated
         cartoons, musical accompaniment, and a "circus-type barker"
         in white-face.  "Poetry readings with a jazz background
         are nothing new.  On any given afternoon a half-dozen
         'poets' and lethargic trios wait to spring into strident

1965

discourse in a half-dozen New York coffee houses, as soon
as an out-of-towner wanders in.
Yesterday's effort was something else."

42  HOFFMAN, FREDERICK J.  "Theodore Roethke:  The Poetic Shape
of Death."  Theodore Roethke:  Essays on the Poetry.
Edited by Arnold Stein.  Seattle:  University of Washington Press, pp. 94–114.
There are four agonizing and over-lapping stages of
growth in Roethke's poetry:  from the prenatal, to childhood, through movement toward maturity, to the contemplation of the conditions and implications of death.  Roethke
needs to define each stage while evolving and expanding
toward the next.  In maturity, love looks forward to
annihilation.  The womb, the past, offer no solace.
Roethke's later work is a definition of death as he, the
poet, maneuvers through mortality.  See also 1970.B11.

43  HOUGH, HENRY W.  "'The Far Field' Short but Sweet Volume of
Theodore Roethke's Poems."  Denver Post, March 28, page
unknown (from the Roethke collection, University of
Washington).
This book of "musical and nostalgic poetry" is a good
introduction to Roethke's work.

44  HUGHES, TED.  "Wind and Weather."  Listening and Writing,
Autumn, pp. 32–34.
The author discusses Roethke's poem "The Storm (Forio
d'Ischia)" under the general heading of weather.

45  JARRELL, RANDALL.  "Fifty Years of American Poetry."  The
Third Book of Criticism.  New York:  Farrar, Straus,
Giroux, pp. 326–327.
Reprint of 1963.B47.

JONES, NARD.  "A View from Sunday...."  Northwest Today
(Seattle Post-Intelligencer), September 19, p. 2.
Review of On the Poet and His Craft, edited by Ralph J.
Mills, Jr.  Roethke's photo is on the cover of this maga-
46    zine, p. 1.  The reviewer stresses the fact that Roethke
"suffered periods when life became too much and (he)
sought to escape."  "Here is a shy but great man, quite
possibly the greatest who ever lived here, self-revealed."

47  KESSLER, JASCHA.  "Practitioner of the Poet's Curse."  Los
Angeles Times, July 11, page unknown (from the Roethke
collection, University of Washington).

1965

Review of On The Poet and His Craft, edited by Ralph J. Mills, Jr. This collection fails to clear up the mystery of Theodore Roethke; and this is as it should be.

48   KIRSCH, ROBERT B. "National Awards Reflect Better Caliber of Judges." Los Angeles Times, March 12, page unknown (from the Roethke collection, University of Washington).
      "It was a good year for poetry. But Roethke's work transcended the chronological measure. He was until the final moment a poet in growth, one who rejected the faddish and the obscure, who refreshed the older disciplines of language with a keen and perceiving eye."

49   KUNITZ, STANLEY. "Theodore Roethke." Atlantic Brief Lives: A Biographical Companion to the Arts. Edited by Louis Kronenberger, Assoc. Editor Emily Morison Beck. Boston, Toronto: Atlantic-Little, Brown, 1965, 1967, 1968, 1969, 1970, 1971, pp. 649-651.
      The author discusses Roethke's stature as a poet of the generation following Frost, Pound, Eliot, etc.; his serious, competitive nature; their first meeting; Roethke's physical appearance and unusual agility; his periodic mental breakdowns; his ability as a teacher; The Lost Son, Roethke's "great" book; and his later years when "he divined himself."

50   _____. "Roethke: Poet of Transformations." New Republic, CLII (January 23), 23-29.
      Roethke was a Protean figure, with "cunning to match his daemonic energy." "He had schooled himself so well in the formal disciplines that he could turn even his stammerings into art." His "imagination is populated with shape-shifters, who turn into the protagonists of his poems." The author discusses in some depth Open House, in which Roethke searched for his idiom; Roethke's "most heroic enterprise," The Lost Son sequence that continued into Praise to the End!; his knowledge of Jung or his disciple, Maud Bodkin; the beloved, another shapeshifter; Negative Capability in the early poems, love poems, and the Yeatsian poems; and the sequences in The Far Field. See also 1971.B27.

51   _____. "Roethke Remembered." Show, V (May), 10.
      Reprint of Kunitz's speech made while accepting the National Book Award for Roethke's posthumous volume, The Far Field. Roethke "had cunning to match his demonic energy and he had schooled himself so well in the formal disciplines that he could turn even his stammerings into art." A few comments on the book itself stress the presence of death, but with an unusual radiance.

1965

52  LONG, CLAYTON. "Argumentum Ad Hominem, 1963, For Theodore
      Roethke." Prairie Schooner, XXXIX (Fall), 243.
      A poem in tribute to Roethke.

53  LONGLEY, MICHAEL. "Recent Poetry." Irish Times (Dublin),
      November 27, p. 9.
        Review of The Far Field. "Though few pieces in 'The
      Far Field' completely satisfy, the sensibility which
      emerges is irresistible.... The poems' continual and
      natural concern is death: the rambling prolix free verse
      is a frantic last minute inventory where everything must
      be named and celebrated before it is too late, before the
      end."

54  MacKENZIE, NANCY K. "End Papers." New York Times,
      November 19, p. 37.
        Review of Theodore Roethke: Essays on the Poetry,
      edited by Arnold Stein. Favorable brief review.

55  MALKOFF, KARL. "Cleansing the Doors of Perception."
      Minnesota Review, V (October-December), 342-348.
        Review of On the Poet and His Craft. As a prose writer,
      Roethke fails to get outside himself and make valid criti-
      cisms of poets he reviewed or add significantly to the
      critical theory of his time. What his writings do empha-
      size, though Mills' arrangement of them neglects, is his
      own developing conception of the manner and matter of his
      poetry.

56  _____. Review of Theodore Roethke: Essays on the Poetry,
      edited by Arnold Stein. New Mexico Quarterly, XXXV
      (Winter 1965-1966), 379-380.
        These essays amount to private assessments, surveys,
      unrelated to the body of Roethke criticism and frequently
      covering the same ground inefficiently. Roethke's change
      of styles is left unexploited. Some of the excellent
      pioneering work could have more successfully helped ful-
      fill the book's aim, to acquaint the reader with a some-
      times difficult poet.

57  MARTIN, ROBERT B. Review of The Far Field. Princeton Alumni
      Weekly, LXV: 18 (February 23), page unknown (from the
      Roethke collection, University of Washington).
        For all their passion, these poems are filled with a
      "receptive serenity."

58  MARTZ, LOUIS L. "A Greenhouse Eden." Theodore Roethke:
      Essays on the Poetry. Edited by Arnold Stein. Seattle:
      University of Washington Press, pp. 14-35.

The "Greenhouse Eden" is a place or state of mind that
Roethke could sometimes attain in his poetry. The Lost
Son and The Far Field contain the best examples of it,
poems that are different from, or react against, his early
"metaphysical" vein, resulting in "Roethke's truest manner,
the cultivation of the inner force of memory." See also
1966.B62.

59 _____. "Recent Poetry: The Eligiac Mode." Yale Review, LIV
(December), 294-297.
    Review of The Far Field. "Roethke is clearly aware that
he is writing his own long elegy here and in the process
paying tribute to his masters and his best-loved ones."
He is a "creative" imitator, conscious of "the wonder of
human apprehension."

60 MEREDITH, WILLIAM. "A Steady Storm of Correspondences:
Theodore Roethke's Long Journey Out of the Self." Theodore
Roethke: Essays on the Poetry. Edited by Arnold Stein.
Seattle: University of Washington Press, pp. 36-53.
    Reprint of 1964.B39.

61 _____. "Cogitating with His Finger Tips." Book Week (Washington Post), July 18, pp. 4, 15.
    Review of The Far Field and On the Poet and His Craft.
Roethke's is a willful poetic identity, whose identification with things and creatures was not mere observation,
but a sentient act. The "North American Sequence" is
uneven, with imperfections stemming "from his passion for
sincerity and his trust in his feelings, the same forces
that made his best poems what they are." Roethke's prose
statements can sometimes be used as glosses for his poetry.

62 MILLS, RALPH J., JR. "In the Way of Becoming: Roethke's Last
Poems." Theodore Roethke: Essays on the Poetry. Edited
by Arnold Stein. Seattle: University of Washington Press,
pp. 115-135.
    In The Far Field Roethke sets forth on a "quest for
mystical illumination," necessarily requiring the divesting
of the very self that labored long to mature. The manner
and matter of "North American Sequence" and "Sequence,
Sometimes Metaphysical" are not new, but rather the cul-
mination of his work. The soul seeks to get outside itself, sometimes facing formidable odds, thus paralleling
the retreats and advances of the self. Though the call to
communion is clear, the realization is not so simple. The
soul's journey involves Roethke in a strong sense of place,
the source of powerful descriptive writing. There are
periods of knowing (rational) and not-knowing (mystical);

and objects culminating in the symbol of the rose. The more formal poems of "Sequence, Sometimes Metaphysical" strike "inwardly steadily with little recourse to external affairs." Roethke here approximates "the instant of naked revelation." The last self is one "born of the spirit, purged of dross and yet keeping its attachment to creation. So the poet celebrates this spiritual birth by joining in a dance of cosmic proportions with all creatures and things."

63 _____. "A Note on the Personal Element in Recent American Poetry." Chicago Circle Studies, I (December), 9.
Only two paragraphs are devoted to Roethke in this essay. The material was later expanded and incorporated by Mills in Creation's Very Self: On the Personal Element In Recent American Poetry. For annotation, See 1969.B39.

64 MUELLER, LISEL. "An Exacting Poet's Astute, Witty Essays on His Craft." Panorama--Chicago Daily News, August 7, p. 8.
Review of On The Poet and His Craft. A favorable review stressing Roethke's own words that he was a poet of love and praise who wished to be read aloud. Beyond comments on Roethke's conscious effort to perfect his craft, not much of a critical nature is said.

65 MUGGERIDGE, MALCOLM. "Books." Esquire, LXIV (August), 46.
Review of On the Poet and His Craft. "The thought... was thin, and the conclusions for the most part banal."

66 ORIGO, IRIS. "Marguerite Caetani." Atlantic Monthly, CCXV (February), 86.
Roethke's letter to Princess Caetani, founder and editor of Botteghe Oscure, reprinted in The Glass House, is quoted here. Also mentioned is his letter accompanying "Where Knock Is Open Wide" when submitted for publication.

67 PEARCE, ROY HARVEY. "Theodore Roethke: The Power of Sympathy." Theodore Roethke: Essays on the Poetry. Edited by Arnold Stein. Seattle: University of Washington Press, pp. 167-199.
"Theodore Roethke's achievement takes on its special meaning from the fact that he single-mindedly searched out violence in its very sources and strove mightily to find such modes of order as would transform it into power--the power of sympathy, the means to reach across the gulf which separates the sources of violence within from those of the violence without. The paradigm for his poetry is this: violence transformed into power through order." The author

discusses each of Roethke's books demonstrating the relation of this conception to the evolution of style and
theme. He concludes that Roethke did not live to achieve
his final style or statement of theme, but "To have revealed the sacredness of the second person, of all persons
(and places and things) as they in truth are second--this
is Roethke's achievement. And more than that: to have
made known that our world of third persons is one in which
the power of sympathy, if it exists outside the order of
nature, becomes one of violence, now murderous, now suici-
dal, now both; to have transformed suicide into a means of
rebirth and discovery; to have 'undone' death, and to have
dared to 'do' love. Freed in the process, Roethke might
have indeed become his own kind of Blake." See also
1969.B43.

68  PINSKER, SANFORD. "Theodore Roethke/The Poet in Prose."
    Tyee Magazine (University of Washington), I (Autumn),
    22-23, 29.
        Review of On the Poet and His Craft, edited by Ralph J.
    Mills, Jr. After questioning the nation's failure to
    recognize Roethke as a significant poetic presence, the
    reviewer looks closely at many of Roethke's essays, quoting
    liberally, explaining, and always stressing their openness
    and honesty.

69  PRESS, JOHN "Recent Poems." Punch, CCXLIX (November 3), 665.
        Review of The Far Field. "Roethke...was, within his
    limits, a poet of rare gifts." The Far Field "constitutes
    one long hymn to radiance and stillness."

70  PRYCE-JONES, ALAN. "Roetke (sic): A Poet Who Takes His Voca-
    tion Very Seriously." New York Herald Tribune, July 10,
    page unknown (from the Roethke collection, University of
    Washington).
        Review of On the Poet and His Craft, edited by Ralph J.
    Mills, Jr. Summary of contents with little critical
    comment.

71  QUINN, SISTER BERNETTA M. "A Fresh Approach to Poetic Flights."
    Boston Herald, September 26, page unknown (from the Roethke
    collection, University of Washington).
        Review of Connoisseurs of Chaos, by Denis Donoghue. The
    best section of this book is the discussion of Roethke.
    The author elaborates.

72  READ, DAVID W. "Roethke: A Poet Who Lived Deeply in Nature."
    St. Louis Post-Dispatch, March 7, page unknown (from the
    Roethke collection, University of Washington).

1965

Review of The Far Field. The reviewer deals with a
large variety of subjects, each reflecting favorably on
Roethke.

73 ROBERTS, PERCIVAL R., III. "Death of Theodore Roethke
Inestimable Loss to Poetry." Wilmington (Del.) Journal,
April 14, page unknown (from the Roethke collection,
University of Washington).
Review of The Far Field. "Roethke is a nature poet and
his involvement with the subject is complete, compelling
and consummate." His least success occurs in the love
poems.

74 ROREM, NED. Poems of Love and the Rain. Oceanside, N.Y.:
Boosey and Hawkes.
"A Song Cycle for Mezzo Soprano and Piano," this work
includes two Roethke poems: "The Apparition," part 5
(pp. 13-15) and part 13 (pp. 37-39); and "Interlude,"
part 9 (pp. 28-29).

75 ROSENTHAL, M. L. "Throes of Creation." New York Times Book
Review, July 18, p. 4.
Review of On the Poet and His Craft. Many of Roethke's
prose pieces are not worth reprinting, though some (on
Bogan, Thomas, Belitt and Lewis) "are exemplary in their
justice and detailed attentiveness." He was "acutely
aware of the problem of derivativeness" and ultimately
tried to make something out of his own weaknesses.

76 _____. "The Couch and Poetic Insight." Reporter, XXXII
(March 25), 52-53.
Review of The Far Field. This is an uneven book. The
poems touch because of their feeling of imminent death and
their "inability to cope with the old, still unresolved
hysteria...and of a consequent resort to the stock cosmic
pieties of sagedom from Chuang-tzu on down." There is a
complacency despite partial success and the work in general
"is marred by verbosity, cliché, and derivativeness."

77 SCHEVILL, JAMES. "The Modern Poets' Terrible Honesty of
Imagination." This World (San Francisco Chronicle),
January 31, page unknown (from the Roethke collection,
University of Washington).
Review of The Far Field. "In this book Roethke achieved
the mature perception of a great poet who survived many
personal agonies and transformed them into a loving percep-
tion of the balanced nature of experience."

78  SEYMOUR-SMITH, MARTIN. "Two from America." The Scotsman
       (Edinburgh), November 13, page unknown (from the Roethke
       collection, University of Washington).
          Review of The Far Field. Roethke never found his own
       voice: "I would say rather that he was an imitator--
       sometimes even a parodist--of Yeats." "What seemed golden
       at first reading turns out on closer examination to be
       lifted from other poets, or merely glib."

79  SIFTON, PAUL G. "Acquisition Notes: Theodore Roethke Manu-
       scripts." Information Bulletin (U.S. Library of Congress),
       XXIV:49 (December 6), 641-642.
          Rolfe Humphries has given the Library of Congress a
       "group of early letters and peoms (sic)" from the years
       1934-1941. "The collection provides illuminating insight
       into the difficulties the poet underwent as a college
       teacher during the great depression, his self-doubts as
       to his abilities as a poet, and his hopes for critical
       recognition and popular acclaim."

80  SMART, ELIZABETH. "Books." The Queen (London), October 6,
       page unknown (from the Roethke collection, University of
       Washington).
          Review of The Far Field. Roethke deserves the National
       Book Award.

81  SMITH, JOHN. "Editor's Choice." Poetry Review (London), LVI
       (Winter), 248-249.
          Review of The Far Field. Roethke's work is "delightful,"
       but his method has pitfalls: childishness instead of
       childlikeness. But in his many variations he displayed a
       true lyric voice with "curious mystical simplicity" much
       like Blake's.

82  SNODGRASS, W. D. "'That Anguish of Concreteness'--Theodore
       Roethke's Career." Theodore Roethke: Essays on the
       Poetry. Edited by Arnold Stein. Seattle: University of
       Washington, pp. 78-93.
          Roethke "managed to sum up in his work this culture's
       war against form and even to advance that attack several
       steps further than anyone in his art had previously done,"
       yet he failed to capitalize on his success. Open House
       is pre-revolutionary; The Lost Son "a beautiful balance
       between lyricism and prosiness"; Praise to the End! wild
       and experimental, an "achieved style" that Roethke never
       seriously engaged again; the reversal to more formal poems
       in The Waking and Words for the Wind, almost indistinguish-
       able from the voice of Yeats; The Far Field with its "sense

1965

of failure, or failure of desire," suffering from
Roethke's longing for death. He wanted to be free from
the self, but he chose to do it by means of a woman "not
affirmed as herself," and in Yeats' voice. The late poems
show slackness and expectability because Roethke's rejec-
tion has become stylized, formalized and dissolute.

83    SPENDER, STEPHEN. "The Objective Ego." Theodore Roethke:
      Essays on the Poetry. Edited by Arnold Stein. Seattle:
      University of Washington Press, pp. 3-13.
         "Paradoxical as it may seem in The Lost Son and Praise to
      the End!, Roethke in his concentration on his own experi-
      ence, his complete identification of the 'I' with the
      surrounding objects seems nearer than any other poet but
      Rimbaud himself to what Rimbaud called 'objective poetry.'"
      Roethke's poems in the grand manner of Yeats are egotistic
      and not his best. He is best when "the 'I' becomes the
      medium, the conveyor of the material of the not-I."

84    STANFORD, ANN. "High Noon for a Hothouse Poet." Los Angeles
      Times, December 26, page unknown (from the Roethke collec-
      tion, University of Washington).
         Review of Theodore Roethke: Essays on the Poetry,
      edited by Arnold Stein. Little more than a summary of the
      essays.

85    THOMPSON, FRANCIS J. "Professional 'Strategies' of a Gifted
      Poet-Teacher." Roanoke (Va.) Times, August 22, page
      unknown (from the Roethke collection, University of
      Washington).
         Review of On The Poet and His Craft, edited by Ralph J.
      Mills, Jr. Favorable review that summarizes the contents
      of the book at length and makes frequent evaluations.

86    _____. "His Standards Rivaled Those of the Greatest."
      Roanoke (Va.) Times, December 5, page unknown (from the
      Roethke collection, University of Washington). Review of
      Theodore Roethke: Essays on the Poetry, edited by Arnold
      Stein.
         The author regrets that the essays included do not do
      justice to Roethke's work.

87    WAIN, JOHN. "The Monocle of My Sea-Faced Uncle." Theodore
      Roethke: Essays on the Poetry. Edited by Arnold Stein.
      Seattle: University of Washington Press, pp. 54-77.
         Reprint of 1964.B59.

88   WALSH, CHAD.  "A Cadence for Our Time."  Saturday Review,
        XLVIII (January 2), 28.
            Review of The Far Field.  Roethke's last book is a
        feast.  Maybe now, since his death, critics will be able
        to grapple with this "mixed choir."

89   ZINNES, HARRIET.  "Books in English."  Books Abroad, XXXIX
        (Summer), 353.
            Review of The Far Field.  Death hovers throughout the
        posthumous volume.  Also reviewed is The Contemporary Poet
        as Artist and Critic:  Eight Symposia, which the reviewer
        feels throws much light on Roethke's work.


## 1966 A BOOKS

1    MALKOFF, KARL.  Theodore Roethke:  An Introduction to the
        Poetry.  New York:  Columbia University Press.  Foreward
        by John Unterecker.
            Malkoff's book is an attempt at a comprehensive survey
        of Roethke's work to place "each poem in the context of
        the poet's total development."  A denial of some British
        critics' contention that Roethke's poems are "low-grade
        nonsense verse" quickly comes forth.  And he concludes by
        saying that "Roethke's poetic techniques developed hand
        in hand with his thought; the organic growth of his work
        provides a convenient, and 'natural,' basis of organiza-
        tion for studying it."

2    MARTZ, WILLIAM J., Ed.  The Achievement of Theodore Roethke:
        A Comprehensive Selection of His Poems with a Critical
        Introduction.  Glenview, Ill.:  Scott, Foresman.
            Roethke is a Romantic, speaking for individuality and
        the anti-rational.  But a basic question is, How does he
        "absorb that tradition in terms of his own originality?"
        And how deep is his experience?  In absorbing the Romantic
        tradition, what are the qualities of Roethke's style?
        Answers begin with the journey metaphor and Roethke's
        persistent wishing, his reliance on paradox, on a formi-
        dable talent at dramatizing the quality of his experience.
        He is nature poet, love poet and philosophical poet in the
        tradition of the religious meditation.

3    WOLFF, GEORGE A.  "The Productions of Time:  Themes and Images
        in the Poetry of Theodore Roethke."  DA 27:3023A-3024A
        (Michigan State University, 1966).

# THEODORE ROETHKE'S CAREER: AN ANNOTATED BIBLIOGRAPHY

1966

## 1966 B SHORTER WRITINGS

1 ALEXANDER, FLOYCE M. "Roethke, Two Years Later." Western Humanities Review, XX (Winter), 76-78.
Review of The Far Field. Unlike earlier books, The Far Field "contains little of the experimental Joycean language" and is closely knit to the central theme of death. Roethke's early life in Michigan parallels that of Hemingway in Illinois and how he "may have unearthed the essence of that peculiar quality of American life that fluctuates between the peak of hope and the abyss of despair." Death, in Roethke, reaches its most developed expression. The themes of Life and Death in the work of both Roethke and Hemingway are seen as running on parallel tracks for some distance.

2 ANON. "Renewed by Death." London Times Literary Supplement, January 27, p. 65.
Review of The Far Field. (James McLeod, in Theodore Roethke: A Bibliography, attributes this review to Howard Moss.) The prevailing tone is that of Eliot. "The power of these final poems lies in the fact that Roethke's hold on life was always too full-blooded for him to renounce it easily." But nature alone is not enough. Without a personal philosophy, Roethke finds chaos hard to face. See also 1967.B15.

3 ANON. "Recent Acquisitions." Wilson Library Bulletin, XL (February), 484.
Refers to group of early letters and poems of Roethke presented to the Library of Congress by Rolfe Humphries. "These manuscripts constitute an important primary source for the study of Roethke's formative years."

4 ANON. Review of Theodore Roethke: Essays on the Poetry, edited by Arnold Stein. Choice, III (March), 35.
"Nothing yet written about the poetry can provide readers much help until they have been totally immersed in Roethke's 'metre-making argument.' This volume is exploratory; at the present stage of study, every critic must find a language of his own to cope with his experiences of the poetry, for Roethke was an extremely personal poet and a special kind of nature-mystic."

5 ANON. Review of Theodore Roethke: Essays on the Poetry, edited by Arnold Stein. Booklist, LXII (March 15), 692.
"Excellent complement to Roethke's own poetic theory in On the Poet and His Craft;" a book aimed at "extending and

creating understanding of Roethke as a poet and of honor-
ing his memory."

6    ANON.    "Roethke Book Wins Award." University of Washington
      Daily, April 8, p. 14.
         On the Poet and His Craft has been selected as an Amer-
      ican Library Association Notable Book of 1965.

7    ANON.    "Library Group Honors Roethke, Kayira Books." Seattle
      Times, April 17, p. 19.
         Brief mention of the American Library Association's
      selection of On the Poet and His Craft as an outstanding
      book of the past year.

8    ANON.    "The Collected Poems of Theodore Roethke." Kirkus
      Service, XXXIV (May 1), 502.
         Repeat of September 15, 1965 report; 1965.B12.

9    ANON.    Review of Collected Poems. Playboy, (August), page
      unknown (from the Roethke collection, University of
      Washington).
         This book "represents the poet's sustained effort to
      become whatever is." "We have been lucky:  There is
      nothing like these poems in all literature."

10   ANON.    Review of Collected Poems. Booklist, LXIII
      (September 15), 92.
         Summary of the format of the book, nothing more.

11   ANON.    Review of Collected Poems. Library Journal, XCI
      (September 15), 4374.
         "Roethke's search for essences, his experiments with
      language, and his skill in infusing the familiar with
      'newness' are demonstrated over and over."

12   ANON.    "Verse." New Yorker, XLII (September 24), 239-240.
      Review of Collected Poems. (Attributed to Joseph Slater
      in Theodore Roethke:  A Bibliography, by James McLeod.)
         Roethke's variety of tone is remarkable, from "joyous
      release from despair" to "black hopelessness and angers."
      "Joyce, it now is evident, was often at the center of
      Roethke's wild humor, while he remained almost untouched
      by glum Surrealism." He used the entire range of his
      experience, "often at psychic extremes."

13   ANON.    "Scribblings Recall Roethke:  Noted Poet, Former
      Professor." The Daily Collegian (Penn State University),
      September 25, p. 3.

1966

An account of Roethke material found in an old desk by
Jack B. McManis, a Penn State English professor. The
material included notes, examinations, jottings and the
poem "Saturday Eight O'Clock."

14   ANON.   Review of Collected Poems. Choice, III (October), 651.
"Roethke, master of the conventional tone, probably influenced more post-World War II poets through his verse
and On The Poet and His Craft...than any other American
poet in his time; this alone recommends him."

15   ANON.   Review of Collected Poems. Milwaukee Journal.
October 2, page unknown (from the Roethke collection,
University of Washington).
Favorable brief review.

16   ANON.   "Roethke Material on Display." Centre Daily Times
(State College, Pa.), November 15, p. 6.
Ernest Hemingway and Roethke material (memorabilia,
letters and manuscripts) are displayed at the Penn State
University Pattee Library.

17   BANNON, BARBARA.   "Forecast of Paperbacks." Publisher's
Weekly, CLXXXIX (February 14), 149.
Review of On the Poet and His Craft. Brief generaliza-
tion as to the book's contents. No evaluation.

18   BECKER, JANE M.   "Watching a Poet's Development." Tampa (Fla.)
Tribune, September 11, page unknown (from the Roethke
collection, University of Washington).
Review of Collected Poems. Roethke's "oftentimes extrav-
agant imagery may be a matter of taste, but his failure to
say something meaningful with such images is a justifiable
point of attack."

19   BILLINGS, CLAUDE.   "Books: Collection Displays Poet Roethke's
Range." Indianapolis Star, July 3, page unknown (from the
Roethke collection, University of Washington).
Review of Collected Poems. Many of Roethke's poems are
"'exquisite.'"

20   BOYERS, ROBERT.   "A Very Separate Peace." Kenyon Review,
XXVIII (November), 683-691.
Review of Collected Poems. Roethke's is "a poetry which
invigorates precisely in proportion as Roethke insistently
attempts to console both himself and his readers." His
work makes us grasp the principle of change at the root of
stability. The direction his consolation takes is a basic

question, which involves the examination of his ideas on love, death, etc. Yet ultimately Roethke's work lacks "vitality of context" that, for example, Lowell's poems possess.

21  BRACKER, JOHN. "Variety, Sensitivity Mark Roethke's Poems." Wichita Falls (Tex.) Times, July 31, page unknown (from the Roethke collection, University of Washington).
    Review of Collected Poems. Favorable review that stresses the qualities in Roethke's work of "versatility, experimentation and development."

22  BURKE, KENNETH. "The Vegetal Radicalism of Theodore Roethke." Language as Symbolic Action. Berkeley: University of California Press, pp. 254-281.
    Reprint of 1950.B7; See also 1971.B7.

23  BUTTEL, HELEN T. "Roethke's 'I Knew a Woman.'" Explicator, XXIV (May), Item 78.
    Response to Virginia Peck's treatment of the poem in an earlier issue of Explicator. The author wishes to make the point that the woman is dead and the poem represents an "extravagant eulogy."

24  "C. A. B." "Roethke Poems--Love Songs to Mother Nature." Buffalo (N.Y.) Evening News, August 6, page unknown (from the Roethke collection, University of Washington).
    Review of Collected Poems. Roethke grew more American as he aged.

25  CARRUTH, HAYDEN. "In Spite of Artifice." Hudson Review, XIX (Winter 1966/1967), 689-693.
    Review of Collected Poems. Some Roethke qualities persist throughout: love of detail, generosity, affection, and insistent, absorbing curiosity. Yet the later poems are extremely difficult, "absolute conundrums jammed together." Certain ideas are important to Roethke: edge, the cave, the river, roots, fish, birds, women, the eye, the dance. Roethke's anguish lay in the knowledge that he hadn't the faintest notion where the path led, or whether to go forward or back."

26  CIARDI, JOHN. "A Roethke Memorial." Saturday Review, XLIX (April 9), 16.
    The people of Saginaw, Michigan react to Roethke's death with a memorial. Ciardi contributes a poem, "Was a Man." See also 1967.B21; 1971.B9.

27  _____. "Was a Man." This Strangest Everything. New Brunswick, N.J.: Rutgers University Press.
    A poem in tribute to Roethke; often reprinted.

1966

28   CONQUEST, ROBERT. "A Seattle Parkland." Encounter, XXVII
        (October), 52-53.
           A poem in tribute to Roethke. See also 1967.B24.

29   COOLEY, FRANKLIN D. "'Cumulative Effect' of Poetry by Roethke."
        Richmond (Va.) Times Dispatch, July 17, page unknown (from
        the Roethke collection, University of Washington).
           Review of Collected Poems. Favorable brief review.

30   CURLEY, DOROTHY. Review of Theodore Roethke: Essays on the
        Poetry, edited by Arnold Stein. Library Journal, XCI
        (January 1), 112.
           "The essays are carefully done discreet units, each con-
        sidering Roethke from a different point of view."

31   _____. Review of Collected Poems. Library Journal, XCI
        (June 15), 3219.
           "Love poems, comment on urban life, gay nonsense, bitter
        nonsense, all are here, but the heart of the work is the
        poetry of nature, the indoor nature of greenhouses and the
        outdoor nature of small creatures and flowing water. The
        great-hearted, the completely sentient Mr. Roethke wrote
        from the center of his violent calm with a total control
        of his own range of symbols and rhythms and a total com-
        mitment to humane values."

32   _____. Review of Theodore Roethke, by Karl Malkoff. Library
        Journal, XCI (October 1), 4664, 4666.
           Malkoff's emphasis is on the content of Roethke's work
        rather than the technique. "The critical approach is
        methodical, disciplined, and respectful."

33   DANIELL, ROSEMARY. "Work Collected: Poet Roethke Was Engaged
        with All Life." Atlanta Constitution & Journal, July 24,
        page unknown (from the Roethke collection, University of
        Washington).
           Review of Collected Poems. Roethke was totally immersed
        in life, "making motion through all of its parts, the good
        and the bad."

34   DAVISON, P. "Some Recent Poetry." Atlantic Monthly, CCXVIII
        (November), 163.
           Review of Collected Poems. "Theodore Roethke's Collected
        Poems...constitute the most powerful body of work yet pub-
        lished by any American born in this century."

35   DONOGHUE, DENIS. "Aboriginal Poet." New York Review of Books,
        VII (September 22), 14-16.

Review of Collected Poems and Theodore Roethke: An Introduction to the Poetry, by Karl Malkoff. Roethke had
good reason to leave out from earlier collections the
seventeen new poems printed here. Malkoff is useful on
Jung, but there is more to look at in regard to Roethke's
aboriginal destructive element. Malkoff also helps with
the "spiritual" poems, using Evelyn Underhill's Mysticism
as a gloss. Roethke's "feeling for the specifically human
dimension is insecure." His poems are not pastoral, as
Lawrence's, "putting complex things into a simple con-
tainer." The later poems, however, show movement into a
"human idiom," freedom from a strong sense of abstraction,
and lengthened cadences.

36  DOUGLAS, DENNIS. "End of an Era." The Age Literary Supplement
    (London), February 19, page unknown (from the Roethke
    collection, University of Washington).
       Review of The Far Field. Roethke is placed at the end
    of a poetic revolution that began with Whitman; one that
    may not have been meant to succeed.

37  FIELDS, KENNETH. "Strategies of Criticism." Southern Review,
    NS II (Autumn), 974-975.
       Review of On the Poet and His Craft. This book is sty-
    listically uneven, of course. But there are valuable re-
    marks on technique for anyone interested in teaching poetry
    or creative writing.

38  FOSTER, STEVEN. "Roethke: Poet of Plenitude." Sage, XI
    (Fall), 161-163.
       Review of The Achievement of Theodore Roethke by William
    Martz. Martz's treatment of Roethke's achievement is too
    narrowly restrictive. For "the sort of lovely mishmash
    one might expect from a man who exhibited so many sides of
    himself and who granted life its inconceivable variety"
    cannot be contained in Martz's three categories of Roethke
    as "nature poet, love poet, and meditative poet." Roethke's
    "was a whole vision of plenitude--infinitude, finitude--
    of mutability forever bathed in rain; and to section him
    into neat pieces so as to put him back together is to
    thwart the bigness and variety of his vision, which was
    always at term, and which, like a Mark Tobey painting,
    admits of nothing so much as controlled and fecund
    explosion."

39  FULLER, EDMUND. "A Poet of Love." Wall Street Journal,
    August 5, p. 6.
       Review of Collected Poems and On the Poet and His Craft.
    "Roethke worked in a fine balance between the traditional

1966

and the experimental, never content to rest within a narrow range of forms or modes, reaching outward always in
both conception and craft, capable of exalted celebration,
wrath, satire, gentle humor, and childlike play. His
spirit is profoundly religious in its view of man and the
whole order of creation." In addition to this kind of
generalization, some biographical information is given as
well as brief excerpts from the essays to emphasize
Roethke's roles as teacher and critic.

40  GEIGER, DON. Review of On the Poet and His Craft. Quarterly
Journal of Speech, LII (April), 202.
"An implicitly commemorative book, its critical impor-
tance is doubtless less intrinsic than relational, illuminating various aspects of the thought and character of
an accomplished American poet."

41  GELPI, ALBERT J. "Roethke's Heritage." Christian Science
Monitor, October 6, p. 11.
Review of Collected Poems. Roethke's roots are in nineteenth century transcendentalism; "...his pulse beats with
the same throb which Emerson transmitted to Whitman to
constitute an indigenous American poetry." Support for
this view, with Whitman as his bard, is found in Roethke's
use of the catalogue, his orchestrated free verse with "an
organic inner structure." The difference between Roethke
and his forbears is his more complex development, his
consciousness of his own modernity.

42  GUSTAFSON, RICHARD. "In Roethkeland." Midwest Quarterly, VII
(January), 167-174.
"Roethke's poetry can be considered a quest out of fear.
It began with the wide-eyed pathos of a lonely child who
feared the big and perhaps feared himself because he was
bigger than he wanted to be. The child seeks the comfort
of the small and celebrates their ways. But he grows up,
falls in love to a depth that expands him, and reaches
middle age with a philosophic calm.
"It is Roethke's basicness that gives him his genius.
There is little complicated symbolism; there are no eso-
teric struggles with ideas. There is only the tightness
of huddling soul, the teeming life of nature, and the
coming serenity of death. But what one remembers most
about Roethke's work is his love for the small, his botan-
ical closeness with plants, his kinship with little animals,
and the way he brought them all together in a place so
unique it can only be called Roethkeland."

43    "H. A. K." "No Escape." <u>Boston Globe</u>, July 3, page unknown
      (from the Roethke collection, University of Washington).
         Review of <u>Collected Poems</u>. Favorable review that la-
      ments Roethke's inability to return from "the molten
      center."

44    HALL, DOUGLAS KENT. Review of <u>Collected Poems</u>. <u>Portland</u>
      (Ore.) <u>Journal</u>, July 16, page unknown (from the Roethke
      collection, University of Washington).
         Roethke's "imagery speaks with the power of a man trying
      desperately to put the past into the future."

45    HINTERBERGER, JOHN. "At Playhouse: Actors Read Northwest
      Poets." <u>Seattle Times</u>, April 18, p. 21.
         Four of Roethke's poems were included on the program by
      local actors. Little comment is specifically aimed at
      Roethke.

46    HOSKINS, KATHERINE. "Roethke in his Prose." <u>Poetry</u>, CVII
      (March), 400-401.
         Review of <u>On the Poet and His Craft</u>. Roethke had "the
      generosity and modesty that we like to associate with
      strength.... Even by 1960 he didn't seem aware that he
      was not only one of our noblest savages but, in many
      respects, the most delicate." Mills' book is a fitting
      tribute to and statement of Roethke's talent as poet and
      teacher.

47    HOWARD, RICHARD. "Carolyn Kizer: 'Our Masks Keep Us in Thrall
      to Ourselves...'." <u>Tri-Quarterly</u>, VI, 109-110, 113.
         Roethke is influential as both a teacher and writer in
      the poetry of Carolyn Kizer. He is also used an an exam-
      ple in a discussion of "charges most frequently leveled
      against poetry written by women." <u>See also</u> 1971.B21.

48    HUFF, ROBERT. "On the Death of Theodore Roethke." <u>Poetry</u>,
      CVII (March), 360.
         A poem in tribute to Roethke. <u>See also</u> 1966.B49;
      1967.B42.

49    _____. "On the Death of Theodore Roethke." <u>The Course</u>.
      Detroit: Wayne State University Press.
         Reprint of 1966.B48; <u>See also</u> 1967.B42.

50    INGE, M. THOMAS. "Poetry Anthology Reflects Mind of 20th
      Century America." <u>Nashville Tennessean</u>, July 17, page
      unknown (from the Roethke collection, University of
      Washington).

1966

> Review of <u>The Achievement of Theodore Roethke</u>, by
> William J. Martz. Martz offers a "perceptive assessment
> of Roethke."

51 JONES, LYN. "The Teaching Poet." <u>Humanist</u>, XXVI (November/
December), 204-205.
> Review of <u>On the Poet and His Craft</u>. Roethke's "approach
> to poetry is basically descriptive and demonstrative."
> There are liberal quotations, but nothing more analytical
> than this is said.

52 KIRBY-SMITH, TOM. "After Roethke." <u>Southern Review</u>, NS II
(January), 110-111.
> A poem in tribute to Roethke.

53 KITCHING, JESSIE B. "Forecasts." <u>Publisher's Weekly</u>,
CLXXXIX (June 27), 98.
> Review of <u>Collected Poems</u>. Brief mention of format with
> this evaluation: "Great contemporary lyric poetry."

54 LANDINI, RICHARD G. "Roethke's Contemporary Poetry Collection
Reveals Single Theme: the Self." <u>The Arizona Republic</u>
(Phoenix), August 28, page unknown (from the Roethke
collection, University of Washington).
> Review of <u>Collected Poems</u>. With Roethke's "sudden death
> a formidable civilizing force was rudely taken from us.
> Our time and our condition need lines like these to keep
> us from each other's pockets, from each other's throats...."

55 LASK, THOMAS. "Celebration and Defeats." <u>New York Times</u>,
August 2, p. 31.
> Review of <u>Collected Poems</u>. Roethke's work has wide
> appeal for those both interested and not interested in the
> technique of poetry. The contention among some critics
> that Roethke's voice was not his own is discussed here, in
> a generalized manner as the reviewer concludes that "with
> nature as his fountain and source, Roethke moved away from
> the reasoned and rational."

56 LAZARUS, A. L. "Book Reviews." <u>College English</u>, XXVII
(May), 647-648.
> Review of <u>On the Poet and His Craft</u>. "Roethke propounds
> no original poetic (his originality remains in his poems)
> but does light up some of the ways in which the writing
> of poetry is a discipline. He thus contributes to the
> dialogue between tradition and revolt, with the Establish-
> ment winning most of the arguments."

57    LEHERR, DAVID A. Untitled. <u>The Pennsylvania State University Department of Public Information News</u>, September 11, pp. 1-3 (unpaginated).
        An account of Roethke notes, jottings and examinations found by Jack B. McManis, assistant professor at Penn State, in a desk used by Roethke from 1936 to 1947. Some of the remarks are printed here, as well as comments by McManis and Roethke's poem "Saturday Eight O'Clock."

58    LEWISOHN, JAMES. "'There Once Was a Girl Named Myrtle....'" <u>Portland</u> (Me.) <u>Telegram</u>, July 24, page unknown (from the Roethke collection, University of Washington).
        Review of <u>Collected Poems</u>. Favorable review that quotes Roethke's lines extensively.

59    _____. "Theodore Roethke." <u>Beloit Poetry Journal</u>, XVII (Winter 1966/1967), 1.
        A poem in tribute to Roethke. <u>See also</u> 1967.B51.

60    LONGLEY, MICHAEL. Review of <u>The Far Field</u>. <u>Outposts</u> (England), No. 69 (Summer), p. 21.
        "The best poems...take the form of huge accumulations of factual observations. They are like frantic last-minute inventories and succeed most where their urgency precludes any attempt to graft on a philosophical solution. When Roethke allows himself pause his chief weakness emerges all too clearly as a kind of hysterical pantheism." Roethke has extended and orchestrated Whitman's phrase. His "charity is overwhelming. He has redirected poetry to its proper concerns...."

61    LOWELL, ROBERT. "For Theodore Roethke." <u>Partisan Review</u>, XXXIII (Fall), 573.
        A poem in tribute to Roethke. <u>See also</u> 1967.B52; 1967.B53.

62    MARTZ, LOUIS L. "Theodore Roethke: A Greenhouse Eden." <u>The Poem of the Mind: Essays on Poetry--English and American</u>. New York: Oxford University Press, pp. 162-182.
        Reprint of 1965.B58.

63    _____. "Recent Poetry: Roethke, Warren and Others." <u>Yale Review</u>, LVI (December), 275.
        Review of <u>Collected Poems</u>. Roethke's work shows the arrangement of earlier volumes and some struggle to gain the proper effect. But "as the whole volume stands, we have a sense of serene finality."

1966

64    MAY, JAMES BOYER. "Towards Print (Further Observations on
      'Living Literature')." Trace, LIX (Winter), 326, 409-410.
          Review of On the Poet and His Craft and Theodore Roethke:
      Essays on the Poetry, edited by Arnold Stein. "For all
      the elements in his work deserving of praise, he (Roethke)
      will not be looked back upon as a major voice of the Twen-
      tieth Century. He dwelt almost exclusively on personal
      themes, providing no wide view or revelation of the world
      of his day..., he was a larger man than he was a poet....
      He dealt with major themes only from an underside. His
      importance lies in lesser areas of technical achievement
      and unique explorations of his own states of mind."

65    McDONNELL, THOMAS P. "New Poetry & Criticism." The Pilot
      (Boston), November 19, page unknown (from the Roethke
      collection, University of Washington).
          Review of Collected Poems. The work is unquestionably
      fine, but Doubleday produces a cheap product.

66    McINTIRE, LUCY B. "Poetry." Savannah (Ga.) News, July 17, page
      unknown (from the Roethke collection, University of
      Washington).
          Review of Collected Poems. Favorable brief review.

67    McMANIS, JACK. Title unknown (though entitled "Theodore
      Roethke as a Poetry Teacher at Penn State, 1936-1947" by
      McLeod in Theodore Roethke: A Bibliography. My photo-
      copy includes no title. KM). Penn State English Notes,
      VI:1 (Spring), 19-21.
          The author, Professor of English at Penn State, was the
      discoverer of much Roethke material in an old desk. The
      notes, commentaries and jottings show the diligence and
      concern that Roethke showed as a teacher of verse writing.
      There are examples of examinations and Roethke's poem
      "Saturday Eight O'Clock."

68    MILLS, RALPH J., JR. "Theodore Roethke." Contemporary Amer-
      ican Poetry. New York: Random House, pp. 48-71.
          Slightly revised reprint of 1958.B30; See also 1967.B57.

69    _____. "Recognition." New York Times Book Review, July 17,
      pp. 5, 30-31.
          Review of Collected Poems and Theodore Roethke: Essays
      on the Poetry, edited by Arnold Stein. The reviewer
      traces Roethke's development briefly and generally through
      his poems. Beginning with The Lost Son Roethke produces
      a "unique verse" of a truly fluid psychic life. The re-
      turn to formal verse in the 1950's complements that just

1966

mentioned "by treating different aspects of the same mystical theme." Echoed here are John Wain's comments from
Stein's book about Roethke's sympathy for poets he admired.
This "explains" the imitation-of-Yeats syndrome popular
with so many critics. The question is dismissed as finally
academic.

70   MUELLER, LISEL. "A Poetic Pilgrimage: The Life Work of
     Roethke." Panorama--Chicago Daily News, July 23, p. 7.
       Review of Collected Poems. Roethke's total body of work
     is "a pilgrimage, a quest for the soul. What sets Roethke
     apart from the two or three contemporaries whose individual
     poems are as fine as his is the coherence of·his work, the
     continuity and evolution of his struggle toward a vision,
     a knowledge of order and wholeness, which could release
     the caged self from the consciousness of violence, greed,
     separateness, spiritual emptiness." Roethke's first orig-
     inal work is in The Lost Son. His father's "authority and
     order made a small universe, one the poet never ceased to
     long for." Roethke, a mystic, comes to the knowledge that
     all life is one "obscurely and painfully." The Far Field
     attains the destination all the other poems are heading
     for, it is a summing-up.

71   NELSON, DALE. "Spirit of Roethke Moves, Yet Still Remains."
     Northwest Today (Seattle Post-Intelligencer), July 24,
     p. 20.
       An article in praise of Roethke for his perception and
     awareness. The author begins by summarizing some recent
     critics on Roethke's stature as a poet. He then discusses
     hallucinogenics to emphasize Roethke's capacity for aware-
     ness without such artificial aids.

72   NICHOLSON, NORMAN. "Two American Poets." Church Times
     (London), August 26, page unknown (from the Roethke col-
     lection, University of Washington).
       Review of The Far Field. "The best of Roethke should
     not quickly be overwhelmed by time, though I do not think
     he ever quite became the major poet that his American
     admirers claim him to be."

73   PERRINE, LAURENCE and JAMES M. REID, eds. 100 American Poems
     of the Twentieth Century. New York: Harcourt, Brace and
     World, pp. 204-207.
       Brief comments on "Elegy for Jane" and "My Papa's Waltz."

74   PETERSON, CLELL T. Review of Theodore Roethke: Essays on the
     Poetry, edited by Arnold Stein. College English, XXVIII
     (November), 185.

1966

In these essays "there is a recurrent uneasy concern for
Roethke's achievement, a feeling that in his constant ex-
perimenting with verbal and metrical effects he never
found his proper voice. And this implies, perhaps, another failure; of the poet's quest of self, found only in
the inviolable voice, was also one of his principal themes."
But the concensus confirms Roethke's stature and his poetry, "much of which is as good as the best of our time."

75    PINSKER, SANFORD. "Nine Roads Lead to Theodore Roethke."
University of Washington Daily, March 8, p. 11. Review
of Theodore Roethke: Essays on the Poetry, edited by
Arnold Stein.
Stein's introduction to Roethke "the man" is especially
revealing. Some of the essayists' personal relationships
with Roethke are here given space as well as summaries of
their critical positions.

76    RAGAN, SAM. "Southern Accent." Raleigh (N.C.) Observer,
July 17, page unknown (from the Roethke collection, University of Washington).
Review of Collected Poems. "One feels...that the world
of Theodore Roethke had been mastered, or at least mastered as far as any man can master and understand himself."

77    RETTEW, THOMAS M. "Roethke's Poems." Wilmington (Del.) News,
July 26, page unknown (from the Roethke collection, University of Washington).
Review of Collected Poems. "Roethke lacks the excite-
ment of an Eliot, the fiery erudition of a Pound and the
brilliant sheen of Wallace Stevens. But he has a sincere
empathetic awareness that he communicates."

78    ROSS, ALAN. "Selected Books." London Magazine, NS X
(January), 91.
Review of The Far Field. Not his best book, "something
more than concentration having been lost in the extension
of hothouse to prairie." The poems of "North American
Sequence" show a "rhetorical windyness" not deriving
mainly from their subject matters, though the "Mixed
Sequence" and "Sequence, Sometimes Metaphysical" show
"his old taste."

79    SCARBOROUGH, GEORGE. "Half Poet and Half Academician."
Chattanooga Times, July 24, page unknown (from the
Roethke collection, University of Washington).
Review of Collected Poems. Roethke used "subjects, not
themes." Though occasionally too conventional, much of
the poetry is beautiful.

1966

80    SCHEVILL, JAMES.  "For Theodore Roethke."  Southern Review,
         NS II (October), 911-912.
             A poem in tribute to Roethke.

81    _____.  "'A Joyous Poet' Shaped by Extremes."  This World
         (San Francisco Sunday Examiner & Chronicle), October 2,
         pp. 38, 40.
             Review of Collected Poems.  The author discusses how
         Roethke's poetic development mirrored the man.

82    SCOTT, WINFIELD TOWNLEY.  "Roethke."  Poetry, CVIII (August),
         287-288.
             A poem in tribute to Roethke.  See also 1967.B70.

83    SERGEANT, HOWARD.  "Poetry Review."  English (England), XVI
         (Spring), 31.
             Review of The Far Field.  The book "contains some of
         Roethke's most substantial poems."

84    SERRIN, BILL.  "The Wild Men's Leader, Looking into Life's
         Gullet."  Detroit Free Press, August 21, page unknown
         (from the Roethke collection, University of Washington).
             Review of Collected Poems.  The article speaks little of
         the book.  It is primarily biographical and personal.

85    SEXTON, ANNE.  "The Barfly Ought to Sing."  Tri-Quarterly, VII
         (Fall), 92.
             Both Sexton and Plath recognize, in correspondence, the
         latter's debt to Roethke's poetry.  Sexton refers to him
         as the "image-ridden-darer, Roethke."  See also 1970.B20.

86    SLATER, JOSEPH.  "Immortal Bard and Others."  Saturday Review,
         XLIX (December 31), 24.
             Review of Collected Poems.  Roethke "now seems an immor-
         tal poet:  a virtuoso of form and melody; a seer of the
         inner world and the outer one, whose visions shake and
         sustain the heart."  All the variety in one volume makes
         it very powerful.

87    SOUTHWORTH, JAMES G.  "Theodore Roethke's The Far Field."
         College English, XXVII (February), 413-418.
             Each section of The Far Field is discussed in some depth.
         "The total effect of Roethke's poetry is epical and The
         Far Field describes the final stages in the fight between
         the angels and the devils for the poet's soul with tempo-
         rary victories on both sides until the angels are trium-
         phant in the end."

1966

88 _____. "Books." <u>Western Humanities Review</u>, XX (Winter),
79–80.
Review of <u>On the Poet and His Craft</u>. "It is clear that
Roethke early understood himself and never deviated from
or compromised with his intense integrity." The reviewer
excerpts revealing passages from each section of the book
concluding that there is nothing new here, only "amplifica-
tion and corroboration of many ideas and characteristics."

89 SPENDER, STEPHEN. "Roethke: The Lost Son." <u>New Republic</u>,
CLV (August 27), 23–25.
Review of <u>Collected Poems</u>. Roethke is a poet of "the
ego of the alluvial slime." He echoes Wordsworth, but
more than making us <u>feel</u> nature, he <u>becomes</u> it. He is
closer to Wagner. "Roethke's greenhouse poetry is not
solipsist, because it is about a world in which the
objective becomes the subjective," and finally universal.
But there is a gap between "insideness and outsideness."
Love bridges it. There are three phases in Roethke's
poetry: "the poetry of isolation; the poetry of bridging
the gulf of self and not-self; and, thirdly, the poetry of
more generally shared experience." Despite precarious
moments of triumph, Roethke never really escapes isolation.

90 STEFANILE, FELIX. "Profiles and Presences." <u>Poetry</u>, CIX
(December), 200. Review of <u>Theodore Roethke: Essays on
the Poetry</u>, edited by Arnold Stein.
Roethke challenges our "traditional attitudes towards
reality." Wain's essay is perhaps the best as he senses
that "Roethke's structural experiments and deviations...
are related to his feeling for what is universal and what
is real." "Roethke's self-investigations uniquely speak
to us, in clearly structural terms. He veered between
structure, as Yeats might have maneuvered it, for a poet's
need, and structure as its own search."

91 STEPHENS, MEIC. Review of <u>The Far Field</u>. <u>Poetry Wales</u>,
Spring, pp. 39–40.
In these poems "there is the realization that Roethke
was a sick man who contemplated life's tides for the sake
of the intensely personal horror and fascination that he
found in them." Roethke is at his best in the "acute,
penetrating studies of small animals, fish and flowers...."

92 STILWELL, ROBERT L. "Books in English." <u>Books Abroad</u>, XL
(Autumn), 460.
Review of <u>On the Poet and His Craft</u>. A valuable collec-
tion, well edited, in which the best pieces display

"Roethke's generosity of spirit, respect for language, and rich joy of life."

93   SUDLER, BARBARA. "Roethke Collection Shows His Virtuosity."
     Denver Post, August 14, page unknown (from the Roethke
     collection, University of Washington).
        Review of Collected Poems. Favorable brief review.

94   THOMAS, DYLAN. Letter to Theodore Roethke, March 31, 1953.
     Selected Letters of Dylan Thomas. Edited by Constantine
     Fitzgibbon. London: J. M. Dent & Sons, pp. 400-401.
        Thomas comments on the effects of his reading of Roethke's
     poems over the BBC. "You still have a grotesquely small
     audience here, but very fierce."

95   _____. Letter to Theodore Roethke, June 15, 1953. Selected
     Letters of Dylan Thomas. Edited by Constantine Fitzgibbon.
     London: J. M. Dent & Sons, pp. 403-406.
        Thomas speaks of his American tour (on which he failed
     to meet Roethke due to the latter's marriage and honey-
     moon), Roethke's recent poetry, English publication for
     The Waking, and reading over the BBC, as well as personal
     wishes for a Roethke visit in Ireland.

96   TURCO, LEWIS. "Aspects." December Magazine, VIII:1, 158-159.
        A poem in tribute to Roethke. See also 1967.B80.

97   WAGGONER, HYATT H. "Book Reviews." American Literature,
     XXXVIII (November), 417-418. Review of Theodore Roethke:
     Essays on the Poetry, edited by Arnold Stein.
        The reviewer finds seven of the articles in the book
     "rewarding" and very helpful in a study of Roethke's work.
     The other three range from "trifling" to "an exercise in
     fashionable critical jargon." But overall, the book is a
     must for Roethke scholars.

98   WAIN, JOHN. "Nature's Golden Age." Observer Weekend Review.
     (London), August 21, Books p. 17.
        Review of The Poetry of Earth, edited by E. D. H.
     Johnson. Roethke is mentioned as a modern counterpart to
     such English writers as Gilbert White, Clare and Coleridge.

99   WALSH, CHAD. "Plant and Phantom." Book Week (Washington
     Post), July 31, pp. 1, 12.
        Review of Collected Poems. Roethke does not possess the
     social awareness of Auden, the "sense of all civilizations
     as one civilization" of Eliot, the psychic distance from
     nature of Frost, nor is he like the "Confessional" poets.

1966

Roethke's poems give us the "I" of mankind, as well as the one poet. The reviewer then examines the stylistic evolution through Roethke's books, discussing his affinities to other poets, and how his poems have the effect of building up.

100   WARFEL, HARRY R. "Language Patterns and Literature: A Note on Roethke's Poetry." Topic: A Journal of the Liberal Arts, XII (Fall), 21-29.
       Roethke's work exhibits a "compositional strategy" that few critics understand or comment on. Syntax is an important element of his artistry--"The special originality of Roethke lay not in subject matter, theme, or tone but in the artistic maneuvering of his sentences within the limits of a traditional metrical pattern."

101   WEBER, R. B. "Through Dark and Light." Louisville (Ky.) Courier-Journal, October 2, p. D5.
       Review of Collected Poems. Moderately favorable review that sees in the later poems strengths lacking in the earlier ones.

102   WHARTON, WILL. "A Tragic Poetess in Need of Psychiatrist, Not Critic." St. Louis Globe-Democrat, July 10, page unknown (from the Roethke collection, University of Washington).
       Review of Collected Poems. Favorable brief review.

*103  WHITE, GEORGE ABBOTT. "Weeds Too: The Poetry of Theodore Roethke." Generation, XVII, 56-80.
       This citation is taken from the Charles Wright thesis on Roethke found in Box 2, Folder 17, of the Roethke collection at the University of Washington. I am uncertain as to the contents because I was unable to locate the journal.

104   WISEMAN, CHRISTOPHER. "New Verse: A Silenced Voice." Glasgow Herald, January 8, page unknown (from the Roethke collection, University of Washington).
       Review of The Far Field. "Roethke's style is a unique mixture of riddles, spare lyricism and discursive incantation." "Roethke is basically a simple unintellectual poet whose strength is more clearly shown in his short lyrics, where his delight in language pleases in a pure, almost child-like way. Some of these poems are banal but most are moving and individual. We have lost an important poet and a distinctive voice."

105   WITHERUP, WILLIAM. "On the Death of Theodore Roethke." Prairie Schooner, XL (Spring), 67.
       A poem in tribute to Roethke.

106   WOESTENDICK, JO.  "More Than a Sneeze."  Houston Chronicle,
      July 10, page unknown (from the Roethke collection, Uni-
      versity of Washington).
         Review of Collected Poems.  Favorable brief review.

107   WOLFF, GEORGE.  "'Sequences' Have Diverse Appeal."  Michigan
      State University News, May 23, page unknown (from the
      Roethke collection, University of Washington).
         Review of The Far Field.  A sketchy, but favorable,
      review that is disappointed by the love poems: "Rather
      than being passionate and convincing they are mostly luke-
      warm comments on loneliness."

108   WOLVERTON, CHARLES.  "The Man Who Made Himself an Island."
      Vancouver (B.C.) Province, August 5, page unknown (from
      the Roethke collection, University of Washington).
         Review of Collected Poems.  "Roethke was indeed a great
      poet, but his muse was lost in a non-poetic age."

109   WOODCOCK, GEORGE.  "Daring Greatness."  New Leader, (New York),
      September 12, pp. 21-22.
         Review of Collected Poems.  Roethke "was a writer of
      exceptional self-containment."  It is with great "sureness"
      that he establishes a dialog with poets like Dickinson,
      Blake, Yeats and Donne.  This is not imitation.  "He is
      not afraid to appear traditional, since, for the most part,
      familiar forms and rhythms suit his voice."  This is free-
      dom that allows him to concentrate on other aspects of his
      work, the "epigrammatic neatness" of the early poems to
      facing "the dark side of existence" in his later poems.
      "...a wardrobe of personas, a gallery of self-portraits;
      and in every class some of the most intense, the most
      protean and the most superbly crafted writing of a
      generation."

110   *YOULE-WHITE, MICHAEL J.  "Theodore Roethke:  Or Lost in His
      Father's Great Greenhouse in the Floral Gardens."  The
      Citadel, volume unknown (Fall), page unknown.
         A poem in tribute to Roethke.  See also 1967.B85.


1967 A BOOKS

  1   HEYEN, WILLIAM H.  "Essays on the Later Poetry of Theodore
      Roethke."  DA 28:3185A (Ohio University, 1967).

  2   REICHERTZ, RONALD R.  "'Once More, The Round':  An Introduc-
      tion to the Poetry of Theodore Roethke."  DA 28:4643A-
      4644A (University of Wisconsin, 1967).

# Theodore Roethke's Career: An Annotated Bibliography

1967

## 1967 B SHORTER WRITINGS

1    ANON. "'And So Much I Have Missed.'" Penn State Alumni News,
LIII (February), 18-19.
An account of the Roethke material found by Professor
Jack B. McManis of the Penn State English Department. This
article is much the same as that by David A. Leherr in
The Pennsylvania State University Department of Public
Information News, September 11, 1966 (1966.B57) but ex-
panded to print more of the material.

2    ANON. Review of Theodore Roethke: An Introduction to the
Poetry, by Karl Malkoff. Choice, IV (March), 41.
Well-received book on Roethke by "an eclectic critic,
thoroughly informed in previous opinions." His comments
on individual poems "offer excellent notes toward more
thorough interpretations."

3    ANON. "Archibald MacLeish Coming to Read Roethke Poetry."
University of Washington Daily, March 3, p. 11.
MacLeish will present the fourth annual Roethke Memorial
Reading.

4    ANON. "The Lost Son." London Times Literary Supplement,
March 16, p. 215.
Review of Theodore Roethke: An Introduction to the
Poetry, by Karl Malkoff. Malkoff's book is an introduction to Roethke's work. He establishes useful patterns of
imagery, shows Roethke's Jungian strain, and provides
"interesting pages on the influence of Evelyn Underhill's
Mysticism and Tillich's theological essays." But he does
not follow deeply the influence of Christopher Smart.

5    ANON. "Roethke Foundation Planning Award." Publisher's
Weekly, CXCI (March 20), 40.
Announcement that the Theodore Roethke Memorial Founda-
tion has been established for the purpose of presenting a
cash award every three years to a book of poetry by an
American poet.

6    ANON. "Award in Memory of Roethke." New York Times,
March 23, p. 32.
Notice of the establishing of the Theodore Roethke
Memorial Foundation to make a $6,000 award every three
years by the Saginaw, Michigan Women of the Friday Book
Club.

1967

7    ANON.    "$6,000 Prize Due to Honor Roethke."  Seattle Post-
        Intelligencer, March 24, p. 3.
            Announcement of the Roethke Memorial Foundation plans
        for an award every three years.

8    ANON.    "Roethke Prize to be Largest Poetry Award."  Univer-
        sity of Washington Daily, March 31, p. 13.
            The Roethke Memorial Foundation, of Saginaw, Michigan,
        plans a $6,000 award every three years.

9    ANON.    "Roethke Poetry Prize."  Christian Science Monitor,
        April 27, p. 5.
            Announcement of the establishment of a $6000 prize to be
        offered every three years, and the hope that a sufficient
        endowment can be raised to support the prize.

*10   ANON.    "Nemerov Named Winner of First Roethke Award."  New
        York Times, May 21, p. 44 (as cited in Theodore Roethke:
        A Bibliography, by James McLeod).
            Unable to locate on this date.

11   ANON.    "Speakers to Present Ted Roethke."  The Saginaw News,
        May 21, Section C, p. 4.
            Stanley Kunitz, John Ciardi and Allan Seager will dis-
        cuss Roethke and his work.  The Theodore Roethke Memorial
        Poetry Prize will be inaugurated by the Roethke Foundation.
        Most of this article discusses the careers of the three
        speakers.

12   ANON.    "Editorial Viewpoint:  Let All Saginaw Recognize
        Roethke."  The Saginaw News, May 22, Section A, p. 6.
            In Saginaw Roethke's greatness was not recognized.  He
        will be honored at "An Evening with Ted Roethke" at
        Arthur Hill High School.  "...maybe we can atone for that
        (not recognizing the boy) by recognizing the man."

13   ANON.    "Archibald MacLeish to Recite Thursday."  University
        of Washington Daily, May 24, p. 1.
            The poet will give the fourth annual Roethke Memorial
        Reading.

14   ANON.    "Crystal Forms on Display."  Centre Daily Times
        (State College, Pa.), July 28, p. 11.
            Cited by McLeod in Theodore Roethke: A Bibliography
        (B16, p. 52), this article does not mention Roethke.

15   ANON.    "Theodore Roethke:  The Far Field."  T.L.S. Essays and
        Reviews from The Times Literary Supplement--1966.  London:
        Oxford University Press, pp. 150-152.
            Reprint of 1966.B2.

1967

16    BAUER, ROBERT V. "Saginaw Plans Recognition for Famed Poet
         Roethke." Centre Daily Times (State College, Pa.),
         June 9, p. 10.
            Roethke is compared to the prophet, but one honored in
         his own town. Saginaw has honored him by establishing the
         Theodore Roethke Memorial Poetry Prize. Stanley Kunitz,
         John Ciardi and Allan Seager were on the inaugural program.
         Comments by people of Saginaw are excerpted from an arti-
         cle appearing in The Saginaw News.

17    BENEDIKT, MICHAEL. "The Completed Pattern." Poetry, CXIV
         (January), 262-266.
            Review of Collected Poems. Roethke's mystic vision has,
         in these poems, the sense of being earned. Here is more
         experience than literature. "In his ability to meditate
         convincingly upon the mystical realities of natural exis-
         tence, in seizing the unseen, Roethke has few parallels
         among poets in English."

18    BERRYMAN, JOHN. "A Strut for Roethke." In "A Garland for
         Theodore Roethke." Michigan Quarterly Review, VI (Fall),
         255-256.
            Reprint of 1963.B31; See also 1964.B12.

19    BOYERS, ROBERT. "A Very Separate Peace." The Young American
         Writers. Edited by Richard Kostelanetz. New York:  Funk
         and Wagnalls, pp. 27-34.
            Roethke has always tried to recapture the remembered
         childhood past and the archetypal past "as means to accept-
         ing the inevitabilities of change, the dying of passion,
         the ultimate finitude." His shifting moods are of prin-
         ciple importance. To be questioned is the "direction of
         his consoling qualities." "Roethke's nostalgia for youth
         is a complex element which somewhat resembles the longing
         of the nineteenth-century Romantic poets." His personality
         is "essentially anarchic." In his surrender to sensualism,
         Roethke refuses to intellectualize his condition. In over-
         looking some elements of the human condition (as Lowell
         has not), Roethke has narrowed his scope and weakened his
         art.

20    CASPER, LEONARD. Review of Theodore Roethke:  An Introduction
         to the Poetry, by Karl Malkoff. Thought, XLII (Autumn),
         450-451.
            "Roethke is inverting the psychoanalytic order:  not all
         acts and attitudes are sexual in origin:  rather, sexual
         behavior is used to symbolize the primacy of extra-
         rational impulses, including the spiritual, in man."

Excluding Open House, this thinking is pursued through
each of Roethke's books, concluding with: "Malkoff argues
persuasively that, under the discipline of his craft and
especially by his reliance on natural leitmotivs to make
complex sequences coherent, Roethke was able to convert a
pathological uncertainty into an expression of existential
horror."

21   CIARDI, JOHN. "An Evening with Theodore Roethke." Michigan
     Quarterly Review, VI (Fall), 238-242.
        This essay is to a large extent a combination of Ciardi's
     previous thoughts on Roethke that had appeared in Saturday
     Review. See also 1966.B26 and 1971.B9.

22   COBLENTZ, STANTON A. The Poetry Circus. New York: Hawthorn
     Books, 1967. Various pages.
        Roethke is grouped with the "modernist" poets who show
     no respect for the values of "traditional" poetry. On
     page 78, the author comments specifically on "The Shape
     of the Fire."

23   COLE, JAMES. "Christmas Eve." In "A Garland for Theodore
     Roethke." Michigan Quarterly Review, VI (Fall), 252.
     Reprint of 1964.B17.

24   CONQUEST, ROBERT. "A Seattle Parkland." In "A Garland for
     Theodore Roethke." Michigan Quarterly Review, VI (Fall),
     267-270.
     Reprint of 1966.B28.

25   COYLE, LEE. "The Journey Out of the Self." The Columbia
     University Owl, January 18, p. 8.
        Review of Collected Poems. Fortunately this work is not
     dominated by social and intellectual exchanges, as has
     been so much poetry of the twentieth century. Roethke has
     music, and more, "a new knowledge, a new peace."

26   DAVIS, DOUGLAS M. "In the Flow of Poetry, the Ladies Flourish."
     National Observer, February 6, p. 31.
        Review of Collected Poems. Roethke's book "shows,
     paradoxically, how madness on its own can almost rescue
     the campus poet from tedium.... Even in his most conven-
     tional verse...there is a sense of desperation, almost of
     fear, that lends Mr. Roethke's work an urgency often mis-
     sing in his peers. He needed no war to come alive; he had
     his own strife to contend with, deep inside."

1967

27    EBELT, ALFRED. "Roethke's Valley," in "A Garland for Theodore
      Roethke." Michigan Quarterly Review, VI (Fall), 272-274.
      A poem in tribute to Roethke.

28    FERRY, DAVID "Roethke's Poetry." Virginia Quarterly Review,
      XLIII (Winter), 169-173.
         Review of Collected Poems and Theodore Roethke: An
      Introduction to the Poetry, by Karl Malkoff. Roethke must
      frequently be faulted for too solemn seriousness, too
      lyrical lyricalness, forced mysticism, and formal obses-
      sions. Yet his experimentations are valuable. His later
      work shows a "promising expansiveness and tentativeness."
      See also 1971.B12.

29    FLINT, R. W. "Poet of the Isolated Self." New York Times
      Book Review, January 15, pp. 4, 41.
         Review of Theodore Roethke: An Introduction to the
      Poetry, by Karl Malkoff. Far more than Frost (with whom,
      because of his debt to nature, he had long been compared),
      Roethke "was a poet of the isolated self or selves." He
      became more self-conscious and philosophical, "aware of
      his bent toward self-destruction," as he struggled against
      the "manic-depressive cycles of our national life."
      "Roethke's other spiritual homeland seems to have been
      Ireland, where the Celtic strain of nonascetic mysticism-
      plus-clowning appealed to him strongly."

30    FREER, COBURN. "Book Reviews." Arizona Quarterly, XXIII
      (Autumn), 280-281.
         Review of Collected Poems. "...it was his conception
      of a poet's different tasks that most sets him (Roethke)
      apart from his contemporaries." His work shows "exuberant
      vulgarity..., high seriousness..., integrity..., and
      colloquial ease." Yet there are faults as Roethke some-
      times tries to make strong single lines and rhythms
      suffice, or he falls into self-imitation.

31    GALVIN, BRENDAN. "For Theodore Roethke." Sage, XI (Fall),
      270.
         A poem in tribute to Roethke.

32    GARDNER, ISABELLA. "This Room Is Full of Clocks," in "A
      Garland for Theodore Roethke." Michigan Quarterly Review,
      VI (Fall), 266-267.
         Reprint of 1963.B39.

33    GILBERT, ISABELLE S. Review of The Far Field. Chicago Jewish
      Forum, Spring, pp. 226-227.

This book is Roethke's "crowning achievement," filled
with his sense of identity with the natural world. The
presences of Emily Dickinson and William Blake are felt,
as well as an affinity, in rhythms, to certain Negro
spirituals. The long and short lines "syncopate with a
steady stream of Debussy-like musical reverie." "His
poetry is written in the Impressionistic vein where mood
and effect are dominant and all is suggested and implied
rather than deliberately stated." Though usually effective,
this impressionism occasionally leaves one with a sense of
"unfinished business, for no conclusions are drawn from
his premises nor are questions resolved."

34   GOLDSTONE, HERBERT and IRVING CUMMINGS, eds. "Theodore
     Roethke." Poets & Poems. Belmont, California: Wadsworth
     Publishing Company, pp. 273-274, 374-376.
        Roethke was "perhaps the greatest American poet to come
     to maturity in the 1940's and early 1950's." His language
     is colloquial, yet distinctive, to present "the direct un-
     mediated sense of childhood, free of any apparent self-
     consciousness or analysis, in order to discover and express
     the most real parts of the self."

35   HALL, DONALD. "The Inward Muse." The Poet as Critic. Edited
     by Frederick P. W. McDowell. Evanston: Northwestern
     University Press, p. 90.
        Roethke is mentioned only incidentally, but seems to
     have assumed in the author's mind the stature of represen-
     tative of a particular kind of poetry that could influence
     his individual expression.

36   HART, DOROTHY. "Theodore Roethke 'Blew' for Seattle." North-
     west Today (Seattle Post-Intelligencer), May 28, p. 17
     (marked p. 7).
        An article in praise of Roethke, "a fierce, forever
     voice of spring." The author quotes at length directly
     from Roethke's work.

37   HENDERSON, JAMES W. "Hometown to Honor Roethke." Saginaw
     News, May 7, Sect. D, p. 2.
        Announcement of "An Evening With Ted Roethke" to be held
     at Arthur Hill High School, featuring Stanley Kunitz, John
     Ciardi and Allan Seager. The author gives an unusually
     long newspaper biography, favorable enough that he would
     be considered among the "small but durable coeterie of
     friends" in Saginaw.

1967

38 _____. "The Poet: Bon Vivant, Whistler, Loner." The Saginaw
News, May 21, Section C, p. 1.
Roethke was a man of many faces. The people who knew
him all remembered something different. Part of his greatness may have been that he never acted as though he should
be taken seriously. Views of him as a poet will be discussed by John Ciardi, Stanley Kunitz and Allan Seager at
Arthur Hill High School's 'An Evening with Ted Roethke.'
The Roethke Memorial Poetry Prize will be inaugurated.

39 HERBERT, TOM. "Fitting Tribute to Theodore Roethke." University of Washington Daily, May 26, p. 12.
Archibald MacLeish read his poems the previous evening.
The occasion (the fourth annual Roethke Memorial Reading)
is not stated.

40 HOFFMAN, FREDERICK J. "Contemporary American Poetry." Patterns of Commitment in American Literature. Edited by
Marston LaFrance. Toronto: University of Toronto Press,
p. 195.
Roethke is here seen as a tradition-bearer who will
endure and whose poetry forms the backdrop for those
younger and truly "contemporary" poets.

41 HOLLENBERG, SUSAN W. "Theodore Roethke: Bibliography."
Twentieth Century Literature, XII (January), 216-221.

42 HUFF, ROBERT. "On the Death of Theodore Roethke," in "A
Garland for Theodore Roethke." Michigan Quarterly Review,
VI (Fall), 252-253.
Reprint of 1966.B48; See also 1966.B49.

43 _____. "Spring Run," in "A Garland for Theodore Roethke."
Michigan Quarterly Review, VI (Fall), 263-264.
Reprint of 1959.B48.

44 HUGHES, TED. Poetry in the Making: An Anthology of Poems and
Programmes from 'Listening and Writing.' London: Faber
and Faber.
Two of Roethke's poems, "The Storm" (34-35) and "Elegy"
(54-55), are presented as illustrations for Hughes' ex-
planation of the writing process. He comments on the
images in "The Storm."

45 JACOBSEN, JOSEPHINE. "Books in Review." Baltimore Evening
Sun, January 12, page unknown (from the Roethke collection,
University of Washington).
Review of Collected Poems. "The basis of Roethke's
poetry lies in the subconscious--there is a sheen of

mystery over the contours of normal objects, and relationships and movements are ambiguous."

46  KEITH, JOSEPH JOEL. "Books in English." Books Abroad, XLI
       (Spring), 223-224.
          Review of Collected Poems. Roethke's achievement ranks
       with the other great contemporary American poet, Richard
       Eberhart. "He is profound, witty, sensitive, mischievous,
       majestic, and reverent." Roethke is "ageless."

47  KOLARS, JOHN. "Roethke," in "A Garland for Theodore Roethke."
       Michigan Quarterly Review, VI (Fall), 257.
          A poem in tribute to Roethke.

48  KUNITZ, STANLEY. "An Evening with Theodore Roethke." Michigan
       Quarterly Review, VI (Fall), 234-238.
          A slightly modified version of the author's essay that
       appeared in the New York Review of Books, 1963.B49. See
       also 1971.B26.

49  LEGGETT, GLENN and HENRY-YORK STEINER. 12 Poets. Alternate
       edition. New York:  Holt, Rinehart and Winston,
       pp. 256-275.
          Short biographical sketch and a selection of Roethke's
       poems. Also included in this unusual anthology, among
       others, are Chaucer, Jonson, Milton, Dryden, Blake, Byron,
       John Crowe Ransom, and Archibald MacLeish.

50  LEWIS, PETER. "The Last Work of Theodore Roethke and Randall
       Jarrell." Stand, IX:2, 57-62.
          Review of The Far Field. In the current "decadent phase
       of 'Modernism,'" the odds are against any poet reaching
       greatness. "Perhaps it is because we have been led to ex-
       pect so much from Roethke that his posthumous book The Far
       Field seems disappointing, a lame and often puzzling con-
       clusion to his poetic career." The technical control re-
       mains, but "Roethke's highly personal idiom that first
       revealed itself in The Lost Son is here often reduced to a
       formula; what once was an original style has degenerated
       into a manner." Some poems, such as "The Abyss," receive
       close looks, but for the most part are found lacking, due
       to Roethke's "rhetorical mannerisms" and the undigested
       presence of Eliot. "Sequence, Sometimes Metaphysical,"
       with Donne's religious poetry undoubtedly behind it, is
       the strongest section of the book, but it too is marred.

51  LEWISOHN, JAMES. "Theodore Roethke," in "A Garland for
       Theodore Roethke." Michigan Quarterly Review, VI (Fall), 274.
          Reprint of 1966.B59.

1967

52    LOWELL, ROBERT.  "For Theodore Roethke," in "A Garland for
          Theodore Roethke."  Michigan Quarterly Review, VI (Fall),
          265.
              Reprint of 1966.B61; See also 1967.B53.

53    _____.  "For Theodore Roethke."  Near the Ocean.  New York:
          Farrar, Straus, Giroux.
              Reprint of 1966.B61; See also 1967.B52.

54    LUPHER, DAVID A.  "The Lost Son:  Theodore Roethke."  Yale
          Literary Magazine, CXXXV (March), 9-12.
              Review of Words for the Wind; Collected Poems; On the
          Poet and His Craft; Theodore Roethke, by Ralph J. Mills, Jr.;
          Theodore Roethke:  An Introduction to the Poetry, by Karl
          Malkoff; and Theodore Roethke:  Essays on the Poetry,
          edited by Arnold Stein.
              Emphasized here is the most original poet who is, para-
          doxically, the most derivative.  Roethke, like Yeats,
          Graves and Blake, had a personal mythology, the green-
          houses, out of which his poems came.  His work will haunt
          the reader, even the one who is most confused.  But there
          will be a revelation.  And it will come fastest and best
          when the poems are read aloud.  This was Roethke's injunc-
          tion:  read the poems aloud and let the rhythms work on
          you.  The books about Roethke are signs of his stature as
          a poet ("probably a great one"), certainly not answering
          satisfactorily the many questions they raise.

55    MALKOFF, KARL.  "Exploring the Boundaries of Self."  Sewanee
          Review, LXXV (Summer), 540-542.
              Review of Collected Poems.  The poems constitute a kind
          of "spiritual autobiography, ...Roethke's desperate attempt
          to come to terms with his world, but also the spectacular
          development of poetic technique that accompanied it."  The
          reviewer goes through each book, summarizing its thematic
          and stylistic importance and relating it to the other
          books.  He concludes with discussion of the misleading
          arrangement of the Collected Poems that sometimes appears
          to contradict Roethke's own final editing.

56    MILLER, ED.  "Evening With Roethke," in "Ed Miller Writes"
          column.  Saginaw News, May 18, Sect. A., p. 6.
              Announcement of "An Evening With Ted Roethke" to be held
          at Arthur Hill High School, featuring Stanley Kunitz, John
          Ciardi and Allan Seager.  The author speaks with an admir-
          ing voice of Roethke's work; and the few personal contacts
          he had with the poet, a youth who could be "uncommonly
          profane."  The article closes with a discussion of Roethke's

ability as a tennis player, with the personal reminiscences
of Al F. Riese, a member of the Saginaw Canoe Club.

57  MILLS, RALPH J., JR.  "Theodore Roethke:  The Lyric of the
    Self."  Poets in Progress.  A reprint, augmented.  Edited
    by Edward Hungerford.  Evanston, Ill.:  Northwestern
    University Press, 1962, 1967, pp. 3-23.
        This is a revised and up-dated version of the author's
    article that appeared in Tri-Quarterly, 1958.B30.  See
    also 1966.B68.

58  _____.  "Book Reviews."  American Literature, XXXIX (May),
    246-247.
        Review of Theodore Roethke:  An Introduction to the
    Poetry, by Karl Malkoff.  The work marks the beginning of
    book-length studies and is a good one.  Malkoff handles
    especially well the "developmental" poems of The Lost Son
    and Praise to the End!, as well as the religious and
    mystical themes.

59  MONTAGUE, JOHN.  "Company," in "A Garland for Theodore Roethke."
    Michigan Quarterly Review, VI (Fall), 256-257.
        A poem in tribute to Roethke.

60  MURPHY, RICHARD.  "The Poet on the Island," in "A Garland for
    Theodore Roethke."  Michigan Quarterly Review, VI (Fall),
    253-254.
        Reprint of 1963.B53.

61  MUSTE, JOHN M.  "American Literature."  The Americana Annual
    1967.  Americana Corporation, p. 56.
        Roethke's Collected Poems "supports the general consensus
    that he was one of the major poets of this century."

62  NELSON, DALE.  "Free in a Tearing Wind."  Northwest Today
    (Seattle Post-Intelligencer), February 26, p. 23.
        Review of Theodore Roethke:  An Introduction to the
    Poetry, by Karl Malkoff.  The reviewer summarizes each
    section of Malkoff's book, complimenting him particularly
    on his treatment of Roethke's reading in philosophy and
    religion.  After Malkoff ranks Roethke with Eliot and
    Stevens among American poets, the reviewer adds Frost to
    the list.

63  POWELL, GROSVENOR E.  "Robert Lowell and Theodore Roethke:
    Two Kinds of Knowing."  Southern Review, NS III (Winter),
    180-185.
        Review of Theodore Roethke:  Essays on the Poetry, edited
    by Arnold Stein.  Roethke is difficult to approach through

1967

exegesis due to the romantic-mystical nature of his work.
Yet these essays contribute much to our understanding.
Roethke follows in the tradition of Wallace Stevens.

64  REICHERTZ, RONALD R. "Roethke's 'Where Knock Is Open Wide,'--
Part I." Explicator, XXVI (December), Item 34.
Mills and Malkoff have overlooked the basic opposition
of birth and death in Part I of this poem.

65  RIDLAND, JOHN. "Two Imitations," in "A Garland for Theodore
Roethke." Michigan Quarterly Review, VI (Fall), 258.
A poem in·tribute to Roethke.

66  ROCHE, PAUL. "The Greenhouse Dionysus," in "A Garland for
Theodore Roethke." Michigan Quarterly Review, VI (Fall),
270.
A poem in tribute to Roethke.

67  ROSENTHAL, M. L. "Theodore Roethke, John Berryman, Anne
Sexton." The New Poets: American and British Poetry
Since World War Two. New York: Oxford University Press,
pp. 112-119.
Roethke is aligned with the "confessional movement" in
American poetry. The later poems, of The Far Field principally, are here discussed in relation to his essay "How
to Write Like Somebody Else." Fragments of these poems,
and his entire work, are found of high quality, but over-
all "the effects are finally unearned."

68  SALTER, ELIZABETH. The Last Years of a Rebel: A Memoir of
Edith Sitwell. Boston: Houghton Mifflin, p. 101.
An account of a meeting between Miss Sitwell and Roethke
sent to the author. In it Roethke's "petrifying manner
like a runaway horse" is described: dancing, weeping,
seemingly contemplating suicide. "Opinions differ as to
what was the matter, some opining that he had been to too
many parties, and was under the spell of the God" (Miss
Sitwell's remark).

69  SCHNEIDER, ELISABETH W., ALBERT L. WALKER and HERBERT E. CHILDS.
The Range of Literature: An Introduction to Prose and
Verse. Second Edition. New York: American Book Co.,
pp. 374-376, 410.
Selection of Roethke poems with question for students
regarding "Elegy" ("Her face like a rain-beaten stone on
the day she rolled off").

1967

70   SCOTT, WINFIELD TOWNLEY.  "Roethke," in "A Garland for Theodore
        Roethke."  Michigan Quarterly Review, VI (Fall), 256.
        Reprint of 1966.B82.

71   SEAGER, ALLAN.  "An Evening with Theodore Roethke."  Michigan
        Quarterly Review, VI (Fall), 227-234, 242-243.
        The outline of Roethke's biography with many of the de-
        tails as they appear later in The Glass House.  See also
        1971.B42.

72   SHAPIRO, KARL.  Randall Jarrell.  Washington, D.C.:  Published
        for the Library of Congress by the Gertrude Clark Whittall
        Poetry and Literature Fund, p. 20.
        In a discussion of American literature as essentially "a
        child literature," the author makes the following remark:
        "Theodore Roethke was a modern kind of nature poet, a
        biology poet with the eyes of a microscope."  Roethke is
        mentioned briefly several other times as one of the prin-
        cipal poets of his generation.  See also 1968.B72.

73   SIMPSON, LOUIS.  "New Books of Poems."  Harper's, CCXXXV
        (August), 90.
        Review of Collected Poems.  Roethke shows "an ear for
        sounds, a talent like an animal, expanding and deepening, in
        the great inheritance of symbolism, ruminating the plants,
        birds, beasts, and women of his psyche.  When he died he
        was one of the few poets capable of conferring happiness
        rather than asking for it."

74   SKELTON, ROBIN.  "The Poetry of Theodore Roethke."  Malahat
        Review, I (January), 141-144.
        Review of Collected Poems.  Though a borrower, Roethke's
        intent was his own, not that of an imitator.  "He attempted
        to fuse the sensual with the mythic perception" in a poetry
        much in the Symbolist tradition.  But "Roethke...was not
        afraid of becoming private."  He was, also, a moral poet,
        issuing warnings in his nonsense and children's poems.

75   STAFFORD, WILLIAM.  "Roethke."  Southern Review, NS III
        (October), 946-947.
        A poem in tribute to Roethke.

76   STEPHENS, ALAN.  "Thinking of Roethke's Death," in "A Garland
        for Theodore Roethke."  Michigan Quarterly Review, VI
        (Fall), 266.
        A poem in tribute to Roethke.

1967

77      ____. "Twelve New Books of Poetry." Denver Quarterly, I
        (Winter), 107–109.
            Review of Collected Poems. Roethke's poems of "visionary
        sensualism" are, in general, flops. "Short bursts--
        entreaty, abrupt narrative statements, exclamation,
        aphorism of a kind Roethke has the patent on." But the
        mode is tiring. It is the meditative poems of solitary
        experience that make Roethke the best poet of his
        generation.

78      STILWELL, ROBERT L. "Books in English." Books Abroad, XLI
        (Spring), 224.
            Review of Theodore Roethke: An Introduction to the
        Poetry, by Karl Malkoff. As a general introduction the
        book survives its occasional superficiality.

79      SUND, ROBERT. "A Day in Summer, 1963," in "A Garland for
        Theodore Roethke." Michigan Quarterly Review, VI (Fall),
        271–272.
            A poem in tribute to Roethke.

80      TURCO, LEWIS. "Aspects," in "A Garland for Theodore Roethke."
        Michigan Quarterly Review, VI (Fall), 254–255.
            Reprint of 1966.B96.

81      TURNER, MYRON. "On the Death of Mr. Roethke," in "A Garland
        for Theodore Roethke." Michigan Quarterly Review, VI
        (Fall), 259.
            A poem in tribute to Roethke. See also 1967.B82.

82      ____. "On the Death of Mr. Roethke." The Literary Review,
        II (Autumn), 64–65.
            Reprint of 1967.B81.

83      ____. "Preludes for Roethke," in "A Garland for Theodore
        Roethke." Michigan Quarterly Review, VI (Fall), 259–263.
            A poem in tribute to Roethke.

84      VENDLER, HELLEN. "Recent American Poetry." Massachusetts
        Review, VIII (Summer), 553–554.
            Review of Collected Poems. "Roethke was a static poet,
        and there is nothing in his last complete volume, A Far
        Field (sic), that was not present almost twenty years
        earlier in his second book." The imitator of Yeats will
        not last, but the greenhouse poet will. "The deliberate
        infantilism of the poetry is its power, and Roethke, not
        Dylan Thomas, is our poet of genesis."

# Writings about Theodore Roethke, 1922-1973

85  YOULE-WHITE, MICHAEL J.  "Theodore Roethke:  Or Lost in His
    Father's Great Greenhouse in the Floral Gardens," in "A
    Garland for Theodore Roethke."  Michigan Quarterly Review,
    VI (Fall), 265.
        Reprint of 1966.B110.


## 1968 A BOOKS

1   FLINT, ROLAND H.  "Many Arrivals Make Us Live:  A Study of the
    Early Poetics of Theodore Roethke, 1941-1953."  DA
    30:318A-319A (University of Minnesota).

2   SEAGER, ALLAN.  The Glass House:  The Life of Theodore Roethke.
    New York:  McGraw-Hill.

3   WALKER, URSULA GENUNG.  Notes on Theodore Roethke.  Charlottes-
    ville:  Bibliographical Society of the University of
    Virginia.
        Contains biographical information under a number of
    headings, including "The Teacher," "The Man," etc.; se-
    lected excerpts from the criticism; a conclusion; a par-
    tial bibliography of Roethke's work and the criticism; and
    a chronology of publications.

## 1968 B SHORTER WRITINGS

1   ALVAREZ, A.  "Sylvia Plath."  The Modern Poet:  Essays from
    The Review.  Edited by Ian Hamilton.  London:  Macdonald,
    p. 76.
        Reprint of 1963.B1; See also 1968.B2 and 1969.B1.

2   _____.  "Sylvia Plath."  Beyond All This Fiddle:  Essays 1955-
    1967.  Allen Lane:  Penguin Press.
        Reprint of 1963.B1; See also 1968.B1 and 1969.B1.

3   ANON.  "Forecasts."  Publisher's Weekly, CXCIII (April 8), 43.
        Review of Selected Letters.  Mills' selection admirably
    illuminates the character of the man, Roethke.  Much of
    the life is here but the previously unpublished drafts of
    poems "provide a valuable, if unsystematic, series of in-
    sights into Roethke's method."

4   ANON.  Review of Selected Letters.  Antiquarian Bookman, XLI
    (June 3), 2198.
        The Letters will serve as a biography for a while.
    Roethke "was a difficult and complex man, and it will be
    a long time before the whole of his personality is put to
    paper."

1968

5   ANON.   "Awards:  Roethke Poetry Award."  Facts on File,
        XXVIII (June 6-12), 239.
            Howard Nemerov won first Roethke prize for The Blue
        Swallows.

6   ANON.   "Pursued by Voices."  London Times Literary Supplement,
        July 4, p. 699.
            Review of Collected Poems.  "All the longer poems in the
        volume and most of the short ones are ruined by Roethke's
        inability to disguise his influences."  Some good work,
        mostly love poems, is original and will survive.  See also
        1969.B5.

7   ANON.   Review of The Glass House, by Allan Seager.  Kirkus
        Reviews, XXXVI (August 1), 875.
            "Seager, like Roethke, tends to take the wish for the
        deed, tends to see mystery and a sense of the marvelous
        where others, including this reviewer, are more apt to find
        an emotional fibbing and mystical pugnacity in what Roethke
        took to be the Blakean-Yeatsian tradition."

8   ANON.   Review of The Glass House, by Allan Seager.  Publisher's
        Weekly, CXCIV (August 26), 270.
            Seager tries again and again to penetrate "the great
        lumbering form of Theodore Roethke (in which) lurked an
        extraordinarily sensitive poet who locked himself in and
        cunningly secreted the key."  The reviewer does not state
        whether or not Seager was successful.

9   ANON.   "Notes on Current Books."  Virginia Quarterly Review,
        XLIV (Autumn), clx.
            Review of Selected Letters.  Roethke's letters are valu-
        able because in them "he often explains and defends his
        poems and his sense of the nature and purpose of poetry.
        The man revealed is sensitive, intelligent, vain, suffer-
        ing, and always intent even to the end upon clawing his
        way to the top."

10  ANON.   "Brief Mention."  American Literature, XL (November),
        436.
            Review of Selected Letters.  (Attributed to Ben W. Fuson
        by McLeod in Theodore Roethke:  A Bibliography.)
        "Mr. Mills selected such letters as are pertinent to
        Roethke's activities as poet, and literary theorist, and
        his handling of them is in accordance with approved
        scholarly practice."

# Writings about Theodore Roethke, 1922-1973

11    ANON.   Review of The Glass House, by Allan Seager.   Star-
        Bulletin & Advertiser (Honolulu), November 24, page unknown
        (from the Roethke collection, University of Washington).
        Seager's insights into the conflict of the soul are
        excellent.

12    BAUER, MALCOLM.   "Portland Elegance; Poet in Travail."
        Portland Oregonian, December 22, page unknown, (from the
        Roethke collection, University of Washington).
        Review of The Glass House, by Allan Seager.  A summary
        discussion of Roethke's periodic mental illness.

13    BEALL, DeWITT.   "Poetic Order in a Life of Chaos."   Chicago
        Daily News, November 16, page unknown (from the Roethke
        collection, University of Washington).
        Review of The Glass House, by Allan Seager.  "I suppose
        the most amazing thing about Roethke is that, out· of the
        chaos of his personal life, out of his manias and depres-
        sions and frequent stays in the bughouse, he could wrest
        poetry that is as sculptured, serene and orderly as any
        in American literature."

14    BLY, ROBERT.   "The Mail."   Atlantic Monthly, CCXXII (December),
        34.
        Response to "The Greatest American Poet," by James
        Dickey, 1968.B29.  Favorable response, but questioning its
        timeliness.

15    BOGER, MARY SNEAD.   "Roethke:  Poet with a Passion for People...
        and Perfection?"   Charlotte (N.C.) Observer, November 10,
        page unknown (from the Roethke collection, University of
        Washington).
        Review of The Glass House, by Allan Seager.  "There was
        an insecurity deep inside the man (Roethke) that is not
        explained satisfactorily by his biographer.  Was it per-
        haps a congenital thing?  Was he not as masculine as he
        strutted?"  Beyond this questioning, and summary of impor-
        tant events in Roethke's life, the review emphasizes the
        paradox of the man.

16    BOYERS, ROBERT.   "The Roethke Letters."   Georgia Review, XXII
        (Winter), 437-445.
        Review of Selected Letters.  "A major figure he (Roethke)
        does still seem to me, ...but I do not think I shall ever
        again regard him as an attractive figure."  These letters
        tell too much of the hack-writer and not enough of the man,
        and others' relationships to him.  The reviewer speaks at
        length about Roethke's attitude toward people who saw "in-
        fluences" in his work and his own emergent voice.

1968

17    BREWSTER, DAVID. "Glimpse into a Poet's Life." Seattle
          Times Magazine, December 29, p. 19.
              Review of The Glass House, by Allan Seager. Favorable
          review of the biography and the way it conveys Roethke's
          exuberance and sense of fun. "Roethke was an academic
          poet, relying on academic praise and taste—dense inward-
          ness and small town memories were the fad—and Seager re-
          marks on his experiences at seven colleges with a sassy
          convincingness."

18    BURKE, KENNETH. "The Mail." Atlantic Monthly, CCXXII
          (December), 36, 41.
              Response to "The Greatest American Poet," by James
          Dickey, 1968.B29. Talks of Roethke's honesty.

19    _____. "Cult of the Breakthrough." New Republic, CLIX
          (September 21), 25-26.
              Review of Selected Letters. Roethke's work represents
          a series of breakthroughs, from his discovery of the green-
          house (earlier called by Burke "vegetal radicalism"), to
          the long poems of "mental tangles" and beyond. His "genius
          was essentially lyrical," though he wanted very much to
          make a dramatic breakthrough. But his career interest
          dominates these Letters, though it is a self-promotion
          "so frank and spontaneous, it has a certain winsomeness."
          The author goes on to discuss Roethke's personality as it
          came through in letters to him, discussing such figures as
          T. S. Eliot and Edward Teller. He concludes with remarks
          on Roethke as an enthusiastic teacher of poetry.

20    BURNS, GERALD. "Poet's Life." Dallas Morning News,
          December 1, page unknown (from the Roethke collection,
          University of Washington).
              Review of The Glass House, by Allan Seager. Favorable
          review that praises Roethke, "a Middle-West Villon who
          dreamed of being the friend of gangsters."

21    BUSH, CLIVE. Review of Theodore Roethke: An Introduction to
          the Poetry, by Karl Malkoff. Notes & Queries, NS XV
          (February), 77-79.
              Roethke "is perhaps best seen as a part of that American
          poetic tradition which concerns itself with the precise
          image as symbol of the natural world.... Roethke's themes
          too are a curious mixture of that uniquely American complex
          of eschatological and romantic preoccupations with the act
          of creation as a paradigm of human consciousness, partic-
          ularly the self's relation to the world which it perceives."
          Malkoff, in quoting from "a wide range of mystics and

psychologists...has mistaken identification for explana-
tion." He fails to correlate theory to the poems; or else
does so superficially.

22    CIARDI, JOHN.   Introduction to "Words for Young Writers--From
      the Notebooks of Theodore Roethke."  Saturday Review, LI
      (June 29), 14.
          Roethke "lived by and to" a primal force that informed
      not only his writing, but his teaching too.  "May young
      writers hear, overhear, and then hear over:  They will not
      soon find a man to say better for them what must be said."

23    COHEN, J. M.  Poetry of this Age 1908-1965.  New York:
      Perrenial Library, Harper and Rowe, pp. 247-249.  (Two
      earlier editions are cited here--London:  Hutchinson &
      Co., 1960, 1966.  Also cited in McLeod, James Richard,
      Theodore Roethke:  A Bibliography, Kent Ohio:  Kent State
      University Press, 1973, p. 155, are Poetry of this Age,
      1908-1958, London:  Arrow Books, 1959, pp. 247-249; and
      Poetry of this Age, 1908-1965, London:  Arrow Books, 1966.
      I have located none of these earlier editions.  KM).
          "Roethke is driven forward by a pulsing lyricism that
      refuses to pause at a single image."  Childhood memories
      and sympathetic responses toward "creatures, insects,
      roots and grasses" supply affirmation absent from the
      world of men.  The awakening is Roethke's chief theme.
      Formal elements receive some mention, mostly as a means
      of discipline.  This seems to be one of Yeats' functions
      in Roethke's development.  Another is the philosophical
      guidance of the older poet, by which Roethke "advanced
      from a dualism by which nature was invoked to combat fear,
      to a vision of unity in which fear is accepted, and eter-
      nity is seen to be man's natural condition."  Roethke "is
      content to be a minor poet, and to speak only for himself."

24    COWLEY, MALCOLM.  "The Mail."  Atlantic Monthly, CCXXII
      (December), 41.
          Response to "The Greatest American Poet," by James
      Dickey, 1968.B29.  Dickey's piece is "brilliant and gen-
      uine," though Roethke was not the greatest American poet.

25    CUTLER, BRUCE.  "Introductions and Conclusions."  Poetry, CXII
      (April), 54-55.
          Review of Theodore Roethke:  An Introduction to the
      Poetry, by Karl Malkoff.  "In what may have been an effort
      to shore up the shakier aspects of Roethke's ideas,
      Malkoff devotes too much effort into organizing them for
      the reader."  This causes a neglect of Roethke as poet

1968

> rather than thinker, "the firmer and more satisfactory"
> area of consideration.

26   DALE, PETER.   "Generosity and Gaiety."   Tribune (London),
     August 16, page unknown (from the Roethke collection,
     University of Washington).
          Review of Collected Poems.  The weakness at the center
     of Roethke's work is "a sentimental attitude to nature and
     a distrust of reason."  It is despite many faults that a
     total man emerges from the poems.

27   DICKEY, JAMES.   "Theodore Roethke."   Babel to Byzantium:  Poets
     and Poetry Now.  New York:  Farrar, Straus and Giroux,
     pp. 148–152.
          Reprint of 1964.B22.

28   _____.   Untitled sub-section of "Theodore Roethke."   Babel to
     Byzantium:  Poets and Poetry Now.  New York:  Farrar,
     Straus and Giroux, pp. 147–148.
          Reprint of 1961.B33.

29   _____.   "The Greatest American Poet."   Atlantic Monthly,
     CCXXII (December), 53–58.
          Review of The Glass House, by Allan Seager.  A memoir/
     review discussing both Roethke and Allan Seager, his biog-
     rapher.  Roethke comes off remote from his poems, common,
     a man Dickey wished had given his work the range it needed
     by writing poems about the stories he told:  prizefighter
     poems, gangster poems and tycoon poems.  But, of what he
     did write, "there is no poetry anywhere that is so valuably
     conscious of the human body as Roethke's; no poetry that
     can place the body in an environment...so vividly and
     evocatively, waking unheard of exchanges between the place
     and human responsiveness at its most creative."  What
     keeps a very good biography from being great is the
     "wavering of purpose" of Roethke's wife.  See also 1971.B11.

30   DODSWORTH, MARTIN.   "Towards the Baseball Poem."   The Listener,
     June 27, p. 842.
          Review of Collected Poems.  "As for Roethke, in so many
     ways a 'natural' poet, he surely did waste his gifts whor-
     ing after Literature--too much philosophy, too much Eliot
     and other voices.  The earliest of his poems remain the
     best."

31   DUNLOP, WILLIAM.   "Roethke's Letters Reveal a Man."   Northwest
     Today (Seattle Post-Intelligencer), May 5, p. 4.

Review of Selected Letters, edited by Ralph J. Mills, Jr.
"...it is the quality of voice throughout this collection
that makes it an important, exciting, continually entertaining, and sometimes deeply moving book." The letters
exhibit Roethke's courage and the great dramas and con-
flicts of his life.

32    EVERETTE, OLIVER. "Theodore Roethke:  The Poet as Teacher."
West Coast Review, III (Spring), 5-11.
The author, former student and sometime Roethke confi-
dante, reminisces about Roethke's teaching methods and
state of mind prior to a period of mental illness, this
one in 1949.

33    FIEDLER, LESLIE A. "Another Nonsense Poet." The Guardian
(London), May 31, page unknown (from the Roethke collection, University of Washington).
Review of Collected Poems. Roethke is many voices, the
best of which the author still considers to be that of the
child in "The Lost Son."

*34    _____. "Poet of Childhood." Manchester Guardian, XCVIII
(June 6), 11.
Review of Collected Poems (as cited in Theodore Roethke:
A Bibliography, by James McLeod). Unable to locate.

35    FULLER, EDMUND. "Poets on Poetry." Wall Street Journal,
August 15, p. 10.
Review of Selected Letters. This review follows that
of James Dickey's From Babel to Byzantium in which Dickey
speaks with great admiration for Roethke's talent. The
reviewer finds here the sadness and fear that Dickey had
pointed out and goes on to stress the earthy and bawdy
humor that matches them.

36    FUSON, BEN W. Review of The Glass House, by Allan Seager, and
Selected Letters. Library Journal, XCIII (September 1),
3006.
"The full-bodied portrait of Roethke limned by Mr. Seager
and Mr. Mills includes the wide range of his attributes:
from vital, idealistic, honest, warm-hearted, incandescent,
intuitive, tender, and penetrating, to arrogant (by turns
with sycophantic), cynical one moment and embarrassingly
self-loathing another, wheedlingly ambitious, over-
apologetic, coarse, and (underneath all his ebullience)
frightened."

# Theodore Roethke's Career: An Annotated Bibliography

37  GOODHEART, E. "The Frailty of the 'I.'" Sewanee Review,
    LXXVI (Summer), 516-519.
        Review of On the Poet and His Craft; Theodore Roethke:
    Essays on the Poetry, edited by Arnold Stein; and Theodore
    Roethke: An Introduction to the Poetry, by Karl Malkoff.
    Roethke's eclecticism is brought out in the Selected Prose.
    Yet his status depends on his acceptance as a confessional
    poet. He managed to preserve a "psychic isolationism,"
    a vision that is, finally, rather pathetic. This is due
    to his special relation to nature.

38  GRANT, DAMIAN. "Centre Court." The Tablet (London), July 6,
    pp. 673-674.
        Review of Collected Poems. If, for this reviewer, John
    Berryman's Sonnets take first seed, Roethke, in his book
    of "reliable things," commits "never a double fault." "We
    can see him maturing...from the competent reproductions of
    Open House...with their firm iambic rhythm, cumbrous wit,
    and moral explicitness to the rich originality of The Far
    Field.... Roethke has profited visibly from many other
    poets, but Whitman, 'maker of catalogues,' is one he is
    especially pleased to invoke as mentor in 'The Abyss,'
    where he leaves us,
        My soul nearly my own,
        My dead selves singing."

39  HALLOCK, P. R. "The Sidelong Pickerel Smile." Alkahest,
    No.2 (Fall), 20-21.
        A poem in tribute to Roethke.

40  HEANY, SEAMUS. "Canticles to the Earth." The Listener,
    August 22, pp. 245-246.
        Review of Collected Poems. Roethke had a strong trust in
    his own creative instincts, "but the most remarkable thing
    about this watery spirit of his is that for all its motion,
    it never altogether finds its final bed and course." The
    reviewer goes on to discuss the early poems, "toned down
    and contained in well-behaved couplets and quatrains."
    Roethke's "real achievement arrives from the boundaries"
    of his experience: childhood and death. Some discussion
    of The Lost Son and The Far Field follows. Praise to the
    End! gives us "an apocalyptic straining towards unity."
    The love poems and meditations are in "direct contrast to
    these wandering tides of the spirit." The longer cata-
    loguing poems are his best, "all of which exhale something
    of a Franciscan love of every living thing, and at the
    same time invoke the notion of a divine unity working
    through them." When "he is not in full possession of his

emotion, when tranquility is missing because in Roethke
tranquility can only arrive through an act of praise, then
he employs the artificer's resources of metre, stanza and
rhyme to conduct himself and the poem towards a provisional
statement." Roethke "seems destined to grudging notice
because he echoes the voices of other poets, or because
people have grown afraid of the gentle note that was his
own."

41  HEYEN, WILLIAM. "Theodore Roethke's Minimals." Minnesota
    Review, VIII:4, 359-375.
        Roethke's "desire, with Whitman, is to confront the ele-
    ments and achieve the harmony, the oneness with nature
    exhibited by minimals." What the small things do, there-
    fore, is unify the poet's fragmented identity. In Open
    House minimals "bear the burden of only traditional asso-
    ciations." The "Greenhouse" poems of The Lost Son initi-
    ate the conscious personal symbolism of minimals. They
    are both fearful and beautiful; finite and infinite;
    symbols of Becoming and Being; and distinctive of sensual
    and sensuous perception. The author pursues these thoughts
    primarily through "The Lost Son" and "Meditations of an Old
    Woman."

42  _____. "He Blusters, Sorrows and Laughs." Saturday Review,
    LI (June 22), 78.
        Review of Selected Letters. Roethke's "duel with
    society" is well captured.

43  HOGAN, WILLIAM. "The Roethke Letters: 'Renaissance Readings.'"
    San Francisco Chronicle, May 23, page unknown (from the
    Roethke collection, University of Washington).
        Review of Selected Letters, edited by Ralph J. Mills, Jr.
    Favorable brief review.

44  JAFFE, DAN. "Inner Turmoil Came Out in Poems." Kansas City
    Star, November 24, p. 3E.
        Review of The Glass House, by Allan Seager. "In this
    remarkable book Allan Seager provides us with a real
    sense of the enormous inner turmoil Theodore Roethke har-
    nessed into some of the most successful poems in the
    language."

45  JENNINGS, ELIZABETH. "Inspiration and Ideas." Twentieth Cen-
    tury (London), CLXXVII (Third), 52-53.
        Review of Collected Poems. Yeats' influence is clear
    enough. But Roethke also wrote "a questing, brooding
    poetry of search and discovery." In these poems he

1968

examines "how beasts move and work," using the long line to good advantage. His poems of the "identity and the significance of the ego" are not as successful. But Roethke is "a truly important American poet, certainly to be ranked with Richard Wilbur, perhaps higher."

46   KENNEDY, X. J. "The Mail." Atlantic Monthly, CCXXII (December), 41.
      Response to "The Greatest American Poet," by James Dickey, 1968.B29. Questions Roethke's stature and Dickey's treatment of Mrs. Roethke.

47   KERMODE, FRANK. "The Mail." Atlantic Monthly, CCXXII (December), 34.
      Response to "The Greatest American Poet," by James Dickey, 1968.B29. Favorable response though he disagrees about Roethke's stature.

48   KIRSCH, ROBERT. "Novelist's Vivid Biography of Poet Theodore Roethke." Los Angeles Times, November 4, page unknown (from the Roethke collection, University of Washington).
      Review of The Glass House, by Allan Seager. This review dwells on the gulf between the biography and the real poet and his work, that is, "the mystery of talent."

49   KOCH, STEPHEN. "The Poet's Scene." New York Times Book Review, September 29, p. 34.
      Review of Selected Letters. Roethke was the "hypertense, 6-foot, noisy poet of neurosis and love." He was not as good as the other big-name poets of the twentieth century (Yeats, Eliot, Moore, etc.), but he was author of some fine poems. But he comes across very dully, as the "Serious Writer of the forties and fifties, dependent on teaching for his livelihood." And that age was one of "inwardness" and "provincialism," which, fortunately, Roethke's poems survive. The letters never let us forget the "Academy," where he was out of touch, with only himself and language. And, they have nothing to say.

50   KUHLMAN, THOMAS A. Review of Theodore Roethke: An Introduction to the Poetry, by Karl Malkoff. American Literature Abstracts, II (December), 158-159.
      Summary of book reviews, with excerpts, showing the responses to be, generally, favorable.

51   KUNITZ, STANLEY. "The Mail." Atlantic Monthly, CCXXII (December), 34.

Response to "The Greatest American Poet," by James
Dickey, 1968.B29. Dickey's account "is undeniably true as
far as it goes."

52 LEIMBACHER, ED. "Epistolary Roethke." Seattle Magazine,
July, pp. 10-11.
Review of Selected Letters. A man motivated by money,
comfort and fame, Roethke still comes through in his letters as a poet, albeit one with an obviously practical
side. "He worked exhaustingly hard to become one of the
greatest modern poets, and for his efforts, he expected
fame and, if not fortune, at least comfort." The author
sees much to appreciate as Roethke speaks of his fellow
poets, places, and "things he liked--writing and drinking
in particular." But the over-all effect, even from a
poet consciously plumbing the terrifying depths of the
psychic interior, is haughty rather than fearful.

53 LEVERTOV, DENISE. "The Mail." Atlantic Monthly, CCXXII
(December), 34-35.
Response to "The Greatest American Poet," by James
Dickey, 1968.B29. Dickey's views are not supportable.
But the article has autobiographical value as Dickey
identifies with Roethke.

54 LOWELL, ROBERT. Paris Review interview by Frederick Seidel.
Robert Lowell: A Collection of Critical Essays. Edited
by Thomas Parkinson. Englewood Cliffs, N.J.: Prentice-
Hall, pp. 30-31.
Reprint of 1961.B56; See also 1963.B52.

55 LUCAS, JOHN. "The Poetry of Theodore Roethke." Oxford Review,
VIII (Trinity), 39-64.
Under discussion are Roethke's reputation; his role-
playing vs. genuineness; his "voice" in the poems (especially The Lost Son), poems where little seems to take
place; the privacy of his language (especially in Praise
to the End!), and its "tricksiness"; breakdowns in meaning
out of fear of sexual involvement; his failure because of
"misunderstanding or misinterpretation of his difficulties";
the factitious result of combined Stevens and Eliot influences in The Far Field.

56 MATHER, BOBBY. "A Capstone Biography of a Tortured Poet."
Detroit Free Press, November 10, page unknown (from the
Roethke collection, University of Washington).
Review of The Glass House, by Allan Seager. The reviewer
regrets the "gray area" that covers Roethke's dealings with

1968

women.  The article is favorable and devotes considerable
space to previous meetings between the reviewer and Seager.

57   MEINKE, PETER.  Howard Nemerov.  (UMPAW #70.)  Minneapolis:
     University of Minnesota Press, p. 16.
         Roethke is spoken of as an influence on Nemerov's
     poetry.

58   MEYERS, DUANE H.  "Roethke Praised in Seager Book."  Daily
     Oklahoman (Oklahoma City), December 29, page unknown (from
     the Roethke collection, University of Washington).
         Review of The Glass House, by Allan Seager.  In a low-
     key manner "Seager succeeds in convincing the reader that
     Roethke was an honest human and a very good poet; perhaps
     the best American poet of the post-war period."

59   MIRANDA, GARY.  "The Pig."  Minnesota Review, VIII:4, 358.
         A poem in tribute to Roethke.

60   MORGAN, MURRAY.  "The New Books."  The Argus (Seattle), LXXV
     (May 24), 8.
         Review of Selected Letters.  "The Roethke of these let-
     ters is less exposed than the artist of the poems.  In
     most he affects a posture, a conscious stance."  The re-
     viewer sees similarities, not in the letters, but the lives,
     between Roethke and Dylan Thomas, despite the former's
     disclaimer:  "'I never went to school to him.'"  "One
     suspects that among letters not selected for publication
     are some that reflect more fully the wild, witty, bawdy,
     melancholy man whose campus personality was that of a
     tornado on a long leash."

61   MURRAY, JAMES G.  "Words--good, bad, indifferent."  Long
     Island (N.Y.) Catholic, November 21, page unknown (from
     the Roethke collection, University of Washington).
         Review of The Glass House, by Allan Seager.  "...poor
     tragic Roethke relied on words as a crutch, using them as
     a prescription for mental health.  They finally tripped
     him up, the ultimate irony being that, whereas the words
     of the poems marvelously succeeded, the life without words
     (the state of the soul, the feelings, relationships, all
     the unspoken acts and postures of a man) sadly failed."

62   NEMEROV, HOWARD.  "The Mail."  Atlantic Monthly, CCXXII
     (December), 34.
         Response to "The Greatest American Poet," by James
     Dickey, 1968.B29.  Entire note:  "I enjoyed Jim Dickey's
     candor, and trust his essay is as judicious as candid."

63  PHILBRICK, CHARLES. "A Poet Out of Eden." Providence (R.I.)
    Journal, December 8, page unknown (from the Roethke collec-
    tion, University of Washington).
        Review of The Glass House, by Allan Seager. Among dis-
    cussions of what biographies of poets are and should do,
    and a sketchy outline of events in Roethke's life, the
    reviewer says: "I suppose that the main connection between
    the Roethke in this book and the writer of the poems lies
    in the apparent fact that he sought a series of surrogate
    fathers, at the same time wanting to be a 'father'--big
    and rich."

64  RILEY, PETER. "New English Poetry." Levende Talen (Nether-
    lands), CCXXXIV, 228-229.
        Review of The Far Field. Roethke's insistence on writing
    the short lyric, or his failure to see how his style is
    unsuited to the short line, lowers his stature as a poet.
    The "long-lined expansive poems" are best, full of accumu-
    lated detail of description. Though "uneconomical," they
    are genuinely felt. "It is when Roethke goes beyond
    description that he fails." He philosophizes and "so
    often reduces the value of his poems by fastening onto
    nature his own dissatisfaction with human life"; or he
    "cheats" reality with rhetoric.

65  RILLIE, JOHN A. M. "Menagerie and Greenhouse." Glasgow
    Herald, May 2, page unknown (from the Roethke collection,
    University of Washington).
        Review of Collected Poems. Roethke will "tax and tear
    you," despite the fact that "his sensibility makes a
    strange and stark world bereft of others."

66  ROETHKE, BEATRICE. "The Mail." Atlantic Monthly, CCXXII
    (December), 41-42.
        Response to "The Greatest American Poet," by James Dickey,
    1968.B29. Points out Dickey's "errors" in his treatment of
    the Roethke-Seager relationship; Roethke's "lies"; the autho-
    rization for Seager to write the biography; the supposed
    withheld permission; and Seager's freedom of material.

67  ROSENTHAL, M. L. "Poet's Story." New York Times Book Review,
    November 24, pp. 12, 16, 18.
        Review of The Glass House, by Allan Seager. Roethke was
    "a casualty of the general War on Nerves," and the review-
    er's first thought was that Seager's book only mismanaged
    privy information. Yet there are valuable revelations
    about Roethke's relation to his father and his work. Some
    reminiscences explain the reviewer's personal image of the

developing poet, extremes of confidence in himself that
made a lasting impression. Many friends, such as A. J. M.
Smith, Stanley Kunitz, Caroline Kizer and Rolfe Humphries,
protected him from the "philistines."

68  RUMLEY, LARRY. "Theodore Roethke's Letters Published by U.W.
Press." Seattle Times Magazine, May 5, p. 1.
Review of Selected Letters. Brief outline of Roethke's
life as evident from Ralph Mills' selection of the letters.
Some excerpts are included, but little critical comment.

69  SCHEVILL, JAMES. "The Mail." Atlantic Monthly, CCXXII
(December), 34.
Response to "The Greatest American Poet," by James
Dickey, 1968.B29. Questions the manner of the article and
treatment of Seager and Mrs. Roethke.

70  SEAMON, RICHARD. "The Mail." Atlantic Monthly, CCXXII
(December), 35-36.
Response to "The Greatest American Poet," by James
Dickey, 1968.B29. What Roethke told were not lies, but
fantasies.

71  SHAPIRO, KARL. "Case History of a Poet's Crack-Ups." Book
World (Chicago Tribune), October 13, p. 7.
"Here, with almost Flemish detail, we are treated to the
paltry minutiae of the poet Getting Ahead, the prideless
transactions of the poet as ninny. Was this necessary?"
Roethke played the poet to the hilt. "He knew romantically
that life is elsewhere but could never find Elsewhere on
the map."

72  _____. "The Death of Randall Jarrell." To Abolish Children/
And Other Essays. Chicago: Quadrangle Books, p. 154.
Reprint of 1967.B72.

73  _____. "Is Poetry an American Art?" To Abolish Children/
And Other Essays. Chicago: Quadrangle Books, p. 60.
Reprint of 1964.B52.

74  _____. "A Malebolge of Fourteen Hundred Books." To Abolish
Children/ And Other Essays. Chicago: Quadrangle Books,
p. 248.
Reprint of 1964.B53.

75  SLAUGHTER, WILLIAM R. "Roethke's 'Song.'" Minnesota Review,
VIII:4, 342-344.
The author sees this poem as representative of the crea-
tive act in each of several modes, the sexual, the

religious and the artistic. The lover, worshipper and
poet plumb their own personalities for "the human-child of
the sexual act, the Christ-child of the religious act, and
the poem-child of the artistic act (all of which are holy
objects)." The result is a "song," the product of creation, that endures.

76  SNODGRASS, W. D. "The Mail." Atlantic Monthly, CCXXII
      (December), 34.
        Response to "The Greatest American Poet," by James
      Dickey, 1968.B29. Support for Dickey's ideas, though
      questioning Roethke's stature.

77  STAFFORD, WILLIAM. "The Mail." Atlantic Monthly, CCXXII
      (December), 36.
        Response to "The Greatest American Poet," by James
      Dickey, 1968.B29. Talks of northwest poets, Dickey's own
      deserved status and the psychology of the word "greatest."

78  SUGGINS, CLARA M. "Theodore Roethke: Poet of Symbols."
      Boston Evening Globe, November 20, page unknown (from the
      Roethke collection, University of Washington).
        Review of The Glass House, by Allan Seager. Seager's
      book is a plea for understanding and appreciation. The
      review dwells primarily on Roethke's periods of mental
      illness, but with the recognition that he returned from
      these "bouts" to productive writing and teaching.

79  SWIFT, JOAN. "John Crowe Ransom Reads Theodore Roethke."
      Southern Review, NS IV (April), 339.
        A poem in tribute to Roethke.

80  SYMONS, JULIAN. "New Poetry." Punch, CCLIV (June 19), 902.
        Review of Collected Poems. Roethke was a garrulous and
      naive poet, with a remarkable ability to personify nature.
      "I suppose it would be fair to say that he never found a
      fully personal style, but his continual experiments have
      their own virtues."

81  THWAITE, ANTHONY. "Guts, Brain, Nerves." New Statesman,
      May 17, p. 659.
        Review of Collected Poems. "Roethke, all guts.... His
      best poems, written in the late Forties and early Fifties,
      were an odd elemental compound of worms's-eye-view,
      infant's sing-song and clumsiness--the clumsiness itself
      imposing a kind of artifice, a style, on the lowly, prim-
      itive, incoherent matter." Roethke's love affairs with
      others' style was "chameleon-like" and he was rightly

1968

angered by critics' dismissal of him as an imitator, "for underneath the adopted masks and cadences a vivid and original poet was eager to be released." But the gut level of experience was a limitation because "willed insights into mindless flux can't be indulged too often by an urban, literary, 20th-century man, without playing up a kind of falsity. Roethke's primitivism sorted oddly with his sophistication; at his best, both go together without one being awkwardly aware of the second."

82   TOYNBEE, PHILIP   "Not Among Her Admirers."   Observer (London), May 5, p. 26.
       Review of Collected Poems.  "Roethke was buffeted by influences for the whole of his writing life."  "And in every case Roethke's verse suffered agonies of indigestion at the start; yet in every case he managed to assimilate the new master and make something original out of the new mixture."  As he bewails his lost innocence, Roethke is never more than a "superb minor poet."

83   TRUESDALE, C. W.   "Theodore Roethke and the Landscape of American Poetry."   Minnesota Review, VIII:4, 345-358.
       The author suggests "that Roethke is a distinctly 'American' poet, that he strikes me as being very firmly within the continuing traditions of American Romanticism, that his return to the Greenhouse world of his childhood was comparable in many essential ways to the extraordinary prevalence in our literature of similar journeys, and that, in his own way, he has, like Thoreau and Melville and Twain, restored to the great American motherland its vitality, freshness, and immediacy. His poetry is as thoroughly Romantic (and limited) as Whitman's, in the sense that it is deeply subjective and self-absorbed; but it is deeply universal too in its amazing ability to create out of his own character a sacred experience wholly consistent with the great religious poetry of the world. His sensibility grows like a flower through the American soil towards the universal light."

84   UNTERMEYER, LOUIS.   "Multifaceted Portrait of a Multifaceted Poet."   Saturday Review, LI (November 9), 36, 39.
       Review of The Glass House, by Allan Seager. The treatment of Roethke's life is passable. But what the reviewer wants is some insight into the poetry from the life and its influences. "Poetry was Roethke's therapy."

85   WAGER, WILLIS.   "Return: Wilbur, Albee, Morris."   American Literature: A World View. New York: New York University Press; London: University of London Press, pp. 250-251.

1969

Capsule account of Roethke's major works and themes, teaching career and some biographical information.

86  WAGGONER, HYATT.  American Poets:  From the Puritans to the Present.  Boston:  Houghton Mifflin, pp. 563-577.
    Roethke comes close to the American tradition of Emerson, Whitman and Dickinson in his transcendentalism.  He sought to see by "embracing, incorporating."  There are both philosophical and verbal parallels.  The tradition goes further back, to Vaughan, Traherne and Blake.

87  WHARTON, WILL.  "Roethke:  'Ragging Discontent with Self.'"  St. Louis Globe-Democrat, November 2, page unknown (from the Roethke collection, University of Washington).
    Review of The Glass House, by Allan Seager.  After calling Roethke "the representative American poet," the author proceeds briefly to summarize some of the major incidents of Roethke's life.

88  WIGGINS, ALLEN.  "Roethke...About His Life."  Cleveland Plain Dealer, December 22, page unknown (from the Roethke collection, University of Washington).
    Review of The Glass House, by Allan Seager.  "Theodore Roethke was probably the least gifted important poet America has produced.  Throughout his career, Roethke's subjects, his words, his meters were versions of his own body--big, fat, awkward and weak in the knees."  Yet "In the end, Roethke made some of the most haunting poetry of nature mysticism in the language, and he became, in this industrialized country, a kind of desolate oracle of the simple, prodigal earth.  We are in his debt."

## 1969 A BOOKS

1  GLOEGE, RANDALL G.  "Suspension of Belief in the Poetry of Theodore Roethke."  DAI 31:757A (Bowling Green State University).

2  LaBELLE, JENIJOY.  "Theodore Roethke and Tradition:  'The Pure Serene of Memory in One Man.'"  DAI 30:  2029A (University of California at San Diego).

3  LEWANDOWSKI, MARYLOU.  "Tradition and the Original Talent of Theodore Roethke."  DAI 31:  4170A (State University of New York at Binghamton).

1969

1969 B SHORTER WRITINGS

1    ALVAREZ, A.  "Sylvia Plath."  Beyond All This Fiddle:  Essays
     1955-1967.  New York:  Random House, p. 47.
        Reprint of 1963.B1; See also 1968.B1, 1968.B2.

2    ANON.  Reveiw of Selected Letters.  Choice, V (January), 1446.
        This is a valuable volume even though Roethke's letters
     are not as informative of his poetic personality as other
     documents.

3    ANON.  Review of The Glass House, by Allan Seager.  Booklist,
     LXV (February 15), 633.
        "Roethke's poetic method, teaching enthusiasm, recogni-
     tions, friendships, and erratic behavior are fully covered.
     The reasons for his occasional mental illness are not
     fully solved, but the personality of a difficult and oddly
     appealing man and poet is presented with clarity."

4    ANON.  "Profiles of American Authors:  Roethke, Ciardi,
     Wagoner:  Poets Who Are Also Teachers."  English Teaching
     Forum (United States Information Agency), VII (May-June),
     11-16.
        Roethke's "Words for Young Writers--from the Notes of
     Theodore Roethke," arranged by David Wagoner, is reprinted,
     with John Ciardi's introduction, from the Saturday Review.
     This makes up Part I (pp. 11-14).  Part II (pp. 15-16) con-
     sists of excerpts from Theodore Roethke, by Ralph J.
     Mills, Jr.

5    ANON.  "Theodore Roethke:  Collected Poems."  T.L.S. Essays
     and Reviews from The Times Literary Supplement--1968.
     London:  Oxford University Press, pp. 99-102.
        Reprint of 1968.B6.

6    ATLAS, JAMES.  "Roethke's Boswell."  Poetry, CXIV (August),
     327-330.
        Review of The Glass House, by Allan Seager.  Roethke
     never relinquished his origins.  And though Seager does
     capture much of the early Saginaw years, he fails to do
     much with Roethke as poet.  He does not reconcile the poems
     to the life.  What emerges "is a confusing image of a poet
     lost in the turmoil of his own pre-occupations, yearning
     for the recognition which he thought would appease his ego
     and his guilt, contriving to win the Nobel Prize even after
     he had won the Pulitzer, and dreaming of his father's
     resurrection from an early death."

7   BOWERMAN, DONALD.  "Theodore Roethke:  A Houseman Echo."
      Notes & Queries, NS XVI (July), 266.
        Houseman's "The Immortal Part," XLII, A Shropshire Lad,
      is heard in Roethke's "Death Piece."

8   BOYERS, ROBERT.  "The Roethke Puzzle."  New Republic, CLX
      (January 18), 32-34.
        Review of The Glass House, by Allan Seager.  "Theodore
      Roethke, certainly a major American poet, was to an almost
      unbelievable degree a liar and a boor."  His continuous
      mental illness is not satisfactorily explained, either by
      Seager, or in his poems.  The biography does not show the
      relation of Roethke's poems to his life, nor the life's
      relation to its time.  But the latter is a failing of
      Roethke, not Seager.  The book is crucial, despite its
      distance.  But, perhaps, "Roethke needs this handling if
      he is to remain tolerable at all."

9   CIARDI, JOHN.  "Comments on Theodore Roethke."  Cimarron Review,
      No. 7 (March), pp. 6-8.
        A reminiscence that stresses Roethke's violently compet-
      itive nature at sports and his fantasies about mobsters.
      Ciardi's poem, "Was a Man," is reprinted here.

10  CLARK, JON.  "On the Diagonal."  Michigan Quarterly Review,
      VIII (Winter), 1.
        A sketch on the life and works of Allan Seager, with
      special mention of his last book, The Glass House.  The
      book was to have been published the previous year (1967),
      but instead was delayed (because of objections made by
      Mrs. Roethke) until after Seager's death (May 10, 1968).
      In Seager's final months, "with failing health and energy,
      he had to tone down and discard passage after passage
      against his insistent sense of integrity, against the un-
      usually strong urge for accurate detail that pervades all
      his fiction, against his own deep involvement in writing
      what he now knew to be his last work on earth, this life
      of a man in whom he saw his own life and creative turmoil."

11  COLUSSI, D. L.  "Roethke's 'The Gentle.'"  Explicator, XXVII
      (May), Item 73.
        At question is the shallowness/depth of Roethke's dream.
      Horace is the dream persona, perhaps a "caricature of that
      true poet, the gentile (pagan) and often-walking Roman."
      "Bunion" is the central image and dominates the theme of
      attempting to write poetry, or "hiking."

# Theodore Roethke's Career: An Annotated Bibliography

1969

12  COTT, JONATHAN. "Two Dream Poets: Theodore Roethke and John
    Berryman." On Contemporary Literature. Edited by Richard
    Kostelanetz. Second, Expanded, Edition. New York: Avon
    Books, 1964, 1969, pp. 520-531.
        Roethke is linked with Berryman with each being a dis-
    tinct kind of "dream" poet. Roethke's search for the self
    is so obvious that Freud and Jung are superfluous. His
    province is of "minimals." "In Roethke's poems, the ideal
    is delineated only by the identity the poet makes between
    his psyche and the world. Both are the same—as in the
    womb or in dreams—and this is the world of Roethke's
    poetry."

13  CURLEY, DOROTHY NYREN, with MAURICE KRAMER and ELAINE FIALKA
    KRAMER, eds. A Library of Literary Criticism, Volume III.
    New York: Frederick Ungar Publishing Co., pp. 86-93.
        Excerpts from reviews by many of Roethke's most notable
    critics, including Auden, Kunitz, Burke, Schwartz, James
    Dickey, etc.

14  DEMBO, L. S. Review of The Glass House, by Allan Seager.
    American Literature, XLI (May), 305.
        Despite the exhaustive research involved in Seager's
    book, "it is not really a literary biography." He has not
    explored the poet in psychological depth, not in his sig-
    nificant cultural role as teacher, settling, rather, for
    a "heavily documented character study."

15  DEUTSCH, BABETTE. "Lament for the Makers: 1964." The Col-
    lected Poems of Babette Deutsch. New York: Doubleday &
    Co., pp. 5-6.
        Reprint of 1964.B21.

16  DeVANY, JULIA C. Review of The Glass House, by Allan Seager;
    and Selected Letters. Spirit, XXXVI (Spring), 37-39.
        Though a highly favorable portrait, Allan Seager's biog-
    raphy of Theodore Roethke is successful in the creation of
    a life, and the creation of an entire poetic era. Roethke
    is accurately depicted as a man viewing his circle "with
    the objectivity of an outsider." There is, in Ralph Mills'
    selection of Roethke's letters, "despite its professional
    slant, the emergence of an intensely emotional, witty,
    honest and plain-spoken man." Here too, however, Roethke
    seems an unusually likeable individual.

17  EDWARDS, THOMAS "Roethke." Alkahest, No. 3 (Fall), pp. 22-23.
        A poem in tribute to Roethke.

1969

18   FREER, COBURN. "Book Reviews." Arizona Quarterly, XXV
      (Spring), 83-85.
         Review of The Glass House, by Allan Seager. "The extent
      to which Roethke willingly created his own history is both
      interesting and appalling." The biography comes off well
      as a "well-researched memoir." Roethke's attitude toward
      himself as a thug, a criminal, is briefly discussed in
      Freudian terms.

19   GARMON, GERALD M. "Roethke's 'Open House.'" Explicator,
      XXVIII (November), Item 27.
         Roethke's expression of love is by a poet for his work,
      not a man for a woman. His poetic purpose is clarity.

20   GELPI, ALBERT. "He Wrote Searching, and Found." Christian
      Science Monitor, January 23, p. 11.
         Review of The Glass House, by Allan Seager. His native
      Saginaw, the greenhouses and his father's death, leaving
      him in isolation, are seen as the sources of Roethke's
      poetry. He was an extremely vulnerable man. Yet he
      "learned to use his anxieties as the source of his poems
      and conversely to use poetry to delve beneath the conscious
      surface of the psyche to those dark and turbid depths
      where contradictions lay locked in conflict." Seager's
      view that Roethke came to see his father as the Father
      "does not explain, or explain away, Roethke's profound
      religious sense, his involvement with mystical and theo-
      logical thought, and his deepening vision of a God not
      just transcendent but incarnate." Seager's account re-
      mains too external.

21   HAMBURGER, MICHAEL. The Truth of Poetry: Tensions in Modern
      Poetry from Baudelaire to the 1960s. New York: Harcourt,
      Brace & World, pp. 282-283.
         The "early flower poems" ("Orchids" is the example cited
      here) are, in a sense, "part of Roethke's autobiography,
      an exploration of those subconscious layers of the person-
      ality which remain intimately related to the animal,
      vegetable and even mineral orders." The author uses this
      discussion to define modern nature poetry in distinction
      from Romantic nature poetry.

22   HARPER, GEORGE. "A Study Sensitive to a Fault." St. Peters-
      burg (Fla.) Times, January 12, p. 5G.
         Review of The Glass House, by Allan Seager. The author
      takes exception to Seager's treatment of "academics" and
      recounts his personal experience with Roethke at the award
      dinner of the Poetry Society of America in 1962.

1969

23  HARRINGTON, MICHAEL. "No Half-Baked Bacchus from Saginaw."
     Commonweal, LXXXIX (February 21), 656-657.
          Review of The Glass House, by Allan Seager. Seager's
     biography is not probing, but perhaps is acceptable.
     Harrington deals primarily with Roethke's Americanness and
     modernity.

24  HAYMAN, RONALD. "From Hart Crane to Gary Snyder." Encounter,
     XXXII (February), 73-76.
          Review of Collected Poems. Two principle questions:
     1. Did Roethke digest his borrowings from Eliot, Yeats,
     Dylan Thomas and Whitman?; 2. Did he go beyond the achieve-
     ment of the "greenhouse" poems? Roethke's undefined vision
     causes failure in some of his poems, such as "Four for Sir
     John Davies." The worst failures "come in trying to endow
     all three kinds of natural life with an aura of super-
     natural significance." Too, he lacks humor.

25  HENRY, NAT. "Roethke's 'I Knew a Woman.'" Explicator, XXVII
     (January), Item 31.
          Previous Explicator writers "have been entrapped in the
     assumption of a dance metaphor." "Working a subliminal
     welter of figures from hunting and farming, Roethke implies
     that for him the woman was a combination of Artemis
     (huntress), Demeter (Earth Mother), and Venus in her
     tutorial role."

26  HEYEN, WILLIAM. "The Divine Abyss: Theodore Roethke's
     Mysticism." Texas Studies in Literature and Language, XI
     (Summer), 1051-1068.
          Under discussion is Roethke's realization of the role his
     madness plays in his art: "the divine abyss becomes for
     Roethke a symbol of man's fortunate fall." Roethke prob-
     ably knew and felt drawn to Evelyn Underhill's Mysticism:
     A Study of Man's Spiritual Consciousness. "The Abyss" is
     examined as "a striking summary of Roethke's mysticism."
     See also 1971.B18.

27  HOCHMAN, SANDRA. "Letter--Dickey on Seager on Roethke."
     Atlantic Monthly, CCXXIII (February), 38.
          A request for more work like Dickey's. See 1968.B29.

28  HOWARD, RICHARD. Review of Selected Letters. Poetry, CXIII
     (February), 359-360.
          "It was when he stood outside himself, 'beyond becoming
     and perishing,' that Roethke was himself most rewardingly....
     But in these anxious griping letters, compounded of sorry
     gossip and simple need, the poet is only one. The wrong
     one."

29   JOHNSON, KENNETH.   Review of Selected Letters.   Midcontinent
        American Studies Journal, X (Fall), 81-82.
            A Roethke letter of 1958 to John Holmes says "This is
        at once a word of greeting and a cry for help."   The re-
        viewer understands this statement as symptomatic of
        Roethke's life and letters.   The insights provided into the
        poems make the book valuable.

30   LASK, THOMAS.   "Life Was as Difficult as Art."   New York Times,
        January 1, p. 19.
            Review of Selected Letters and The Glass House, by Allan
        Seager.   "You would never gather from these letters that
        Roethke was a successful and recognized poet."   "That
        surge for fame moved forward like a clumsy, unstoppable
        tank."   Seager minimizes none of the complexities of
        Roethke and it is only side by side, complementing each
        other, that the two books can be wholly successful.

31   LONGLEY, MICHAEL.   Review of Collected Poems.   Dublin Magazine,
        VIII (Spring/Summer), 86-88.
            After Frost, Roethke is the finest twentieth century
        American poet because he accepted the "great tradition of
        poetry in English."   He was one of the few "who have
        tackled profoundly the schizophrenic tensions which result
        when a European inheritance pulls against an American lo-
        cale."   Roethke's Collected Poems is a paradigm of this
        massive effort:   early poems of unselfconscious childhood
        experiences; the uncertain middle poems reaching out to
        absorb disparate influences, such as Clare, Yeats, Whitman
        and Blake; and the final synthesis apparent in, particu-
        larly, the 'North American Sequence' from The Far Field.

32   MAGNUSON, KRISTIN.   "Poet-Teachers Blend Verse and Lectures in
        Dual Role."   University of Washington Daily, April 17,
        p. 12.
            Roethke's name is incidentally mentioned as a reason for
        the University of Washington's high place as a poetry cen-
        ter.   The article is about five teaching poets currently
        on the faculty.

33   MALKOFF, KARL.   "For Theodore Roethke."   Southwest Review,
        LIV (Summer), 247.
            A poem in tribute to Roethke.

34   _____.   "Roethke:   The Poet as Albatross."   Southwest Review,
        LIV (Summer), 329-332.
            Review of The Glass House, by Allan Seager and Selected
        Letters.   Roethke's "work, at its best, communicates the

215

full terror of the specifically human struggle to exist."
Seager in his account of Otto Roethke's death, "gives
further significance to the sense of guilt and the need
for reconciliation that mark Roethke's treatment of his
father in verse." Roethke was not a "confessional" poet.
He carefully selected, and even distorted, details to
create "a private myth specifically calculated to bear the
weight of his public vision." Though not proving, the
biography evokes sympathy for a terrified man. Though
primarily self-centered and concerned with the "business"
of poetry, Roethke's letters do show his "frenzied energy."

35    MARTZ, WILLIAM J.  John Berryman.  UMPAW # 85.  Minneapolis:
      University of Minnesota Press, p. 35.
         Roethke is here mentioned with Berryman as the creators
      of the "only" two great long poems to emerge in American
      poetry following World War II, "North American Sequence"
      and Homage to Mistress Bradstreet.

36    MAXWELL, J. C.  "Notes on Theodore Roethke."  Notes & Queries,
      NS XVI (July), 265-266.
         A number of items of Roethke criticism are questioned:
      a variant reading of "Big Wind"; supposed mistakes by
      Ursula Genung Walker and Karl Malkoff in their respective
      books on Roethke; Karl Malkoff's interpretation of an
      ambiguous line in "The Waking"; Roethke's reliance on
      John Heath-Stubbs for his final line in "The Dying Man";
      and the use of the rare word "roundy," which Hopkins may
      well be behind.

37    McCLELLAN, ELWOOD.  "Theodore Roethke:  A Review Article."
      Michigan History, LIII (Winter), 319-322.
         Review of The Glass House, by Allan Seager and Selected
      Letters.  Neither the Letters nor The Glass House do much
      to "shed light on the relationship between his (Roethke's)
      life and his poetry."  The reviewer, a former student of
      Allan Seager, finds the Letters "sophomoric and self-
      pitying," and the biography assuming much more about
      Roethke's relationship to his father than can realistically
      be assumed.

38    McMICHAEL, JAMES.  "The Poetry of Theodore Roethke."  Southern
      Review, NS V (Winter), 4-25.
         Roethke's work is a journey out of the self.  Discussing
      it leads to considerations of the nature of his God, meta-
      phor, mindlessness, sexual desires, the unity of experience,
      the relation of body and soul.  There is a close examina-
      tion of the "North American Sequence" from The Far Field
      and its final symbol, the rose.

39  MILLS, RALPH J., JR. <u>Creation's Very Self: On the Personal</u>
    <u>Element in Recent American Poetry</u>. Fort Worth: Texas
    Christian University Press, pp. 8–13.
       The author distinguishes "modernist" from "contemporary"
    poets by the relation the poet chooses his own personality
    to have to his poem. Roethke, a contemporary, seeks "a
    personal mode of utterance to embody perceivings and
    intuitions very much" his own. The self cannot, should
    not, be separated from the poem. The process of develop-
    ing a style and idiom is one of "Second Birth" (James
    Dickey's term) and Roethke's progress toward his own voice
    is just this. It can be, and in his case was, a painful
    experience. But, speaking of the more intense self-
    examination in "The Lost Son," "past experience which came
    alive then in his imagination finds a language that car-
    ries it to the page with the urgency and sensuous immediacy
    of life itself." The later love poems and meditations con-
    tinue "his relentless pursuit of personal unity of being
    through the relation of self to the beloved, to the cosmos,
    and finally to God." In the act of writing Roethke remakes
    himself into a distinctive poetic personality. <u>See also</u>
    1965.B63.

40  MOODY, MINNIE HITE. "A Friend's-Eye View of a Tormented Poet."
    <u>Columbus</u> (Ohio) <u>Sunday Dispatch</u>, January 5, page unknown
    (from the Roethke collection, University of Washington).
       Review of <u>The Glass House</u>, by Allan Seager. Roethke is
    "the big, vain, introverted, clumsy, neurotic, tormented
    man who desperately needed friends but all too often ten-
    dered their friendship a shabby response."

41  O'GORMAN, NED. "Theodore Roethke and Paddy Flynn." <u>Columbia</u>
    <u>University Forum</u>, XII (Spring), 34–36.
       Review of <u>The Glass House</u>, by Allan Seager. Considering
    Roethke's poetic vitality, Seager's "ungainly detachment"
    in his biography is disconcerting. O'Gorman proceeds to
    give his own evaluation of Roethke as man and poet. "He
    was too large a man for English departments and their in-
    trigues." "There is a Vergilian music to his poetry, so
    rooted in the landscape of his youth, so troubled by the
    shades." Lowell, Stevens, and Dickinson are poets close
    to Roethke in spirit, but with Yeats there is a trouble-
    some kinship. Roethke's work, unlike Yeats', frequently
    points to an event that is not there. From this point
    O'Gorman generalizes about the weaknesses of American
    poetry.

1969

42  PAUL, SHERMAN. "Making It as a Poet." Nation, CCVIII
        (January 6), 27.
            Review of The Glass House, by Allan Seager and Selected
        Letters. The letters "record an education, in Roethke's
        case a maturation--obliquely, however, at a distinct re-
        move from the mind that made the poems." But the biography
        seems only the "scenario of the life." "The critical re-
        ception of Roethke's books interests him more than the
        forces within and without that enabled Roethke, time after
        time, to go beyond his past performances certainly, a
        variety of forces and not only his breakdowns are respon-
        sible for his poetic progress." Roethke as a performer;
        as a writer of children's books; as one obsessed with the
        theme of "the writhing forms of his secret life"; each of
        these deserves more in-depth treatment.

43  PEARCE, ROY HARVEY. "Theodore Roethke: The Power of Sympathy."
        Historicism Once More: Problems and Occasions for the
        American Scholar. Princeton, N.J.: Princeton University
        Press, pp. 294-326.
            Reprint of 1965.B67.

44  PFEIFFER, TED. "Theodore Roethke Was a Poet--All the Way."
        Louisville (Ky.) Times, January 7, page unknown (from the
        Roethke collection, University of Washington).
            Review of The Glass House, by Allan Seager. Roethke was
        better as a teacher than poet. The reviewer says little
        more in the way of evaluation, except that the book "is a
        fascinating study of the working of the creative poetic
        mind."

45  ROTHERMEL, J. F. "Roethke Walked the Fine Line Between Insan-
        ity and Genius." Birmingham (Alabama) News, January 26,
        page unknown (from the Roethke collection, University of
        Washington).
            Review of The Glass House, by Allan Seager. Roethke's
        complex personality is emphasized.

46  SCOTT, WINFIELD TOWNLEY. "a dirty hand": The Literary Note-
        books of Winfield Townley Scott. Forward by Merle
        Armitage. Austin & London: University of Texas Press,
        pp. 39, 88.
            Scott talks of Roethke's book, Praise to the End!, being
        considered for the National Book Award (Wallace Stevens
        said "It's terrible!"); and a "collected poems," probably
        The Waking, being considered for the Bollingen Prize.

47  SEAGER, JOAN. "Letter--Dickey on Seager on Roethke." Atlantic
    Monthly, CCXXIII (February), 38.
        Mrs. Seager comes to her husband's defense against
    Mrs. Roethke. See 1968.B29.

48  SERGEANT, HOWARD. "Poetry Review." English, XVIII (Spring),
    34.
        Review of Collected Poems. "Roethke...exhibits his in-
    fluences (Auden, Ransom, Thomas, Lowell, and especially
    Yeats) like battle-scars at the beginning of each new
    phase of development as if to mark the intensity of the
    struggle for sovereignty over his material. Yet for all
    that..., it is to Roethke that one turns for sheer creative
    zest, for deep personal concern and commitment, and for
    the celebration of life in all its rich complexity."

49  STEIN, ARNOLD. "Roethke: Man and Poet." Virginia Quarterly
    Review, XLV (Spring), 361-365.
        Review of The Glass House, by Allan Seager. "In short,
    though we end the book knowing a great deal more about
    Roethke the ordinary man, the effect of our knowledge is
    to make it clear that Roethke the extraordinary man slips
    through the laborious network of external evidence, a
    'shape-changer' from way back."

50  STYRON, NELL. "Roethke's Stormy Career Presented by Colleague."
    Columbia Missourian, January 26, page unknown (from the
    Roethke collection, University of Washington).
        Review of The Glass House, by Allan Seager. Favorable
    review that touches on a variety of aspects of Roethke's
    life for purposes of summary, but makes little critical
    comment.

51  TILLINGHAST, RICHARD. "Worlds of Their Own." Southern Review,
    NS V (Spring), 594-596.
        Review of Collected Poems. Roethke worried strangely
    about his reputation at the end--his heart was not in the
    later Eliotesque poems. Yet the 'North American Sequence'
    probably contains his greatest poems. The variety of
    poems, many successful, is remarkable.

52  VANDERHAAR, MARGARET. Review of The Glass House, by Allan
    Seager. New Orleans Review, I (Spring), 285-286.
        Even Seager's "loving bias cannot obscure the reader's
    impression that Theodore Roethke was coarse, self-centered,
    vain, boorish, petty, guilt-ridden, and totally uninter-
    ested in anything but his own career. It may be that for
    the more admirable side of the poet, we must indeed, as
    Mallarmé suggests, look to the poems."

1969

53   WEINIG, S. M. ANTHONY, S. H. C. J.   Review of The Glass House, by Allan Seager.  Best Sellers, XXVIII (January 1), 417.
      "Holding its chosen course between official and revelatory, the document is a reliable chart from which to plot further studies that can spare the details and develop the insights which Allan Seager lines up with precision and assurance."  The Roethke family's "German qualities" receive special mention, as does the poet's relation to his father, Otto.  What held Roethke together, even after periods of mental illness, was his "integrity as artist." His was a "hard-won wholeness" that made his poems what they are and contributed to an inspired teaching talent.

54   WESLING, DONALD.  "The Inevitable Ear:  Freedom and Necessity in Lyric Form, Wordsworth and After."  Journal of English Literary History (ELH), XXXVI (September), 544-561.
      Roethke is discussed as the author of "meditative poems, in which internalized speech is designed to represent a process of thought."  "Meditation at Oyster River" and "The Abyss" are examined in over-all structuring.  Roethke has come "further than Wordsworth in a fascination with dissolving identities, ...(he) longs to experience the pre-history of consciousness itself."

55   WILDER, AMOS N.  The New Voice:  Religion, Literature, Hermeneutics.  New York:  Herder and Herder.  Various pages, see index.
      Roethke is cited in discussion of several themes, especially love and transcendence.


1970 A BOOKS

1   BULLIS, JERALD.  "Theodore Roethke:  A Study of His Poetry."
     DAI 31:6593A (Cornell University).

2   GALVIN, BRENDAN JAMES.  "What the Grave Says, the Nest Denies: Burkean Strategies in Theodore Roethke's 'Lost Son' Poems."
     DAI 31:2384A-2385A (University of Massachusetts).

3   HAYDEN, MARY H.  "Theodore Roethke:  A Poetics of Space."
     DAI 31:4163A (University of California at Irvine).

4   KAIYALA, MARGUERITE L.  "The Poetic Development of Theodore Roethke in Relation to the Emersonian-Thoreauvian Tradition of Nature."  DAI 31:3507A-3508A (University of Washington).

# Writings about Theodore Roethke, 1922-1973

5 McDADE, GERARD F. "The Primitive Vision of Theodore Roethke: A Study of Aboriginal Elements in His Poetry." DAI 31:1806A (Temple University).

6 STEVENS, PHILIP BOYD. "A Study of Kinesthetic Imagery in Selected Poetry of Theodore Roethke." DAI 31:5560A (Northwestern University).

## 1970 B SHORTER WRITINGS

1 ANON. "Regents Do Their Thing (Again)...Building Named...." University of Washington Daily, February 17, p. 11.
A new auditorium under construction at the university will be named after Roethke.

2 ANON. "Mistakable Identity." London Times Literary Supplement, July 23, p. 790. Review of Selected Letters.
Roethke's letter-writing style is weak--"there is little sense of care and liking for the letter as a form." Also discussed are Roethke's manic-depressive psychology and his "I-love-me" syndrome. Even his comments on other poets illuminate little, descending to the "level of the merely competitive." His main achievement lies in the "flower, vegetable, and greenhouse poems," full of childhood. The letters are of a harried man.

3 ANON. "Allan Seager Papers." Bancroftiana, No. 47 (October), p. 5.
Notice of the recent purchase by the Bancroft Library, University of California at Berkeley, of Seager's papers, including the manuscript of The Glass House. "Along with drafts and galleys for the Roethke book are numerous interviews which Seager conducted with persons who had known the poet at various times in his life; as much of this latter material was not included in the text, and as the printed version differs in many ways from the projected biography, the files are indeed valuable to all future Roethke studies."

4 BRINNAN, JOHN MALCOLM. "Roethke Plain." Atlantic Monthly, CCXXV (March), 58-60.
A poem in tribute to Roethke.

5 BROWN, ASHLEY. "Playing for Keeps." Spectator, July 4 and 11, p. 16.
Review of Selected Letters. Roethke was shrewd about his talent, drawing on wholly English and American resources, but depending upon his "personal myth" more than most poets.

1970

He was aggressive about the poets of the preceding generation, constantly competing with them. This is the source
of much of his accomplishment.

6   BULLIS, JERALD.  "Theodore Roethke." Massachusetts Review,
      XI (Winter), 209-212.
         Review of The Glass House, by Allan Seager and Selected
      Letters.  Roethke's letters "show us a man vacillating
      between making it as a poet and making it as a poet, with
      the greater emphasis, finally, on the latter desire."
      Though not a professional critic, Roethke showed a "keen,
      if idiosyncratic, critical judgement."  The biography is
      a credible, "novelistic" book.

7   GANGEWERE, R. J.  "Theodore Roethke:  The Future of a Reputa-
      tion."  Carnegie Series in English, XI.  Pittsburgh:
      Carnegie-Mellon University, pp. 65-73.
         Though consistently interesting as a poet, Roethke's
      sphere of influence has not expanded since his death.  The
      author predicts such expansion in the approaches to poetry
      offered by Freudian and Jungian psychology; the recogni-
      tion of the affinity between Roethke and Eastern mystics,
      a more "transcendent" symbolism to supplement that of
      traditional Christianity; and the technical means employed
      by Roethke to extend his consciousness.  Finally, Roethke
      must be more clearly placed in the tradition of "confes-
      sional" poetry.

8   HARMON, WILLIAM.  "From 'Van Diemen's Land' (Book V of 'Looms')."
      Antioch Review, XXX (Fall/Winter 1970-1971), 445.
         A poem in tribute to Roethke.

9   HERON, PHILIP E.  "The Vision of Meaning:  Theodore Roethke's
      'Frau Bauman, Frau Schmidt, and Frau Schwartze.'"  Western
      Speech, XXXIV (Winter), 29-33.
         After much talk of nineteenth and twentieth century
      theories of "vision," Roethke's images of the three women,
      who are not really present, are discussed.  The author
      sees in the poem a "creation within and of a garden (that)
      resembles all creation."  The women are like witches,
      "mediators between the biological forces of life and
      individual instances of life."  In Roethke's vision, they
      change shapes in the place of the poem where "all experi-
      ence is provisional, shifting, all hypotheses, tentative,
      all meaning neither within, nor without, but between,
      precisely in the flux of perception."

10   HEYEN, WILLIAM. "In Memoriam: Theodore Roethke." <u>Southern Review</u>, NS VI (Winter), 181-184. (Reprinted in <u>Depth of Field</u>. Baton Rouge: Louisiana State University Press, 1970.)
     A poem in tribute to Roethke.

11   HOFFMAN, FREDERICK J. "Theodore Roethke: The Poetic Shape of Death." <u>Modern American Poetry</u>. Edited by Jerome Mazzaro. New York: David McKay Co., pp. 301-320.
     Reprint of 1965.B42.

12   JAFFE, DAN. "Theodore Roethke: 'In a Slow Up-Sway.'" <u>The Fifties: Fiction, Poetry, Drama</u>. Edited by Warren French. Deland, Fla.: Everett/Edwards, pp. 199-207.
     Despite receiving both a Pulitzer Prize and a National Book Award in the 1950's Roethke remained relatively anonymous among the publicity grabbers associated with the "movements" of the decade. This was true even though he had a desire for a wide audience. His poems reach for the broadest kinds of experience, always balancing energy and control. Roethke felt the need to share life, even the most intimate, and this was, culturally, a threat to the self-assurance of the times.

13   KRIM, SEYMOUR. "Inside the Greenhouse." <u>London Magazine</u>, NS X (September), 91-93.
     Review of <u>Selected Letters</u>. Roethke's "careerism," competition with living and dead poets, is very embarrassing. He "was a professional poet. But he was an amateur man." This is a "fatal vulnerability" in Roethke and most other American writers. Little of the man comes across in his "dry, too-utilitarian prose."

14   LANGBAUM, ROBERT. "The New Nature Poetry." <u>The Modern Spirit: Essays on the Continuity of Nineteenth and Twentieth Century Literature</u>. New York: Oxford University Press, pp. 116-117.
     An updated version of the author's 1959 essay in <u>American Scholar</u>. Roethke, though in the modern tradition of nature poetry with Lawrence, Frost, Moore and Ted Hughes, mines a different territory, that of the "pre-conscious existence of nature." In discussing "Meditation at Oyster River," the author states that Roethke wishes to regress to formlessness: "He longs to dissolve the configuration of self, and be one with the free-running river tides that flow into the bay."

1970

15    MANNER, GEORGE. "The Bear:  A Tribute to Theodore Roethke."
      Southern Review, NS VI (Winter), 170-171.
      A poem in tribute to Roethke.

16    MAZZARO, JEROME. "Theodore Roethke and the Failures of Lan-
      guage." Modern Poetry Studies, (Buffalo, N.Y.), I
      (July), 73-96.
      Roethke's difficulty of establishing a voice is examined
      here.  There is broad support for the idea of "poet-as-
      instrument."  But Mazzaro sees a failure of language
      "caused by linguistic differences between the internalized,
      primal, familial world of the greenhouse, Saginaw, and the
      tradition which Roethke sought to escape in Open House and
      that of Roethke's literary adult life." His management of
      rhetoric is also discussed, as well as the submergence of
      particulars in universals, and his technical influences.
      Roethke never possessed an authoritative language. See
      also 1971.B31.

17    ROSENTHAL, M. L. "Nervous Whale." New Statesman, July 10,
      p. 25.
      Review of Selected Letters.  A poet who went further
      than his natural gifts seemed to allow, Roethke in his
      letters is both "grossly calculating" and "a more touching,
      sympathetic persona."  One gets the impression of the Amer-
      ican literary milieu with Roethke, "a kind of underdeveloped
      Mauberly.  Disguised as a small, very nervous whale, he
      circles and dodges and splashes his way towards some
      heavenly algae-patch where only immortal leviathans feed."
      But a close reading gives a much broader spectrum of
      Roethke's personality even though Mills has scrupulously
      limited the letters to those centered on his literary
      career.

18    SCHUMACHER, PAUL J. "The Unity of Being:  A Study of Theodore
      Roethke's Poetry." Ohio University Review, XII:1, 20-40.
      Roethke "manifests a religious commitment to the unity
      of being as intense as that of the theologians Thomas
      Aquinas and Paul Tillich."  His poetry "constitutes a
      spiritual autobiography--the soul seeking to know itself
      within the ambit of a chaotic but benign world, a dark but
      illuminating subconscious, a silent but encompassing God--
      the quest for authentic existence within being."  There are
      distinguishable periods of this quest and the remainder of
      the essay identifies and expands upon them.  The first, in
      Open House, "is primarily an outer-inner world correlation;"
      then there is a shift, in The Lost Son and Praise to the
      End!, "to poems of subliminal analysis;" the third period,

of Words for the Wind and The Far Field, is devoted to
"consideration of non-being," a "new awareness of death-
time in Roethke's elliptical life-time," that led him to
search for different sanctuaries, such as love, and communion with the small.

19    SCHWARTZ, DELMORE.  "The Cunning and the Craft of the Uncon-
        scious and the Preconscious."  Selected Essays of Delmore
        Schwartz.  Chicago and London:  University of Chicago
        Press, pp. 197-199.
            Reprint of 1959.B60; See also 1971.B40.

20    SEXTON, ANNE.  "The Barfly Ought to Sing."  The Art of Sylvia
        Plath.  Edited by Charles Newman.  London:  Faber and
        Faber, p. 178.
            Reprint of 1965.B85.

21    SHEEHAN, DONALD.  Review of The Glass House, by Allan Seager.
        Modern Philology, LXVIII (August), 123-126.
            Roethke "appears to us in Seager's narrative so stark,
        so stick figure and two dimensional that we cannot even
        believe, let alone understand, the life it is supposed to
        represent--no one outside of exotic myth ever acted in
        this gracelessly simplistic way."  Roethke's mind "must
        have been for students surprising, exhilarating, and, in
        the end, deeply educative."  But Seager fails to convey
        much of it.

22    SPEARS, MONROE K.  Dionysus and the City.  New York:  Oxford
        University Press, pp. 247-250.
            Roethke's poetry, couched in "non-human visionary fears
        and adult madness," is remote and limited, "tending to
        obsessive concern with certain experiences and to incoher-
        ence on the verge of real obscurity."

23    STONE, JOHN H.  "A Note for Theodore Roethke."  Western Human-
        ities Review, XXIV (Summer), 260.
            A poem in tribute to Roethke.

24    THORNE, J. P.  "Generative Grammar and Stylistic Analysis."
        New Horizons in Linguistics, edited by John Lyons.
        Harmondsworth, England:  Penguin Books, pp. 194-196.
            The author examines Roethke's use of a deviant grammar
        in his poem "Dolour."

25    WARD, A. C.  "Roethke, Theodore."  Longman Companion to Twen-
        tieth Century Literature.  London:  Longman, p. 456.
            Two sentence biography.  Open House, Words for the Wind
        mentioned.

# Theodore Roethke's Career: An Annotated Bibliography

1971

## 1971 A BOOKS

1   HEYEN, WILLIAM, Ed. Profile of Theodore Roethke. Columbus,
    Ohio:  Charles E. Merrill.  Compiler's "Preface."
    pp. v–vi.
      The compiler reprints some of the more important, "sub-
    stantial" essays on Roethke and his poetry, thus ignoring
    shorter reviews and notes.  Eight articles, including
    those of Allan Seager, Stanley Kunitz (twice), John Ciardi,
    Kenneth Burke, Jerome Mazzaro, Delmore Schwartz, James
    McMichael, David Ferry and Heyen himself are reprinted.

2   McKENZIE, JAMES J.  "A New American Nature Poetry:  Theodore
    Roethke, James Dickey, and James Wright." DAI 32:2698A
    (University of Notre Dame).

3   McLEOD, JAMES RICHARD.  Theodore Roethke:  A Manuscript Check-
    list.  Kent, Ohio:  Kent State University Press.

## 1971 B SHORTER WRITINGS

1   ANON.  "Prose and Poetry." Saturday Review, LIV (May 22), 35.
      Review of Theodore Roethke, by Karl Malkoff.  Malkoff
    opens the door to, but never intrudes upon, "Roethke's
    special and often private vision."

2   ANON.  "A Conversation with Robert Lowell." The Review,
    XXVI (Summer), 14–15.
      Lowell comments on Roethke and especially his Selected
    Letters, recently published.

3   ALLMAN, JOHN.  "Theodore Roethke's Movie:  The Nightmare of
    Joy." Southern Poetry Review, XI (Spring), 13.
      A poem in tribute to Roethke.

4   BLESSING, RICHARD A.  "The Shaking that Steadies:  Theodore
    Roethke's 'The Waking.'" Ball State University Forum, XII
    (Autumn), 17–19.
      Roethke's poem "is a world in process about a world in
    process."  The question raised is:  What can we "know" of
    a world in flux?  Roethke uses the villanelle, a very
    restrictive form, to give "a movement in which structure
    wavers, shifts, almost vanishes, and finally reappears,
    much altered in meaning and value."

5   BOURDAN, JOSEPH A.  "Phoenix Nest:  Lone Scout." Saturday
    Review, LIV (March 13), 19.

Reminiscences of life in Saginaw, Michigan in 1921 when Roethke preferred the "Lone Scouts" to the "Boy Scouts." The boys could do anything they wanted to do to earn badges, but didn't <u>have</u> to do anything. The author comments on the neighborhood then and the neighborhood now.

6    BOYD, JOHN B.  "Texture and Form in Theodore Roethke's Greenhouse Poems."  <u>Modern Language Quarterly</u>, XXXII (December), 409-424.
     Roethke's "greenhouse" poems are a small part of his production.  Yet much of his stature as poet is based on them. Roethke has made lasting poems out of common material, "<u>largely</u> through their formal and structural properties," but also by the "interpenetration or coalescence of subject and object."  Previous critics, such as Burke, Kunitz and Berryman are cited extensively in this discussion of form.

7    BURKE, KENNETH.  "The Vegetal Radicalism of Theodore Roethke." <u>Profile of Theodore Roethke</u>.  Columbus, Ohio:  Charles E. Merrill, pp. 18-46.
     Reprint of 1950.B7; <u>See also</u> 1966.B22.

8    BYRD, B.  "I Want a Row of Bright Clean Books."  <u>Southern Poetry Review</u>, XI (Spring), 15-16.
     A poem in tribute to Roethke.

9    CIARDI, JOHN.  "An Evening with Theodore Roethke."  <u>Profile of Theodore Roethke</u>.  Columbus, Ohio:  Charles E. Merrill, pp. 16-18.
     Reprint of 1967.B21.

10   CORRIGAN, MATTHEW.  "A Phenomenological Glance at a Few Lines of Roethke."  <u>Modern Poetry Studies</u>, II:4, 165-174.
     An examination of a passage from "The Lost Son" "would approach a geometry of creative consciousness."  Husserl and Charles Olson are invoked as theorists to make clear the author's thesis.  "What is interesting in such poetry is that the creative instinct moves in terms of consciousness:  the imagery discovered by the poet is phenomenological in the sense that it is continually trying to clarify itself in terms of the basic metaphoric impulse it is then aware of (light--form--movement)."

11   DICKEY, JAMES.  "The Greatest American Poet:  Roethke." <u>Sorties</u>.  Garden City, N.Y.:  Doubleday & Co., pp. 214-224.
     Reprint of 1968.B29.

1971

12   FERRY, DAVID.   "Roethke's Poetry."   Profile of Theodore
       Roethke.   Columbus, Ohio:   Charles E. Merrill, pp. 96-99.
       Reprint of 1967.B28.

13   FIEDLER, LESLIE.   "The New Mutants."   The Collected Essays of
       Leslie Fiedler, Vol. II.   New York:   Stein & Day, p. 399.
       Reprint of 1965.B33.

14   FREER, COBURN.   "Theodore Roethke's Love Poetry."   Northwest
       Review, XI (Summer), 42-66.
         The love poems, though few, are not unprepared for in
       Roethke's poetic experience.   They show the same dominant
       pattern as the other poems, the Lost or Prodigal Son, and
       move toward the same end, the one metaphysical Other, or
       God.   This movement is the central metaphor in Roethke,
       moreso than any emphasis on imagery or process of psycho-
       logical encounter.   The two themes, found most notably in
       Words for the Wind, are Love and Burden.   Rilke's under-
       standing of the Prodigal Son parable is invoked to show
       how Roethke moves from locating the value of experience in
       himself, to and ultimately through woman so "that although
       the burden of being loved was exhausting, it was finally
       restorative."

15   GALVIN, BRENDAN.   "Kenneth Burke and Theodore Roethke's 'Lost
       Son' Poems."   Northwest Review, XI (Summer), 67-96.
         Burke influenced much of the writing of the Greenhouse
       and 'Lost Son' poems, not only by praising them and asking
       Roethke to write more, but also by offering to help get
       them published and providing, in his critical writings,
       their theoretical rationale.   The author goes on to exam-
       ine many of the poems in the 'Lost Son' and 'Praise to the
       End!' sequence to elaborate on this influence.

16   HAYDEN, MARY H.   "Open House:   Poetry of the Constricted Self."
       Northwest Review, XI (Summer), 116-138.
         Roethke's poetry fans out from a "vital point," his
       home, his past and all their associations.   The poems of
       Open House are tightly rhymed and structured, constricted
       in time, of the individual in a tight space seeking the
       means of escape from his past and place.   "Roethke's
       ability to destroy limits and constrictions will center
       in the desire of the self and the body (virtually insepa-
       rable and now friends) to know love and to make a history
       for himself by moving into the general flow of human ex-
       istence.   The desire for love and sexual union entails
       grasping for the Self more of the energy that invigorates
       the world of nature."

228

17   HEYEN, WILLIAM. Review of The Wild Prayer of Longing, by
     Nathan A. Scott, Jr. Saturday Review, LIV (May 22), 33,
     49.
         Scott sees that eternity is now and that a "sacramental
     view of reality holds that the world is responsive, recip-
     rocal." "Roethke, who early knew that he lacked a 'dancing-
     master,' came to conceive of the world is (sic) sacramental
     terms, hailed it and was hailed by it, heard the inner
     songs of snail, continent, and self, and in his poems kept
     coming constantly near to a Being at ease with itself."

18   _____. "The Divine Abyss: Theodore Roethke's Mysticism."
     Profile of Theodore Roethke. Columbus, Ohio: Charles E.
     Merrill, pp. 100-116.
         Reprint of 1969.B26.

19   HOBBS, JOHN. "The Poet as His Own Interpreter: Roethke on
     'In a Dark Time.'" College English, XXXIII (October),
     55-66.
         Roethke only partially succeeds in the prose explication
     of his poem as he attempts to expand the dark strength of
     a former, enigmatic experience. Side by side with the
     poem, the poet's explanation merely verbalizes much good
     that is implicit while highlighting much that is weak.
     Roethke ultimately has little confidence in the language
     of his poem to do its job.

20   HOWARD, RICHARD. "Foreword." Alone With America: Essays on
     the Art of Poetry in the United States Since 1950. New
     York: Atheneum, p. xi.
         Roethke is named as one of six poets (with Berryman,
     Bishop, Jarrell, Lowell and Wilbur) established "at least
     as types and at best as particulars in our literary land-
     scape" whose names recur consistently in the author's dis-
     cussions of more recently recognized writers. Some of the
     more significant references to Roethke are included here.

21   _____. "Carolyn Kizer: 'Our Masks Keep Us in Thrall to Our-
     selves...'." From the same collection as 1971.B20,
     pp. 272-273, 275.
         Reprint of 1966.B47.

22   _____. "W. S. Merwin: 'We Survived the Selves that We Remem-
     bered.'" From the same collection as 1971.B20, pp. 349-350.
         Roethke is discussed as a kind of type for transformation
     of poetic styles that, if accompanied by torment or pain,
     is permissible.

1971

23 _____. "Anne Sexton: 'Some Tribal Female Who Is Known But
Forbidden.'" From the same collection as 1971.B20, p. 442.
The author discusses Roethke's ideas of necessary imaginative "rightness" when writing in "freer forms" in relation to the poetry of Anne Sexton.

24 _____. "David Wagoner: 'It Dawns on Us That We Must Come
Apart.'" From the same collection as 1971.B20, p. 534.
Roethke's influence on Wagoner is pervasive, even in his
novels. "What Wagoner gets from Roethke is a preoccupa-
tion with the movement from external to created reality,
the sense that we awaken in a world possessed and informed
by something in our dream...."

25 KUNITZ, STANLEY. "Journal for My Daughter: 5." The Testing
Tree. Boston: Atlantic, Little, Brown, p. 5.
Part of a poem in tribute to Roethke.

26 _____. "An Evening with Theodore Roethke." Profile of
Theodore Roethke. Columbus, Ohio: Charles E. Merrill,
pp. 10-16.
A slightly modified version of the author's essay that
appeared in the New York Review of Books (1963.B49). See
also 1967.B48.

27 _____. "Roethke: Poet of Transformations." Profile of
Theodore Roethke. Columbus, Ohio: Charles E. Merrill,
pp. 67-77.
Reprint of 1965.B50.

28 LaBELLE, JENIJOY. "Theodore Roethke and Tradition: 'The Pure
Serene of Memory in One Man.'" Northwest Review, XI
(Summer), 1-18.
The conception put forward by many critics of Roethke as
a poet of distinctly original sensibility is wrong. He
was as conscious of tradition as Eliot and believed in it
as firmly. The clues that Roethke leaves to prove this
position can be seen in the titles and sources of his
poems and by examination of individual passages from works
of poets in "his" tradition. Imitation of specific poets,
not general styles and theories of past ages, enlarges the
meaning of his poems. Roethke tried for just such en-
largement by his eclectic responses to various types of
literature. "The Lost Son" and "Praise to the End!"
sequences, as well as "Sequence, Sometimes Metaphysical,"
are dealt with in detail to illustrate these points.

29  MANN, CHARLES W.  Review of Theodore Roethke:  A Manuscript
      Checklist, by James McLeod.  Library Journal, XCVI
      (December 15), 4083.
        "This is a significant work marred only by a few typos."
      Only a summary of the contents.

30  MARTZ, WILLIAM J.  Review of The Glass House, by Allan Seager.
      Journal of Modern Literature, I (Supplement), 911-913.
        This book does what a biography "has to do, get us to
      the man, make us feel through the facts of a life what a
      life can mean."  Roethke's life and poetry remind one of
      the doctrine of purification by trial.  Seager's treatment
      of Roethke as teacher is questioned, implying a lack of
      thoroughness.  Other weaknesses are minor and quickly
      dismissed.

31  MAZZARO, JEROME.  "Theodore Roethke and the Failures of
      Language."  Profile of Theodore Roethke.  Columbus, Ohio:
      Charles E. Merrill, pp. 47-64.
        Reprint of 1970.B16.

32  McCLOSKEY, MARK.  "The Slattern Muse."  Far Point, V (Winter/
      Spring), 55-60.
        Review of Robin Skelton's Selected Poems showing
      Roethke's influence on later poems.

33  McLEOD, JAMES R.  "Bibliographic Notes on the Creative Process
      and Sources of Roethke's 'The Lost Son' Sequence."  North-
      west Review, XI (Summer), 97-111.
        Several critical positions attempt to deal with the
      nature and value of this sequence of poems.  The author
      here describes these positions and puts them into histor-
      ical perspective with excerpts from various essays and
      reviews.  His bibliography includes the first periodical
      appearances of the fourteen poems themselves, Biographical
      and Critical Comment, Comments and Readings by Roethke,
      and Manuscript Locations.

34  McMICHAEL, JAMES.  "Roethke's North America."  Northwest Review,
      XI (Summer), 149-159.
        "...while these poems leave us with a distinct sense of
      Roethke as a person or self, they direct us away from that
      person, away, even, from our own selves and out toward
      North America.  What the poems ask us to find there is
      not so much impersonal as it is depersonalizing.  To come
      to our world as Roethke would have us come to it is to
      experience something that runs counter to the self, that
      forces a cleanliness upon it that is all but obliterating.

1971

And yet at the same time that this world is asserting itself, it is yielding to the individual soul that in its
own special way inheres in it.  It invites that soul to
find its own beauties and terrors in those parts of the
world that are most engaging.  It involves each of us in
his own search for his own soul.  'North American Sequence'
gives us a model for the search and shows us where to look."

35    ____.  "The Poetry of Theodore Roethke."  Profile of Theodore
      Roethke.  Columbus, Ohio:  Charles E. Merrill, pp. 78-95.
      Reprint of 1969.B38.

36    NOLAND, RICHARD W.  "In Search of the Sacred."  American
      Literature, XLI (Winter 1971/1972), 164-169.
      Review of The Wild Prayer of Longing:  Poetry and the
      Sacred, by Nathan A. Scott, Jr.  The reviewer takes issue
      with Scott's view of Roethke as the "poet of sacramentality."

37    PFLUM, RICHARD.  "Dark Festival (An appreciation after reading
      T. Roethke)."  Southern Poetry Review, XI (Spring), 26-27.
      A poem in tribute to Roethke.

38    PORTER, KENNETH.  "Roethke at Harvard, 1930-31 and the Decade
      After."  Northwest Review, XI (Summer), 139-148.
      Included in this reminiscence are excerpts from the
      author's letters about Roethke's early "poems with an in-
      tellectual atmosphere with several layers of meaning," his
      "metaphysical" poems.  A letter by John Holmes with com-
      ments on Roethke, Stanley Kunitz and publishing is also
      included.  Of special interest is an early draft of
      Roethke's poem "Autumnal," later part of "The Coming of
      the Cold."

39    ROACHE, JOEL.  Richard Eberhart:  The Progress of an American
      Poet.  New York:  Oxford University Press, pp. 191-198.
      An account of Eberhart's associations with Roethke:
      first at the Yaddo Colony near Saratoga Springs, New York,
      in 1950; and then as a substitute for Roethke at the Uni-
      versity of Washington, during a period of illness in
      1952-53.

40    SCHWARTZ, DELMORE.  "The Cunning and Craft of the Unconscious
      and the Preconscious."  Profile of Theodore Roethke.
      Columbus, Ohio:  Charles E. Merrill, pp. 64-66.
      Reprint of 1959.B60; See also 1970.B19.

41    SCOTT, NATHAN A., JR.  "The Example of Roethke."  The Wild
      Prayer of Longing:  Poetry and the Sacred.  New Haven:
      Yale University Press, 1971.  Pp. 76-118.

Roethke "offers what is perhaps the crucial instance of a truly sacramental vision of our human inheritance." He knows of another world whose "presence" he hears as a kind of music, not merely self-indulgent primitivism. Roethke's experience of the world is ontological. His response is piety. With this thesis established, the author pursues it through each of Roethke's volumes.

42  SEAGER, ALLAN. "An Evening with Theodore Roethke." Profile of Theodore Roethke. Columbus, Ohio: Charles E. Merrill, p. 3-10.
    Reprint of 1967.B71.

43  SMITH, RAYMOND. "Fondness and Reverence." Modern Poetry Studies, II:1, 41.
    Review of Depth of Field, by William Heyen. The author sees a "readily discernible" affinity to Roethke in Heyen's work, discussing "Winter Solstice" and "In Memoriam: Theodore Roethke" in this connection.

44  SQUIRES, RADCLIFFE. Allen Tate: A Literary Biography. New York: Pegasus/Bobbs-Merrill, pp. 124-125.
    An account of a writers' conference at Olivet College in July, 1937, when Roethke, along with Robert Lowell, was a student of Tate. "Both Roethke and Lowell became firm admirers of Tate's poetry and established personal friendships with him: Roethke as a life-long correspondent, or perhaps more appropriately, as a life-long long distance telephonant...."

45  STEIN, ARNOLD. "Roethke's Memory: Actions, Visions, and Revisions." Northwest Review, XI (Summer), 19-31.
    An examination of early ideas and drafts from the Notebooks as compared with the final material of the poems shows much about Roethke's method of experiencing his own past, weighing the impact of remembered childhood experience against the attitudes of his maturity in order to do more than merely describe the difference, but to establish its meaning. The author has much to say about the evocation of images of "joy," the nature of opposites, and the constant and important presence of "movement" in Roethke's poems.

46  VERNON, JOHN. "Theodore Roethke's Praise to the End! Poems." Iowa Review, II (Fall), 60-79.
    Under discussion are the sequences of long poems from The Lost Son, Praise to the End! and The Waking. These works deal with the child's loss of the "undifferentiated

1971

whole" through the maturation process. This can be spoken
of in terms of space and time. Elements of style such as
ambiguity, irony, image patterns, etc. are discussed under
this general conception. There is a unity of opposites
that indicates the way in "which Roethke's world is a total
alternative to the dualistic structures of classical Western thought." See also 1973.B28.

47   WOLFF, GEORGE. "Roethke's 'Root Cellar.'" Explicator, XXXIX
     (February), Item 47.
        For Roethke in The Lost Son volume, the rejection of the
     child gives rise to "container" images, sometimes threaten-
     ing, sometimes trustworthy. The poem 'Root Cellar' "pre-
     sents an equilibrium between the stifling enclosures of
     parental neglect and the forces of procreation that goad
     even the dirt into life."

48   _____. "Roethke, Theodore." Encyclopedia of World Literature
     in the 20th Century. Edited by Wolfgang Bernard Fleischman.
     New York:  Frederick Ungar Publishing Co., III, pp. 176-
     177.  Enlarged and updated edition of the Herder Lexikon
     der Weltliteratur im 20. Jahrhundert.
        Roethke's manic-depressive disorder effected his poems,
     "though not to their detriment." A "sense of soilure" is
     at the center of Roethke's work, compelling him toward
     "otherworldliness." Thematic and technical advances are
     discussed, leading to the conclusion that Roethke was not
     a major poet.


1972 A BOOKS

1    ABRAMS, WILLIAM G.  "'Private Substance Into Green':  Nature as
     Substance and Structure in the Poetry of Theodore Roethke."
     DAI 33:3627A (University of Nevada).

2    CARLSON, HELEN Z.  "Beyond Heroism:  Mysticism in the Poetry
     of Theodore Roethke."  DAI 33:2924A (University of
     Connecticut).

3    HILL, ROBERT WHITE.  "Nature Imagery in the Poetry of Theodore
     Roethke and James Dickey."  DAI 34:773A-774A (University
     of Illinois at Champaign-Urbana).

4    HUDSON, SISTER SUZANNE HELEN.  "Night Journey Under the Sea:
     Theodore Roethke's Search for the Self."  DAI 33:5681A
     (Marquette University).

# Writings about Theodore Roethke, 1922-1973

5  LANE, GARY.  A Concordance to the Poems of Theodore Roethke.
   Metuchen, N.J.:  The Scarecrow Press.
      For the 209 poems of The Collected Poems of Theodore
   Roethke.

6  SIMONETTI, FRANCIS ANTHONY.  "A Study of the Poetic Technique
   of Theodore Roethke:  The Lost Son and Other Poems."  DAI
   33:765A-766A (Ball State University).

7  STUART, FLOYD CHARLES.  "The Final Man:  The Poetry of Theodore
   Roethke."  DAI 33:767A (State University of New York at
   Binghamton).

## 1972 B SHORTER WRITINGS

1  ANON.  Review of Straw for the Fire.  Kirkus Service, XL
   (January 1), 56.
      The heightened poetry gains by its juxtaposition with
   simple, unelaborated entries.  The book offers a great
   deal of insight into Roethke's psychology.

2  BLESSING, RICHARD A.  "Theodore Roethke:  A Celebration."
   Tulane Studies in English, XX, 169-180.
      Challenging critics such as M. L. Rosenthal who claim
   that Roethke fails to make reference, direct or remote,
   to the experiences of his own age, the author discusses
   three of Roethke's eligiac poems:  "Elegy for Jane," "Frau
   Bauman, Frau Schmidt, and Frau Schwartze," and "Elegy
   (Should every creature be as I have been)."  It is in the
   transference of energy from his subject, through his craft
   of poetry, that Roethke presents the "essential experience
   of modern life."  "In fact, I think the root metaphor in
   all of Roethke's work is the historical event, provided
   that one understands that any action with all of its con-
   text--its total sweep backward into the past and forward
   into the future--is an event in history."

3  BROYARD, ANATOLE.  "A Poet Talking to Himself."  New York
   Times, March 7, p. 37.
      Review of Straw for the Fire.  Perhaps Roethke "wouldn't
   mind being caught groping for poetry in the file cabinets
   of cliché, bathos and mediocrity."  He didn't want to lose
   anything.  He believed in the "Exhorting of Everything,"
   resulting occasionally in something very bad.  Yet his
   issue-taking with Frost's attitude toward free verse is
   insightful, helping to clarify his views on craft.  This
   aspect of the book has value.

1972

4   BURNS, GERALD. "Last Words from Late Poets." Southwest
      Review, LVII (Summer), 255-256.
         Review of Straw for the Fire. "The big reviews are
      wrong. If you like Roethke's prose and verse already,
      this book helps you like them more. The scraps on teaching
      are wonderful if you teach, on writing if you write. Maybe
      it's a book for professionals. But Roethke has a way with
      a journal entry unlike anyone else's--half-casual humble
      curious questioning sound you won't find purely anywhere
      else."

5   CALHOUN, RICHARD. "James Dickey: The Expansive Imagination."
      Modern American Poetry: Essays in Criticism. Edited by
      Guy Owen. Deland, Fla.: Everett/Edwards, pp. 240-241.
         Dickey's admiration for Roethke is here taken as the
      basis of much of his poetic technique. Roethke aimed for
      a "condition of joy" through an "empathetic imagination"
      that moved "downward towards communion with the minimal
      forms of nature, but never quite escaping from the isola-
      tion of the self. Dickey's has progressively become the
      expansive imagination, moving 'upward.'"

6   DONALDSON, SCOTT. Poet in America: Winfield Townley Scott.
      Austin & London: University of Texas Press, pp. 249-250,
      and others.
         Scott's literary notebooks, "a dirty hand," are confusing
      because not dated. The author here repeats and comments on
      material from that work regarding Roethke without doing
      much to clarify it. Roethke's name occurs several times
      in incidental contexts.

7   GALVIN, BRENDAN. "Theodore Roethke's Proverbs." Concerning
      Poetry, V (Spring), 35-47.
         The author first recognizes in Roethke's work an "abun-
      dance of axiomatic material" which he traces to Roethke's
      method of composition, i.e., joining distinct lines and
      conceptions and letting them evolve into something new on
      their own. With reference to Kenneth Burke's discussion
      of proverbs in "Literature as Equipment for Living," in
      The Philosophy of Literary Form, the author then raises
      the question of how Roethke employs the "axiomatic material"
      in his poetry. After examining numerous individual poems,
      including many in "The Lost Son" and "Praise to the End!"
      sequence, the author concludes: "In general these proverbs
      are strategies to keep Roethke's protagonist moving in his
      perpetual quest for higher levels of being. They induce
      his courageous plunges into the mire of the preconscious,
      and his subsequent returns, with their new perspectives on
      his life and greater participation in existence."

1972

8  HERINGMAN, BERNARD. "'How to Write like Somebody Else.'"
   Modern Poetry Studies, III:1, 31-39.
        Roethke consciously employs the work of other writers,
   but for original effect. The author seeks to identify the
   nature of the influence of Blake, Yeats, Eliot and Whitman,
   as well as the stage of Roethke's career in which the influence has its most significant effect.

9  HEYEN, WILLIAM. Review of Straw for the Fire. Saturday Review,
   LV (March 11), 70-71.
        Roethke and James Dickey are reviewed as poets of the
   same type producing books that "are manifestations of the
   essential duplicity of the American poet:  he believes in
   poetry as a moral force, as a way through to affirmation
   and joy, while continent and self are always singing songs
   of chaos and death."

10  HUBBELL, JAY B.  Who Are the Major American Writers?  Durham,
    N.C.:  Duke University Press, p. 326.
        In the Conclusion to his study the author comments
    briefly on contrasting views among poets and professors
    who are their contemporaries as to relative literary stat-
    ure.  "On the Jackson Bryer poll of academic specialists
    Roethke and Robert Lowell got only 8 out of a possible 138
    votes.  James Dickey apparently got not a single vote."

11  KRAMER, VICTOR A.  "Life-and-Death Dialectics."  Modern Poetry
    Studies, III:1, 41.
        Review of Crossing the Water, by Sylvia Plath.  The
    author sees a definite Roethke influence in five of Plath's
    poems, "Who," "Dark House," "Maenad," "The Beast," and
    "Witch Burning."

12  KRETZ, THOMAS.  Review of Straw for the Fire.  America, CXXVI
    (May 13), 521-522.
        Although Roethke's use of light, wind, water and flowers
    demonstrates their availability to him as a poet, the note-
    books show he wished vainly to project himself into other
    human voices.  "Always searching for the center of things,
    he asked impossible questions."  But, for the reviewer,
    this questioning on Roethke's part is not enough.  The book
    offers only "a few ripe plums scattered about a bowl of
    mealy apples, overripe bananas and sour grapes."

13  LaBELLE, JENIJOY.  "Out of These Nothings--All Beginnings
    Come."  Virginia Quarterly Review, XLVIII (Autumn),
    637-640.

1972

> Review of Straw for the Fire. Wagoner works well through
> a difficult task. But, unfortunately, his biases limit
> the perspectives of Roethke's creativity. Wagoner is too
> much present.

14  LEIBOWITZ, HERBERT. "As if haunted by a raging dark angel."
    New York Times Book Review, April 9, pp. 4, 10.
        Review of Straw for the Fire. Roethke was a fanatic
    about poetry and his poems express his need. This book is
    a kind of "verbal compost heap," that he periodically
    raided for images. But most likely this "material did not
    meet Roethke's high artistic standards," because there is
    much tedium here.

15  McCLATCHY, J. D. "Sweating Light from a Stone: Identifying
    Theodore Roethke." Modern Poetry Studies, III:1, 1-24.
        The author takes issue with the trend in Roethke criti-
    cism toward belief that the poet achieves the transforma-
    tion of the self to the soul. Instead, he discerns a
    constant struggle or crisis in Roethke's poetry that can
    be expressed in many dialectical ways but can never be
    fully resolved. The poet oscillates from pole to pole,
    but ends always in the middle, with his own self, in a
    state of frustration. Significant passages from poems of
    each volume are examined in support of this thesis.

16  MILLS, RALPH J., JR. "Theodore Roethke." Modern American
    Poetry: Essays in Criticism. Edited by Guy Owen.
    Deland, Fla.: Everett/Edwards, pp. 185-204.
        A later version of the essay "Theodore Roethke: The
    Lyric of the Self," in which the author concludes his
    earlier discussion with remarks on Sequence, Sometimes
    Metaphysical and The Far Field.

17  MURRAY, MICHELE. "Recalling Roethke: The Poems Will Suffice,
    Thanks." National Observer, July 29, p. 19.
        Review of Straw for the Fire. "...uncritical adulation
    and indiscriminate publication, rather than adding to the
    impression made by the work, dilute it in the mass of
    surrounding trivia."

18  PHILLIPS, ROBERT. "The Dark Funeral: A Reading of Sylvia
    Plath." Modern Poetry Studies, III;2, 59.
        Plath, as do Roethke and Kunitz, searches for both the
    earthly father and the Heavenly Father simultaneously.

19  RAMSEY, JAROLD. "Roethke in the Greenhouse." Western Human-
    ities Review, XXVI (Winter), 35-47.

Roethke's greenhouses in The Lost Son are discussed in terms of Gaston Bachelard's conception, in The Poetics of Space, of "felicitous space"--"space that has been seized by the imagination." In his reverie, Roethke's greenhouse became "a setting where the subtle and sometimes eerie affinities between plant growth and the life of the human spirit could be studied minutely and lovingly, for the instruction of the spirit." But there is threat in the greenhouse also. Each poem contributes to the sequential logic in conveying these notions, with their resolution being "a mood of composed, expectant contemplation of permanent natural forms."

20  ROSENBERG, KENYON C. "Theodore Roethke." American Reference Books Annual 1972. Edited by Bohdan S. Wynar. Third edition. Littleton, Colorado: Libraries Unlimited, p. 509.
    Review of Theodore Roethke: A Manuscript Checklist by James Richard McLeod. This work is valuable but "it does not go beyond being a mere checklist, as the subtitle indicates."

21  SHAPIRO, KARL. "Scraping the Bottom of the Roethke Barrel." New Republic, CLXVI (March 4), 24.
    Review of Straw for the Fire. Roethke "was a poet of conscious limitations and slight range, though one whose limitations shielded him from cant and spared him wasteful effort." The book is "an anthology of wrong starts and jottings" that adds nothing to Roethke, and is in some places "extraordinarily boring and banal." Roethke's whole achievement is the painful construction of a backward and innocent state from which his poetry comes.

22  SMITH, PAMELA A. "The Unitive Urge in the Poetry of Sylvia Plath." New England Quarterly, XLV (September), 333-335.
    The author uses Roethke's metaphor of the descent into the abyss as both an explanation for and an influence on Plath's poetry.

23  SMITH, RAYMOND. "The Poetic Faith of James Dickey." Modern Poetry Studies, II:6, 266.
    Dickey's use of "primitive, instinctual past" is handled with a "Roethke-like paradox" in the poem "The Eye-Beaters."

24  TURCO, LEWIS. "Good Gray Poets and Bad Old Bards." Modern Poetry Studies, III:2, 83.
    Roethke's villanelle, "The Waking," and its line "I learn by going where I have to go," are seen as enunciating "Emerson's central thesis about organic poetry."

# Theodore Roethke's Career: An Annotated Bibliography

1973

## 1973 A BOOKS

1  McLEOD, JAMES. Theodore Roethke: A Bibliography. Kent, Ohio: Kent State University Press.

## 1973 B SHORTER WRITINGS

1  AIRD, EILEEN. Sylvia Plath. New York: Barnes and Noble, pp. 32-38.
    Roethke is frequently mentioned here. The author discusses his Praise to the End! poems in relation to Colossus.

2  ANON. Review of "Theodore Roethke Reads His Poetry." Caedmon Records Phonodisc TC1351, Tape Cassette CDL51351. Booklist, LXIX (May 15), 896.
    His frenetic reading bears out the diagnosis of Roethke as a manic-depressive. "Yet, even if the listener may want the author to slow down to give his lush organic poetry time to sink in, in some unexpected cases, the headlong delivery succeeds."

3  ANON. Review of Dirty Dinky and Other Creatures. Kirkus Reviews, XLI (July 15), 758.
    Favorable review pointing out Roethke's "inspired nonsense" and "wonderful animal poems."

4  ANON. Review of Dirty Dinky. Booklist, LXX (October 15), 240.
    Little critical comment other than that the illustrations "are inappropriately heavy."

5  ANON. "Brief Mention." American Literature, XLV (November), 493.
    Mention, without comment, of Theodore Roethke: A Bibliography, by James Richard McLeod.

6  ANON. "Notable Children's Books, 1973." Childrens' Book World (Washington Post), November 11, p. 2C.
    Review of Dirty Dinky. Briefly mentioned as published.

7  ANON. Review of Dirty Dinky. Bulletin of the Center for Children's Books (University of Chicago), XXVII (December), 70.
    It is as "sheer, lilting fun" that this collection will appeal to readers, "but it gives a canted perspective of the breadth of Roethke's poetry."

1973

8   ATLAS, JAMES. "Letters: Lowell & Grigson." London Magazine,
    NS XIII (October/November), 122.
        Brief mention of Roethke and his inability to win the
    critical acclaim in England the author feels he deserves.

9   BLESSING, RICHARD A. "Theodore Roethke's Sometimes Metaphysical
    Motion." Texas Studies in Literature and Language, XIV
    (Winter), 731-749.
        This essay seeks to explain Roethke's use of the term
    "metaphysical," as well as to establish and explain the
    interrelationships of all the poems in "Sequence, Sometimes
    Metaphysical." "Perpetual beginner, dreamer of journeys
    repeatedly, Roethke found the idea of using a sequence of
    poems to represent the dynamic flow of experience to be a
    happy one. Like the aging instant which forever vanishes
    just ahead of us, each poem in Sequence, Sometimes Meta-
    physical has independent worth and identity, yet each is
    enlarged in meaning and value by its relationship to other
    of the poems and to the whole. And, like that vanishing
    instant, each poem in the Sequence destroys itself to make
    way for the next poem. Ever decaying, never to be decayed;
    ever evolving, never to be evolved; the poems of Sequence,
    Sometimes Metaphysical prove that each ending is a new
    beginning, and that endings and beginnings alike are 'per-
    petual.' The sequence of twelve poems may not wholly mas-
    ter the complexities of a world in process, but taken
    together, the poems represent a remarkable attempt to wed
    the motion of the creative mind to the motion that is life
    itself."

10  BUSH, MARGARET. Review of Dirty Dinky. Library Journal,
    XCVIII (October 15), 3150.
        Without introductory note or biographical sketch, the
    collection is "disappointingly slight."

11  EBERHART, RICHARD. "Literary Death." Granite (Hanover, N.H.),
    No. 6 (Autumn), p. 153.
        The author recalls his feeling at the death of Roethke
    and recounts an experience they shared in a bar in Saratoga.
    He closes with: "We had to restrain him by talk. I felt
    that if he had gone up and accosted the bartender he might
    have got his block knocked off. He often lived in fantasy,
    where he felt power."

12  JACOBSEN, JOSEPHINE. "Hickety-Pickety: Children's Books."
    Book World (Washington Post), September 9, p. 9.
        Review of Dirty Dinky and Other Creatures. "The child
    who listens, really listens, to these poems will have

1973

learned something about the nature of poetry.... It is
good to be haunted by poetry, and this book will do a
little haunting."

13  JANIK, DEL IVAN. "Roethke's 'The Boy and the Bush.'" The
Explicator, XXXII:3 (November), Item 20.
    This poem can be read as a comic tribute to D. H.
Lawrence.

14  KELLER, DEAN H. "Theodore Roethke." American Reference Books
Annual 1973. Edited by Bohdan S. Wynar. Fourth edition.
Littleton, Colorado: Libraries Unlimited, p. 498.
    Review of A Concordance to the Poems of Theodore Roethke
by Gary Lane. A "welcome addition to reference collections
dealing with modern poetry."

15  KENNEDY, X. J. (Xjk). "Arranging the Remains." Counter/
Measures, No. 2, p. 188.
    Review of Straw for the Fire, arranged by David Wagoner.
Roethke does not deserve the stature that some (such as
James Dickey) would confer on him. Though he possessed an
original talent, this work clearly shows a lack of unity,
a disconnectedness that is common to poems arranged by the
poet himself. "Roethke, as his notebooks proclaim, was all
one giant dumpling of sensation, a quivering aardvark of
unconsciousness.... Preferring to let poems grow in the
dark, accepting his art as a natural (wasteful and prolific)
process, he wisely cultivated his greenhouse and for most
of his life...resisted the temptation to puff himself up
and become significant. But his was more of a sprawling
jungle than it appeared."

16  KILLINGER, JOHN. The Fragile Presence:  Transcendence in
Modern Literature. Philadelphia: Fortress Press,
pp. 103-104.
    Brief discussion of "Root Cellar" that relies mainly on
other critics' evaluations of Roethke's work.

17  KNOEPFLE, JOHN. "Crossing the Midwest." Regional Perspectives:
An Examination of America's Literary Heritage. Edited by
John Gordon Burke. Chicago: American Library Association,
pp. 116-117.
    Roethke is dealt with as a product of the Saginaw, Michi-
gan area and the landscape is seen in his poetry.

18  LaBELLE, JENIJOY. "Roethke's 'I Knew a Woman.'" The Explicator,
XXXII:2 (October), Item 15.
    The writer takes issue with several other commentaries
on this poem also published in The Explicator. Roethke's

source for terminology in the poem is Ben Jonson. Andrew
Marvell is also seen behind the mowing metaphor; St.
Augustine behind the concept of Time; and D. H. Lawrence
behind the theme of carnal knowledge.

*19  LIMMER, RUTH, ed.  Letters from Louise Bogan to Theodore
     Roethke.  Antaeus, No, 11 (Autumn), pp. 138-144.
        Uncertain as to the contents of these letters as I was
     unable to locate the journal.

20   MAZZARO, JEROME.  William Carlos Williams:  The Later Poems.
     Ithaca and London:  Cornell University Press, pp. 173-174.
        While discussing Williams' "voyeuristic poet," the
     author suggests a possible debt to Roethke in "Four for
     Sir John Davies," and the article on tradition and the
     "older writers," "How to Write Like Somebody Else."

21   MERCIER, JEAN.  "Children's Books."  Publisher's Weekly, CCIV
     (July 23), 69.
        Review of Dirty Dinky and Other Creatures.  A "charming
     book."

22   PASCHALL, DOUGLAS.  "Roethke Remains."  Sewanee Review, LXXXI
     (Autumn), 859-864.
        Review of Straw for the Fire, arranged by David Wagoner.
     "Roethke's strengths lay in his power to get back, down,
     and through all the dross and dreck, and into his best
     self.  It was perhaps his failing that he rarely got away
     again."  This conclusive statement follows a discussion of
     the aptness of Wagoner's choice of the straw man as a con-
     trolling metaphor for Roethke's conception of creation,
     and this hodgepodge collection of notes.  "But the edges
     will not jibe, and we are left with a shoebox of broken
     rarities."

23   PHILLIPS, ROBERT.  "The Inward Journeys of Theodore Roethke."
     The Confessional Poets.  Carbondale and Edwardsville:
     Southern Illinois University Press; London and Amsterdam:
     Feffer & Sumons, pp. 107-127.
        After establishing the fact that Roethke is the least
     "public" of the "confessional" poets discussed, the author
     explains why, and why Roethke is unique among them, by
     citing his "manifesto":  To go forward it is necessary to
     first go back; and, The poet does not "comment," but ren-
     ders experience, "however condensed or elliptical that
     experience may be."  An examination of the poems from The
     Lost Son consumes most of the author's space.  These poems
     exemplify again and again the method already cited, asking

questions pertinent to childhood. In the later "inward
journey" poems from Praise to the End! and The Waking,
Roethke employs the same method, but now probing deeper
mature reflections on love, death, etc. But, for the
author, Roethke fails to achieve anything resembling peace
of mind from his traumatic questions. Subsequent books
indicate that: "It is true enough that the spirit of man
can gain strength or a renewal of grace in a period of conflict and of trial. And in wanting so desperately to
achieve just such an epiphany or illumination, Roethke
concludes poem after poem with a description of a mystic
or spiritual event. It is a bit like a whore claiming to
have an orgasm with each new customer. The fact that the
poet rarely if ever achieved these visions makes it impos-
sible for the reader to experience them from the printed
page. It is ecstasy unearned, and the unattained vision
cannot be shared." Besides this essay, Roethke's name
appears numerous times in the author's discussions of the
other "confessional" poets.

24    ROBBINS, J. ALBERT. Review of Theodore Roethke: A Manuscript
      Checklist, by James McLeod. Resources for American Liter-
      ary Study, III (Autumn), 267.
         The book is "a superb research tool."

25    ROSENTHAL, M. L. and A. J. M. SMITH. Exploring Poetry.
      Second edition. New York: Macmillan, pp. 73 and 492.
         Brief discussion of "Orchids" and "The Meadow Mouse."

26    SHAW, ROBERT B. "Roethke Rough." Poetry, CXXI (March),
      341-343.
         Review of Straw for the Fire. Wagoner has done a creative
      job of shaping the fragments from Roethke's notebooks.
      The reviewer is confirmed in his belief that Roethke's
      best work is in the middle period of The Lost Son and
      Praise to the End! when he was not self-consciously modu-
      lating the extremes of his experience. His later period
      is "haunted" by voices, especially Yeats'.

27    UNTERMEYER, LOUIS. "Theodore Roethke." 50 Modern American
      & British Poets, 1920-1970. New York: David McKay Co.,
      pp. 277-279.
         A brief introduction to Roethke's life and poetry, his
      only therapy. The author remarks on several of the poems
      included in the anthology, "Cuttings," "Elegy for Jane,"
      and "In a Dark Time."

1973

28   VERNON, JOHN.   "Theodore Roethke," in <u>The Garden and the Map:</u>
        <u>Schizophrenia in Twentieth-Century Literature and Culture</u>.
        Urbana, Chicago, London:   University of Illinois Press,
        pp. 159-190.
          A slightly altered version of the article that appeared
        in the <u>Iowa Review</u>.  <u>See</u> 1971.B46.

29   WILBUR, RICHARD.   "Poetry's Debt to Poetry."  <u>Hudson Review</u>,
        XXVI (Summer), 278-280.
          Roethke, "the most precarious of the fine poets of our
        century," is discussed under this general thesis:   "A
        commanding imagination...steals not from one writer but
        selectively from all writers, taking whatever will help in
        the articulation of its own sense of things."   The author
        discusses <u>Open House</u> and the effect of certain woman poets
        (Leonie Adams especially) on its poems of praise.   The
        middle poems, of the greenhouse and psychic struggle, are
        powerfully original.   The poems so obviously under Yeats'
        influence are, therefore, hard to believe authentic.
        Roethke, newly married, searching for a new vein, needed
        "to broaden his utterance through imposture."   This in
        turn made him "capable of those last poems which are better
        than ever and so much more his own."

# Index

Murray, James G., 1968.B61
Murray, Michele, 1972.B17
Musser, Jean, 1962.B36
Muste, John M., 1967.B61

Napier, John, 1961.B59
Nathan, Norman, 1961.B60
N. B. C., 1941.B35
Nelson, Dale, 1966.B71; 1967.B62
Nemerov, Howard, 1954.B31;
    1963.B54; 1968.B62
N. H., 1961.B61
Nichols, Lewis, 1963.B55
Nicholson, Norman, 1949.B13;
    1966.B72
N. J., 1958.B32
Noland, Richard W., 1971.B36

O'Gorman, Ned, 1969.B41
Oppenheim, Judith, 1960.B19
Origo, Iris, 1965.B66
Ostroff, Anthony, 1961.B62;
    1964.B43

Parkinson, Thomas, 1950.B10
Parsons, Eugene O., 1948.B28
Parsons, Margaret, 1948.B29
Patrick, John, 1954.B32
Patterson, Elizabeth, 1961.B63–
    B64
Paschall, Douglas, 1973.B22
Paul, Sherman, 1969.B42
P. B., 1958.B33
Pearce, Donald, 1955.B8
Pearce, Roy Harvey, 1957.B3;
    1965.B67; 1969.B43
Peck, Virginia, 1964.B44
Pelto, Dick, 1960.B20
Perkins, Francis D., 1960.B21
Perrine, Laurence, 1966.B73
Perry, Ralph, 1948.B30–B31
Peterson, Bob T., 1962.B22
Peterson, Clell T., 1966.B74
Pfeiffer, Ted, 1969.B44
Pflum, Richard, 1971.B37
P. H., 1949.B14
Philbrick, Charles, 1968.B63
Phillips, Douglas, 1957.B4
Phillips, Robert, 1972.B18;
    1973.B23
Pilsk, Adele, 1961.B65

Pinsker, Sanford, 1965.B68;
    1966.B75
P. M. J., 1942.B7
Porter, Kenneth, 1971.B38
Post, Kirby, 1958.B34
Powell, Grosvenor E., 1967.B63
Powers, Dennis, 1964.B45
Press, John, 1965.B69
Pryce-Jones, Alan, 1964.B46–47;
    1965.B70
Purser, John Thibaut, 1963.B14

Quinn, Sister Bernetta M.,
    1965.B71

Ragan, Sam, 1966.B76
Raleigh, Sally, 1958.B35; 1964.B48
Ramsey, Jarold, 1972.B19
Ramsey, Paul, 1964.B49
Ransom, John Crowe, 1961.B66;
    1964.B50
Read, David W., 1965.B72
Reddin, John J., 1963.B56
Reichertz, Ronald R., 1967.A2, B64
Reid, James M., 1966.B73
Reiss, Edmund, 1953.B17
Rendon, Armando, 1961.B67
Rettew, Thomas M., 1966.B77
Rexroth, Kenneth, 1964.B51
Ribner, Irving, 1962.B37
rice, 1963.B57
Richardson, Mary, 1959.B56
Ridland, John M., 1961.B68;
    1967.B65
Riley, Peter, 1968.B64
Rillie, John A. M., 1968.B65
Roache, Joel, 1971.B39
Robbins, J. Albert, 1973.B24
Roberts, Percival R., III,
    1965.B73
Roche, Paul, 1967.B66
Rodman, Seldon, 1948.B32; 1951.B10
Roethke, Beatrice, 1963.B58;
    1968.B66
Rorem, Ned, 1965.B74
Rosenberg, Kenyon C., 1972.B20
Rosenthal, M. L., 1959.B57;
    1960.B22; 1962.B38; 1965.B75–
    B76; 1967.B67; 1968.B67;
    1970.B17; 1973.B25
Ross, Alan, 1958.B36; 1959.B58;
    1966.B78

## DATE DUE

| | | | |
|---|---|---|---|
| | | | |
| | | | |
| | | | |
| | | | |
| | | | |
| | | | |
| | | | |
| | | | |
| | | | |
| | | | |
| | | | |
| | | | |
| | | | |
| | | | |
| | | | |
| | | | |

DEMCO 38-297

MAR 05 1987